TWENTIETH-CENTURY ATTITUDES

TWENTIETH-CENTURY ATTITUDES

Literary Powers in Uncertain Times

Brooke Allen

Ivan R. Dee
CHICAGO

The paperback edition of this book carries the ISBN 1-56663-597-7.

Library of Congress Cataloging-in-Publication Data:
Allen, Brooke.
    Twentieth-century attitudes : literary powers in uncertain times / Brooke Allen.
    p. cm.
    Includes index.
    ISBN 1-56663-520-9 (alk. paper)
    1. English literature—20th century—History and criticism. 2. American literature—20th century—History and criticism. I. Title.

PR471.A44 2003
820.9'0091—dc21   2003040909

To Peter

Acknowledgments

"The Voice of a New Century: Colette" and "Saul Bellow on Top" appeared originally in the *Hudson Review*. Part of "Rohinton Mistry: A Butterfly on the Dung Heap" was first published in the *Atlantic Monthly*. All the other pieces in this book first appeared in *The New Criterion*.

I wish to give many thanks to Roger Kimball, Hilton Kramer, Michael Anderson, Charles McGrath, Paula Dietz, Frederick Morgan, Myron Kolatch, Alexandra Mullen, Christopher Carduff, David Yezzi, Robert Messenger, Alida Becker, Ron Koury, James Panero, Eric Eichman, Mike Kelly, and Ben Schwarz.

Also, to Jay Strick, for his friendship and encouragement, to my parents, Lewis and Jay Allen, my husband, Peter Aaron, and my daughters, Eve and Elizabeth.

B. A.

Hudson, New York
April 2003

Preface

Writing of George Eliot, Virginia Woolf commented that "I think she is a highly feminine and attractive character . . . and I only wish she could have lived nowadays and so been saved all that nonsense. I mean, being so serious, and digging up fossils, and all the rest of it." Yes, possibly; but one could just as easily wish that Woolf herself had been spared the obsessions of her own time—Freud and significant form and doctrinaire pacifism and obligatory sexual frankness. Many of Eliot's and Woolf's interests and preoccupations may seem quaint and dated, unworthy, in retrospect, of their high artistic capacities, but they indicate a necessary vitality, an engagement with the urgent intellectual and philosophical questions of their times. We are all formed by our times as well as our characters and circumstances, and an argument could be made that the most successful artists—and the most successful human beings—are those who participate avidly in the drama of their particular historical moment: "No man," Tocqueville observed, "can struggle with advantage against the spirit of his age."

The measure of a writer's quality can only really be gauged after enough years have gone by for us to view his work outside the distorting mirror of his or her period; many writers who are unconditionally praised today will be forgotten in half a century. Why, for example, do the Sherlock Holmes stories hold up while countless other examples of the detective genre have become, over the decades, unreadable? Why does the fiction of Edith Wharton, which deals with an arcane code of mores that was dying even at the time she wrote, seem so perfectly applicable to our own world? Why do the early novels of Evelyn Waugh, which epitomize his frenetic milieu and helped to create posterity's perception of the 1920s, continue to delight while those of his apparently similar contemporaries have gone hopelessly stale?

Really good writers do not write well *in spite of* the foibles, prejudices, and fallacies of their times; instead they crystallize these oddities into something universal, create archetypes rather than characters or situations. Christopher Isherwood, for example, was a creature of his times to an almost ridiculous degree: pacifist and parlor pink in the thirties, eager disciple of Hollywood mysticism in the forties, high priest of gay liberation in the fifties and sixties. Yet Isherwood managed to turn out a handful of exquisite novels that transcend the parochial issues he so often wrote about. And Tom Wolfe, the most topical and, to his critics, the most basely "journalistic" of writers, is also more than topical or journalistic: just as his *Radical Chic* has survived long past its historical moment as a send-up not only of sixties preoccupations but of mindless intellectual fashion in general, so his *fin-de-siècle* novels *Bonfire of the Vanities* and *A Man in Full* deal with eternal philosophical questions dressed up in trendy American costume.

This collection of essays examines a series of writers who embody, in various ways, the values and attitudes of their time, and the success or failure of their attempts to transcend these values and attitudes. It begins with Colette, perhaps the first truly twentieth-century writer, who set out deliberately to shock and who personified the sort of in-your-face self-promotion that would develop over the course of the century and come to full fruition in the 1980s. (Colette's opposite numbers, but equally effective at getting attention, are those like

Thomas Pynchon or Woody Allen who cultivate a showy reclusivity, an art known as "backing into the spotlight.") Colette was a good writer but not as good as she made people think she was; she was so successful in creating her own image that it has taken a full century for us even to begin to sum up the literary achievement without being distracted by the still-electric force of her personality.

Most of the authors discussed in these essays are English or American, which is perhaps appropriate since, in international terms, it was undoubtedly the Anglo-American century. Most of them in some way typify or encapsulate their historical moment. Some, like James Baldwin and Saul Bellow, were received ecstatically by their contemporaries, and a measure of reevaluation and revisionism has inevitably set in. Others, like Sylvia Townsend Warner and Angus Wilson, created less of a furor during their lifetimes, but now their work seems at least as good as ever, a generation after their deaths.

It was a colorful and grotesque century, and it produced a wide variety of odd attitudes. This collection can only scratch the surface.

Contents

TWENTIETH-CENTURY ATTITUDES

The Voice of a
New Century: Colette

"Biographers generally believe that it is easy to be
a 'monster.' It is even harder than being
a saint."—Colette

"Everything in art is monstrous, and Madame
Colette does not escape this rule."
—Jean Cocteau

*I*f anyone can qualify as an authority on monsters, it is Judith Thurman, who wrote what is generally considered the principal English-language biography of Isak Dinesen. But in taking on the subject of Colette in her biography *Secrets of the Flesh,* the doughty Thurman seems to have bitten off more than even she can swallow. Much as she might admire the *monstre sacre*—and it is impossible not to admire Colette, however instinctively one might recoil from her—Thurman just can't, in the end, quite approve of her subject. And neither will many readers. "In the prize ring of life few of us would have lasted ten rounds with Colette," John Updike once remarked, and it's the God's truth.

Thurman's biography of Colette comes hard on the heels of a two-volume treatment by two Frenchwomen, Claude Francis and Fernande

Gontier. Francis and Gontier's take on Colette is rather different from Thurman's. Without making her out to be less of the bitch she was, they seem to like her in spite of it all; their tone is on balance one of amusement rather than outrage. Their study is marred and handicapped, though, by the central thesis that clearly inspired it: that Colette's mother Sidonie ("Sido") was a lifelong disciple of the philosophy of Charles Fourier, and that her Fourierist beliefs permeated her daughter's being to the point that "it is impossible to understand Colette . . . without an understanding of the ultraradical background of her maternal family."

The two volumes that follow, though, fail to persuade the reader that it is *impossible* to understand Colette without seeing her through the lens of Fourierism or connecting her with radical politics. Colette was above all a force of nature, and while her maternal family's politics might have provided her with a theoretical justification for the moral liberties she took throughout her life, one strongly suspects that she would have taken them anyway. In fact she despised theory, always defining herself as pagan sensualist rather than intellectual; as Thurman wryly observes, "there was not an ideal that was capable of carrying Colette away, or a sensation that couldn't." Late in life, when it was suggested that she produce a version of her thoughts along the lines of Pascal's *Pensées,* she was scornful: "I have no *pensées.* As a matter of fact thanks be to God, perhaps the most praiseworthy thing about me is that I have known how to write like a woman, without anything moralistic or theoretical, without promulgating."

The subject of Fourier's influence on Colette is worthy of a scholarly article or perhaps a slim volume, but as the driving force for a popular two-volume biography it begins to be merely annoying, for it makes up only a minor strand, at best, in her extraordinary story. More than the product of a time or place, Colette was a self-invention, as Francis and Gontier know very well.

Colette's first transformation occurred during World War II, when the Vichy government presented military defeat as a retribution for sins and held the corruption of urban high society responsible. Colette went from high-society corrupt darling to rustic madonna, and in spite of her own assertions that her grandfather was "a quadroon," she downplayed her African ancestry and became pure Burgundian. The stereotype of Colette as a country girl was in place.

After the war, de Gaulle stressed the grandeur of France, while André Malraux, minister of culture, stressed that the greatness of France was best reflected in the greatness of her writers. Colette became an icon. She embodied all the French values: deep country roots, love in its sensuous splendor, a taste for naughtiness, a discriminating knowledge of wine and gourmet cuisine.

They are right about everything except in contending that World War II marked her *first* transformation, for there had been several before that. What about her decision, as a married woman in her thirties, to go on the music hall stage, dancing in pieces that were both avant-garde and scandalously risqué, and even baring a breast in public? At that time becoming an actress was tantamount to taking up prostitution, and at the very least an act of blatant class betrayal. What about her years as a visible member of Parisian lesbos: her high-profile affairs with notorious lesbians like Georgie Raoul-Duval and Natalie Barney, and above all her long-term, almost marital liaison with Mathilde, Marquise de Morny? When in 1912 she married the *haut bourgeois* left-wing politician Henry de Jouvenel she began to obliterate this period of her past as best she could: Jouvenel was widely thought to be a contender for the presidency, but "could anyone," ask Francis and Gontier, "imagine Colette at the Elysée?" Her image makeover succeeded largely but not entirely, and even as late as the 1930s there were objections to her membership in the Legion of

Honor: a member of the Grande Chancellerie remarked that he could remember a time "when Colette wore around her neck not the red *cravate* of the Legion but a choker, where one could clearly read, 'I belong to Madame de Morny.'"

In the end the self-invented Colette prevailed, with a panache one can only envy. After a youth spent flouting not only every unreasonable convention but every reasonable taboo as well, she ended her life so thoroughly rehabilitated as to become a national monument. The woman who had scorned the ways and means of feminism—suffragettes, she memorably declared, deserved the whip and the harem—became, in her old age and in the years since her death, a goddess for late-twentieth-century feminism. The passive collaborationist who had published her work in many of the most pernicious and anti-Semitic organs of the Vichy government was finally perceived as the quintessence of everything the French love best about themselves. The woman who refused to visit her dying mother and left her little daughter to be brought up by servants and friends transformed herself, as she aged, "into an image of Mother Earth. . . . She presented her past as the misfortune of a misguided adolescent, candid and gullible," write Francis and Gontier. "Colette's life," her longtime friend Cocteau commented, amused: "One scandal after another—then everything changes and she becomes an idol. She ends her life of music halls, beauty parlors, old lesbians in an apotheosis of respectability."

The story of Colette's early life is famous: the pastoral childhood; the innocent young girl taken from the country to Paris by her much older husband, a debauched satyr; the husband, Henry Gauthier-Villars (known as Willy), locking her into a room and forcing her to write stories that he published under his own name; his infidelities; his final desertion, leaving the rejected girl to support herself as a music hall actress.

This is the tale that Colette invented and polished in the autobiographical works she wrote in middle age, *Sido, My Mother's House,* and *My Apprenticeships*. These narratives contain a series of shady half-truths, drastically edited events, and downright lies, as both biographies discussed here reveal.

Colette was born Sidonie-Gabrielle Colette on January 28, 1873, in the village of Saint-Sauveur-en-Puisaye in the area known as "the poor Burgundy." She was the fourth child of her mother, Sidonie. "Sido" was the daughter of Henri Marie Landois, a provincial businessman, son of a wealthy mulatto from Martinique. As a young girl with a genteel background and good education but not much money (her father's fortunes were in constant flux), Sido was brought to Saint-Sauveur to be married off to a mentally deficient, alcoholic landowner, Jules Robineau. Robineau was far from appealing, but Sido, to whom marriage had brought money and local influence, was not dissatisfied. She was rumored to have had several lovers, the most serious of whom was a veteran of Napoleon III's wars, Jules Colette, who had lost a leg at Melignano. Colette had been awarded a sinecure as tax collector for Saint-Sauveur, and he arrived in the village as a romantic outsider. Sido's second child during her marriage to Robineau, Achille, is assumed to have been Colette's son, and eleven months after Robineau's providential death in 1865 Sido and Colette were married.

They had two more children: Leo, born in 1866, and Sidonie-Gabrielle, known as Gabri. Gabri's childhood was in many ways a privileged one. The Colettes passed for aristocracy in Saint-Sauveur, and certainly considered themselves to be of the *gratin*: "Sido insisted that she came from a very distinguished family and instilled in her children the belief that they were different from the common people of Saint-Sauveur," write Francis and Gontier. The Colettes sent Gabri to the local lay school, a new and progressive institution brought into being after the Third Republic broke the church's monopoly on elementary education. *Claudine at School*, her first novel, would quite faithfully reflect her experiences there. She received most of her education, though, at home; the Colettes were enthusiastic naturalists and amateur scientists, and as for literature and history they believed in letting the children have the run of the library, even allowing Gabri to read the scandalous Zola. ("After all," Sido said, consideringly, "maybe there are no bad books.") Gabri was clearly born with a powerful ego, and Sido reinforced her daughter's sense of exceptionalism, applauding everything she did that made her stand out from the village and its mediocre inhabitants. Gabri's school report shows that the daughter followed the mother's lead: "She is very imaginative but there is a deliberate will to be different."

Gabri's formal education ended when she was sixteen. Willy later hinted that she eloped with her music teacher, a *fugue* that made her hard to marry off, but her biographers have not been able to verify this allegation. In any case, it was about this time that she first met Willy, who came to the village as a guest of her brother Achille. Willy was the renegade son of France's foremost scientific publisher. The Gauthier-Villars family was part of the Parisian *bourgeoisie absolue*, rich, right-wing, and ultra-Catholic. Willy was a rebel by nature, *louche*, improvident, risk-loving; at the time he met Gabri he was about thirty and already one of the foremost journalists and critics in France.

It appears that Willy thought Gabri an appealing child but was not much interested in her. He was in love with Germaine Servat, by whom he fathered a child, Jacques; the mother died soon after the son's birth, and the grieving Willy asked the Colettes to find the child a wet nurse in their village.

Both Thurman and the Francis-Gontier team believe that it was Gabri and her family who forced the match upon a passive Willy, still laid low after Germaine's death. The brilliant and cosmopolitan Willy was definitely a catch, while for him a union with a dowerless girl, daughter of a provincial and vaguely scandalous family, amounted to a definite *mésalliance*. Willy's parents expressed their disapproval by reducing his inheritance.

Francis and Gontier contend that Sido and Gabri between them more or less trapped Willy. It is hard to be certain of the facts, but a letter Willy wrote to a friend at the time of his marriage displays his lukewarm attitude toward the whole enterprise: "[Y]ou say I marry without great joy. You are right. It is true. I can do nothing about it. Everyone thinks I have forgotten the wound I suffered, it is wrong. Farewell. There will be some hard times ahead."

By his own admission Willy had always been attracted to very young girls, and it is perhaps for this reason that Gabri, from the beginning of their marriage, acted the *gamine* so energetically. At the time of their marriage she was twenty, he thirty-three; the age gap, in fact, was more the norm than the exception, and at twenty Gabri was hardly—or should not have been—the "child" she later described. But as Thurman says, the age difference "was essential to their scenario as a couple, an exchange to which she brought the vitality and he the prestige. Sporting button boots, large muslin collars and a braid down to her knees, Gabri took pains to appear younger than she was, and Willy, as she noted, went to a good deal of trouble to appear old." His many fictional self-portraits, the most characteristic of which is Maugis, who first appears in *Claudine in Paris,* contrast "Willy's high culture with his low appetites, and his sexual charisma with his unprepossessing and, as he aged, gross appearance." Two lifelong exhibitionists, at this stage they very consciously acted out the roles of Beauty and the Beast.

At the time of the marriage Willy, aside from his flourishing career as a journalist and critic, was starting to write novels. In this endeavor he pioneered a production-line technique, using a bevy of minions in a manner eerily prescient of Andy Warhol's Factory. He had a definite formula: "The storyline," say Francis and Gontier, "would be loosely naughty to appeal to a large public and the characters would be thinly veiled portraits of contemporaries; the infratext would be a social satire." Gabrielle was just one of any number of gifted ghostwriters.

One of them, Ernest Lajeunesse, said that "Like everyone else, I made my literary debut by calling myself Willy." (During the Dreyfus affair the refusal of Willy, who inherited his family's conservative notions, to sign a petition urging that Dreyfus was innocent inspired his friend Pierre Veber to quip that "it's the first time Willy has refused to sign something he didn't write.")

According to Colette's version of her life, Willy casually suggested that she try writing about her schooldays, being sure not to leave out the spicy bits. She complied; when he read it, though, he decided there was nothing much there, and relegated the manuscript to a cupboard where it languished until, taking it out years later, he declared himself a fool for not having recognized its potential and hustled it off at once to an eager publisher. The reality is different. For one thing, Willy put a great deal of effort into turning his wife into a writer, as did his friends: "no woman writer," point out Francis and Gontier, "had so many talented godfathers monitoring her debut."

When the manuscript of *Claudine at School* was finished (and contrary to what Colette would later have the world believe, it was improved and refined by her husband), Willy shopped it around to several publishers, none of whom would have anything to do with it. It then went, indeed, into a cupboard, but emerged not because Willy underwent a conversion about its value and a stunned recognition of his own stupidity but because his flair for timing told him that the public was ready for the raunchy, definitely modern Claudine.

Claudine, whom Thurman has dubbed "the century's first teenage girl," was a harbinger of the world to come. If we look at the year 1900 as a parting of the waters, commented writer and critic Armand Lanoux in 1961, we can see that "with Colette, one is on our shore, just as with Maupassant one is still on the banks of the Second Empire." The robust Colette had been an anomaly in the hothouse atmosphere of 1890s decadence, but with the advancing twentieth century Colette had found her moment—or Willy had found it for her.

Claudine at School was published in March 1900 under Willy's name, not so much because he sought to steal her glory as because both thought it best: Achille Colette had just married into the aristocracy, and something as risqué as *Claudine at School* would not have gone down well with his new in-laws. There was not much initial interest in the novel, but it took off after Willy urged some well-placed friends to write about it. Eventually it became one of France's all-time best-sellers.

Willy milked the success for all it was worth, pioneering the marketing spin-off that has become commonplace today: there were soon Claudine collars, lotion, ice cream, hats, cigarettes, perfume, candies. Every whorehouse in Paris had its resident Claudine. The play, starring the stage phenomenon Polaire, was a smash hit. And Willy titillated public imagination by parading around Paris with Polaire and Colette (now going by the name of Colette Willy), dressed identically as Claudine the schoolgirl. Colette was soon churning out sequels: *Claudine in Paris* (1901), *Claudine Married* (1902), and *Claudine Takes Off* (1903). Willy's name still appeared on the cover, but the couple's friends and acquaintances were made aware of the truth: Colette's authorship was soon "an open secret."

Willy had never been a faithful husband. When Colette first caught him out in an affair—with the *demimondaine* Charlotte Kinceler—she was in an agony of pain and jealousy. The way she chose to cope was one she would repeat throughout her life: she co-opted Charlotte as her own friend. Soon she herself was turning to others for solace, especially other women. In all of her early lesbian affairs Willy not only offered no resistance but was positively encouraging, boosting his jaded libido with voyeurism and threesomes. While Colette later succeeded in covering up most of her lesbian adventures, the number of her feminine conquests was in fact legion.

The most serious of her many girlfriends was the Marquise de Morny, called "Missy," a great-niece of Napoleon III; "her family tree was a resplendent genealogy of illegitimate nobility," say Francis and Gontier. Missy was extremely masculine, dressing almost exclusively in men's clothes. She was very rich, generous and well-bred to a fault, vulnerable and emotionally needy. She soon became "an easy pawn in the intricate game played by Colette and Willy to launch Colette's career."

In 1905, not long after Colette met Missy, she and Willy signed a *séparation des biens,* a legal division of property preliminary to a divorce. Not that the couple appeared to be splitting up; they would continue to live together for a year, maintain frequently passionate relations until 1908, and collaborate after that. Thurman suggests that this was in fact a divorce "of convenience," that Colette could now launder money for the debt-plagued Willy, receiving fees for their collaborations and passing them on. At about the same time Colette embarked on a second career that would prove lucrative and infinitely gratifying to her: the stage.

She started out taking roles in amateur pantomimes staged privately by her wealthy lesbian friends; she so enjoyed the experience that she soon was planning a professional career. She took lessons with the well-known mime Georges Wague and in 1906 made her professional debut, clad in a skimpy tunic, in *L'Amour, le Désir, la Chimère.* Thurman sums up Colette's new choice of career as a radical *geste:* "a complex act of revolt, sexual dissidence, and self-assertion, in which the courage and idealism of a revolutionary were mixed with an adolescent's rage, glee, egotism" (though Colette was by now no adolescent but a woman in her thirties). The vehicles she chose— artsy yet naughty—confirm this opinion. *Rêve d'Egypte* (written by Willy and Wague), in which Colette, as a fleshy and seductive mummy, appeared opposite Missy as the (male) archaeologist who passionately embraces her, caused a hullabaloo so tremendous that it must have gratified even the publicity-happy Colette—though poor Missy was horrified.

By this time Willy had found a replacement for Colette, Meg Villars, and he and Colette were conducting a very noisy, public divorce—though relations between them were as complicated as ever: they even repaired to the beach for a holiday, with Colette and Missy in one house, and Meg and Willy installed next door. In fact Colette and Willy were still a couple, and they made lavish use of Missy's money, influence, and notoriety for all they were worth, a fact of which Missy was dismally aware, writing reproachfully to Willy that "When you put Colette in my arms—which you did completely!—I saw what you wanted, and I didn't flinch, though I could see ahead to what might happen to all three of us. I thus don't merit the reproaches of Colette, who is an impulsive child without much moral feeling, but that certainly isn't her fault!"

Colette's stage career throve: even if, as some of her contemporaries suggested, she wasn't a great performer, she was certainly a great sex symbol, and everyone flocked to see the scandalous Madame Willy. Although she was by now living conjugally with Missy, she continued her ambiguous and frequently passionate relationship with Willy until, strapped for cash, he sold the copyrights to the *Claudine* books in 1907 without consulting her. Her rage knew no bounds— though, contrary to what she led the world to believe, she quickly negotiated an agreement with the publishers and continued to receive royalties for the books; she also succeeded in having her name put on them. From this point on, Willy became more her enemy than her partner in crime, and she would whittle away at his reputation until finally, four years after his death, she got her full revenge with her vicious, libelous portrait of him in *My Apprenticeships*.

In 1910 Colette published *The Vagabond,* a thinly disguised account of her life as a touring actress. It contained a brutal portrait of Willy as an adulterer and artistic fake, a blow that caused him to seek immediate revenge, announcing to the press that he would publish a novel called *Sidonie: or the Perverted Peasant.* (One of the unexpected charms of these books is that it is impossible not to like Willy; he may have been a cynic and a user, but at least he made a worthy opponent.) *Sidonie* was only a joke, but in 1911 he did strike back with *Les Imprudences de Peggy* (published under the name of Meg Villars), which portrayed his ex-wife, in Thurman's words, as "a predatory dyke of forty with a fat behind and a childish pout worked on assiduously in front of the mirror." Colette, abetted by her family, now began circulating rumors that Willy had murdered Germaine Servat.

In 1911 Colette, working as a columnist for *Le Matin,* met and fell in love with the paper's co-editor-in-chief, Henry Bertrand Léon Robert, baron de Jouvenel des Ursins. It was a *coup de foudre.* Jouvenel was still married to his first wife, Claire Boas; he had a son by her and another, illegitimate one by Isabelle de Comminges, Renaud. With Jouvenel finally divorced, he and Colette were married on December 18, 1912, just before her fortieth birthday. Their daughter, Colette Renée—to whom they gave Colette's own childhood nickname of Bel-Gazou—was born in July 1913.

Colette was an appalling mother. "Not only would there never be any contest," writes Thurman; "there would never be any balance between her own well-being and that of her child. Colette and her daughter only lived under the same roof for the odd month in summer. Bel-Gazou was raised at Castel-Nouvel [the Jouvenel estate] by her English nanny, and sometimes half a year would pass without a parental visit. The wild and lonely little girl was sent to boarding school at eight, and when she reached adolescence, farmed out to various women friends who acted as Colette's surrogates."

It is in trying to come to terms with Colette's treatment of Bel-Gazou that Thurman's determination to like Colette is stretched to the breaking point. Francis and Gontier have no such qualms; they take the arrogant, defensive woman that Bel-Gazou—Colette de Jouvenel—became and seem to draw the conclusion that she brought her problems on herself. Colette's own letters, though, tell a different story: it is nauseating to hear the mother rave about the ungratefulness and ignorance of the adolescent daughter. At the same age she herself, she stresses, was erudite and capable. Possibly; but if so, it was because she had a mother to teach her, an advantage poor Bel-Gazou couldn't claim.

With the outbreak of World War I, Henry de Jouvenel joined the infantry as a sergeant and departed to the front. Colette made a halfhearted effort to contribute to the war effort, signing up as a volunteer night nurse. The romantic legend of Colette the nurse has endured, but in fact she stuck to the dull routine less than a week, leaving, at that point, to join her husband at Verdun. From there she wrote firsthand reports for *Le Matin*. "She is the rare writer of her stature," Thurman comments, "who never revolts against the horror, the folly, and the arrogance of World War I, and whose view of human nature is not profoundly blackened by her experience. . . . Even in her letters, she experiences and describes the war with a lyrical exuberance." Thurman excuses this apparent blindness by saying it is "likely that Colette feigns lightheartedness out of patriotism and to keep up the morale of her readers." This seems a weak excuse for a refusal to countenance suffering that she displayed not only during the First World War but during the Second as well, and indeed throughout her life. Pain, illness, sorrow, disfigurement all repelled her, and she turned her back on them resolutely and finally. If there was a scrap of glory to be found in an inglorious slaughter, she would find it and ignore the rest. It is part and parcel with the "disgust" for "mortal frailty" that Thurman detects elsewhere, the cure for which is inevitably to "eat and thrive."

Almost immediately, Henry de Jouvenel proved an unsatisfactory mate. He was a compulsive womanizer who had no intention of curtailing his tomcatting for any wife, however formidable. When he returned to *Le Matin* at the end of the war, the couple led increasingly separate lives. Colette survived and throve. She befriended Henry's chief *amour*, the couturière Germaine Patat, signed on as chief drama critic for *Le Matin*, and began work in 1919 on the novel that would be her masterpiece: *Chéri*, the story of a *demimondaine* in her late forties, Lea, and her love affair with Chéri, a nineteen-year-old boy. "For the first time in my life I felt morally certain of having written a novel for which I need neither blush nor doubt," Colette wrote, and she was right: *Chéri*, with its sequel *The Last of Chéri*, contains all the passion with which she was, in her work as in her life, so profligate, tempered by a measure of delicacy that is not always as evident.

Chéri had been half-serialized in *La Vie Parisienne* when Henry's ex-wife, Claire Boas, sent her sixteen-year-old son Bertrand to Colette on a mission: to persuade the current baronne de Jouvenel to allow her, Claire, to continue using the same title. "Either Claire's strategy was remarkably cynical or it was mythically unconscious," Thurman writes. "Beauty's father acted in the same way when he sent his daughter to the Beast's mansion." Colette, who had never been allowed to meet Bertrand before, was delighted, and she soon drew the pretty young fellow into her orbit. She invited him to her house in Brittany where, alone with Colette and two of her equally avid women friends, he felt uncomfortable under the predatory scrutiny of this "coven." In the event it was Colette herself who initiated him.

According to Bertrand, Colette was "demanding, voracious, expert, and rewarding"; he continued to love her and defend her all his life. The affair lasted five years, and since in middle age Colette was no more discreet than she had been in youth, it created a scandal throughout Paris and threatened Henry's otherwise flourishing political career. It eventually caused the final breakup of the Jouvenels' marriage, a catastrophe for which Colette, rather incredibly, refused to take the rap: "If one must be punished for loving, for loving too simply and too diversely at the same time, I will thus be punished. Nothing remains to me except to be someone who has never acted in her own best interest, and who has never known a greedy passion except one: to cherish."

The audacity takes one's breath away. The angle provided by Henry de Jouvenel's secretary, though, many years later, tells a truer story. Revenge against Jouvenel's infidelity had to have been a motivating factor, he said. Also, he stressed, Colette was above all a *provocatrice*: "She belonged to the first generation of twentieth-century revolutionaries. That revolution was as much if not more intellectual than it was erotic. The more fundamental a taboo, the better to defy it." And not least, there was her irrepressible love of drama. "Her whole life was a theater piece, you know, and *Phèdre* is a classic French role."

Twice divorced, fifty years old, her legendary sexual powers at last on the wane, it seemed as though Colette's love life might now suffer; but at this crucial moment in her life it was her good fortune—or more probably, a manifestation of her powerful gift for self-preservation—to meet a man who would provide the single-hearted devotion she had never received from (or given to) anyone, and who would stick with her for the rest of her life.

Maurice Goudeket was fifteen years her junior, a Dutch-Jewish pearl merchant, intelligent and cultivated, and something of a loner. Their romance began slowly but gathered steam, and by 1931 they were living in adjoining suites at Paris's Claridge Hotel. Thurman describes Colette's love for Goudeket as "profoundly reparative": "His constancy gradually disarms her mistrust. He enjoys her bullying, but they make a game of it—becoming partners and playmates rather than victim and oppressor."

Goudeket's worth was not always evident to her friends. He had to endure endless snobbery as an "obscure Jewish upstart who sold jewelry and aspired to the place in Colette's life once filled by the brilliant Willy, the noble Missy, and the powerful Jouvenel." But

Goudeket had staying power while the others were already retreating into the past. Willy (who for some years had been referring to himself as "the late Willy," to Colette as "my widow"), died in 1931, Henry de Jouvenel four years later. The always depressive Missy shot herself in 1945.

Colette and Goudeket were made of tougher stuff. When the combination of the stock market crash and Chanel's popularization of costume jewelry destroyed the pearl market, the bankrupt Goudeket went to work selling washing machines and toilet plungers; soon he and Colette were embarked on a madcap scheme to start a line of salons and beauty products, with Goudeket running the business end and Colette squeezing the backing out of her rich buddies and providing in notoriety what she lacked in the beautician's arts. The enterprise was a flop, and so, as even Colette had to admit, was her attempt to return to the stage: after watching the aging star in a revival of *The Vagabond*, Natalie Barney dryly commented: "A Vagabond indeed, a walking pedestal topped with a tiny triangle of a face, compactly plump, with an octoroon complexion and the air of an owl in broad daylight."

But as the years went on the couple prospered. They were married in 1935 after ten years together. Goudeket successfully took to journalism, and Colette, secure in his affections, continued the remarkably productive streak that had begun in 1925 with *Chéri*. *The Last of Chéri* was published in 1926; *Break of Day* in 1927; *Sido*, a dishonest but lyrically powerful memoir, in 1930; the treacherous *My Apprenticeships* in 1936. With *La Chatte* (1933), *Duo* (1934), and *Bella-Vista* (1936) she began the exploration of the novella form that would occupy most of the rest of her professional life. During this busy time she was as prolific a journalist as ever, if not more so: among her many other accomplishments, Colette was one of the finest drama critics of her generation.

World War II and the Occupation saw Goudeket, as a Jew, terribly threatened. He was interned in a detention camp at Compiègne for seven weeks in 1941 and 1942, and spent the rest of the war years in and out of hiding. Colette, who turned seventy in 1943, was crippled by arthritis. Still, her work continued to go well; she put out eight books during the course of the war, including two of her most popular works, *The Pure and the Impure* and *Gigi*. Her equanimity about publishing in *P.P.*, *Gringoire*, *La Gerbe*, and Charles Maurras's *Candide*, some of the most virulently pro-Vichy and anti-Semitic journals of the era, is hard to defend, especially when we consider that Bel-Gazou and her half-brother, Renaud, were risking their lives in the Resistance; so is her bitchy novel *Julie de Carneilhan*, a revenge piece against the father of her daughter that resonates with the unsavory political and racial attitudes of Vichy France. If we choose to be generous about Colette and her motivations (and there is no reason we should), we can, like one friend, see her as belonging "to that herd of passive collaborationists who were legion. As the balance of the war began to shift, so did the proportion of those who actively supported the Allies and the Free French forces. But they changed their allegiance out of prudence, because Germany was losing, and not from conviction."

Whatever the rationale, Colette miraculously emerged from the war with her reputation unscathed. In 1945 she was elected to the Académie Goncourt, becoming its president four years later. With the postwar reestablishment of Paris as the center of world culture, Colette gained an international public and became what she has been known as ever since, a sort of personification of *la France*, a literary Marianne. By the time of her death, in 1954, she was a national monument, and received the only state funeral the Republic had ever given to a woman. Maurice Goudeket was with her to the end. Several years later he remarried, fathering a son at the age of seventy-one. He died in 1977.

The perusal of these two rich biographies, whatever their occasional lapses of judgment, taste, and reason, gives an intensely detailed picture of a dramatic and often contradictory life. The Colette that emerges is a far cry from the romantic slave of passion created, to a very large degree, by Colette herself. The real Colette was a supremely selfish, greedy, ruthless, and often ridiculous woman. It is hard to like her much; it is even harder, though, not to admire the brute force with which she grabbed everything she wanted from life, just as one cannot but admire the talent that capricious Nature bestowed, as is so often the case, on a very unlikely recipient. "Neither a great heart nor a great mind," as Thurman pertinently reflects, quoting Laforgue on Baudelaire; "and yet what plaintive nerves, what nostrils open to everything, what a magic voice."

[*2000*]

A Socialist Rivalry:
H. G. Wells and
George Bernard Shaw

*H*orace Walpole claimed that the world is a comedy to those who think, a tragedy to those who feel. The story of George Bernard Shaw and H. G. Wells could be aptly summed up in the dichotomy: Shaw was the thinking man *par excellence,* whose emotional detachment made him seem diabolically cold-blooded to many of his contemporaries, including Wells, while Wells was a man who hardly knew the meaning of the word "detachment"; his intellect, impressive though it was, could always be overruled by his intense emotions.

The two men met at the disastrous premiere of Henry James's play *Guy Domville,* in January 1895. Shaw, thirty-eight years old, was one of London's foremost critics as well as a well-known playwright. Wells, ten years younger, was relatively unknown, but he was poised for an imminent flight to superstardom: *The Time Machine* would appear in May of that year.

That evening saw the beginning of a fifty-year association between the two men that for want of a better word has been called a friendship, though the protagonists' characters were so opposed, their egos so voracious, that they could as easily be considered enemies as friends. They both used their considerable supplies of charm to conceal the extent of their mutual hostility from their public, each other, and even themselves, and the diverting history of their relations can now be followed in a welcome edition of the great men's correspondence, edited by J. Percy Smith.

"The idea must not get around that the Wellsians and Shavians have any differences," Shaw wrote to Wells in old age. "They are in fact the same body." But Shaw was a master of bluff. From 1903, when Wells joined the Fabian Society (of which Shaw had been a member practically since its beginning in 1884), until Wells's death in 1946, the two men struggled for the symbolic leadership of the English socialist movement. To their contemporaries, Wells and Shaw represented very different faces of socialism, and with Shaw's incomparable gift of rhetoric and Wells's of energy, they established the pattern for the two competing strains that are still at odds within British socialism: Shaw, with his comrades-in-arms Sidney and Beatrice Webb, stood for the bureaucratic strain, Wells for the libertarian one, to use a distinction Michael Foot makes in his new biography of Wells, *H. G.*, a study as worshipful as Michael Coren's 1992 biography was derogatory, and therefore equally unreliable.

Shaw had staked everything on the essential Fabian principles of historical process, gradualism, and the organic "permeation" of English society. Indeed, he had practically invented them. Wells took a different approach: he believed quite simply in revolution. He became a Fabian with the express intention of taking over the Society and boldly asserting his own revolutionary aims, and for that he had the mandate of the younger and more radical members. Where the Old Gang—Shaw, the Webbs, Hubert Bland, Edward Pease, Sydney Olivier—were middle-aged, Wells, if not in his own first youth, stood for Youth all over the world. Storm Jameson later described the extraordinary effect Wells had upon her contemporaries: "He formed a whole generation, throwing himself at us in a rage of energy, overwhelming us with his ideas, some absurd, all explosively liberating.

Unlike Bernard Shaw, who did no more than instruct and amuse us, he changed our lives."

Wells began his attack on the Fabians with a public assault on an economic tract of Shaw's, to which the older man responded with characteristic bravado. "Nothing can be more improbable than that I am wrong," Shaw wrote to his critic: "still, even I am not absolutely infallible; and as you are an interesting youth, I may as well hear what babble you may have to offer."

Wells was aware of his value to an organization whose genteel brand of socialism was beginning to be perceived as less than thrilling, and he was determined to make his attacks on the Society matters of public debate, with himself cast in the role of Young Turk. Soon he was talking of throwing all the Society's carefully evolved theories "into the dustbin," and in early 1906 he delivered a paper, "Faults of the Fabians," a devastating attack on the Old Gang's discreet methods.

> We don't advertise, thank you, it's not quite our style. We cry Socialism as the reduced gentlewoman cried oranges—I do so hope no one will hear me. . . .
>
> You know this cryptic socialism is not a little reminiscent of the mouse that set out to kill the cat; violent methods were deprecated. . . . The mouse decided to adopt indirect and inconspicuous methods, not to complicate its proceedings by too many associates, to win over and attract the cat by friendly advances rather than frighten her by a sudden attack. It is believed that in the end the mouse did succeed in permeating the cat, but the cat is still living and the mouse can't be found.

Clearly shaken, Beatrice Webb resorted to the traditional English ploy of invoking class snobbery when bested, explaining that "this is absolutely the first time he has tried to co-operate with his fellow men—and he has neither tradition nor training to fit him to do it. It is a case of 'Kipps' in matters more important than table manners."

Shaw was a wilier customer. He was as determined to keep these Fabian fissures private as Wells was to force them into the open, for he believed deeply in the creed of gradualism, the principle that social change must occur as an organic process rather than a sudden disturbance. He also knew, however, that a number of Wells's points were well taken and that Wells himself, with his tremendous following, was an invaluable asset to the Fabians. He must be kept in his place as a vital but subordinate member of the team. "Generally speaking," Shaw wrote to him, "you must identify yourself frankly with us, and not play the critical outsider and the satirist. We are all very clever; and long ago we have come to understand that we must not play our cleverness off against one another for the mere fun of it."

Wells was pleased by the consternation he had wrought. He quickly followed up his parry with a thrust, a caustic tract called "The Misery of Boots," in which he sneered at the Fabians and their methods. Again, Shaw played the diplomat.

> The whole thing is so ridiculous that if you once let your mind turn from your political object to criticism of the conduct and personality of the men around you, you are lost. Instantly you find them insufferable; they find you the same; and the problem of how to get rid of one another supersedes Socialism, to the great advantage of the capitalist. . . . You must, in short, learn your business as a propagandist and peripatetic philosopher if you are ever to be anything more than a novelist bombinating in vacuo except for a touch of reality gained in your early life.

At Shaw's urging, Wells stood for the executive of the Society and was elected in March 1907. Predictably Wells and his supporters pushed for the Fabians to take a far more active role in the political life of the nation and to seek a large membership across class lines rather than to maintain their current identity as an elite cadre of intellectuals. Shaw argued the Old Gang's purpose. "We have absolutely nothing but our ideas to offer; and to sell them in exchange for votes & subscriptions is 'the idea of gain' at its maddest. If you want a party, there are three or four to choose from; and we hope to see another—a Socialist one—formed."

In the event, when it came to hand-to-hand combat with Shaw, Wells never stood a chance. The history of their relations was to be one of perpetual frustration for the younger man. The battle was in many ways unequal. Shaw had honed his skills as a debater and a rhetorician to a level that few have ever reached; Wells was physically unprepossessing, Cockney, a mediocre public speaker. But what fatally handicapped him was the very same ungovernable passion that made him such an attractive figure. He loved, he hated, he felt. He found it impossible to keep his temper while Shaw repressed his, disguising venom as light sarcasm. Frank Harris spoke of Shaw's "exasperating patience"; he never lost his cool. He defeated Wells by provoking bursts of uncontrolled rage and then behaving like a tolerant adult with a fractious child, tut-tutting about the little one's nasty temper. "I seem to spend my life rescuing the victims of your outrageous onslaughts and seeming to remonstrate with you and make fun of you whilst I have to boost you subtly all the time."

Shaw was victorious against Wells and innumerable lesser opponents in this kind of intellectual gamesmanship largely because of his own unassailable self-control, which Wells was canny enough to recognize as being in fact not so much self-control as lack of appetite. Wells described himself as "a biologist first and foremost," Shaw as having "a physiological disgust at vital activities." This distinction goes far toward accounting for the balance of power between the two: the man who thinks holds a distinct advantage over the man whose body and emotions prevail.

It was Wells's exotic sex life that finally cooked his goose with the more conventional Fabians. He had long advocated complete freedom between the sexes and derided the institution of bourgeois marriage; he preached free love and he practiced it. The Fabians reluctantly tolerated Wells's peccadilloes until he invaded their own turf by trying to elope with Hubert Bland's daughter Rosamund. Shaw, apparently, was moved to remonstrate, and Wells blasted him.

> The more I think you over the more it comes home to me what an unmitigated middle-Victorian ass you are. You play about with ideas like a daring garrulous maiden aunt, but when it comes to an affair like the Bland affair you show the instincts of conscious gentility and the judgement of a hen. . . . The fact is yours is a flimsy intellectual acquisitive sort of mind adrift & chattering brightly in a world you don't understand. You dont know, as I do, in blood & substance, lust, failure, shame, hate, love, and creative passion. You don't understand & you cant understand the rights & wrongs of the case into which you stick your maiden judgement—any more than you can understand the aims of the Fabian Society that your vanity has wrecked.

This is a letter few friendships, or even professional associations, could withstand, but Shaw accepted the rebuke with his customary sangfroid. Little more than a year later Wells offended again, in a far more serious manner, with another Fabian daughter, Amber Reeves. (Their affair resulted in Amber's pregnancy, and is recounted faithfully in Wells's 1909 novel *Ann Veronica,* a shocking and notorious book in its day.) Shaw, who actually was quite nonjudgmental in sexual matters, came to the lovers' defense, and Wells smothered him with gratitude as passionate as the abuse he had heaped on him the previous year. "Occasionally," Wells wrote, "you don't simply rise to a difficult situation but soar above it and I withdraw anything you would like withdrawn from our correspondence of the last two years or so."

Wells stayed married to his Jane, and the pregnant Amber was married off to Blanco White, a young Fabian who generously volunteered to bring up the child as his own. Thus ended Wells's alliance with the Fabians, though he was to aim a final blow at them in his 1910 novel *The New Machiavelli*. But Wells and Shaw continued their association: if anything, they became rather friendlier once they were no longer competing for Fabian turf. A certain distance was maintained, but they acknowledged that in a general sense they were allies, and they kept up a tenuous friendship aided by the fact that each man was genuinely fond of the other's wife.

As Wells passed into his fifties, sixties, and seventies, Shaw's pose continued to be that of the sage lecturing the importunate youth. Characteristic was the advice he offered Wells on how to speak in public.

When you first spoke at a Fabian meeting, I told you to hold up your head & speak to the bracketed bust of Selwyn Image on the back wall. To shew that you were not going to be taught by me, you made the commonest blunder of the tyro: you insisted on having a table; leaning over it on your knuckles; and addressing the contents of your contracted chest to the tablecloth. I will now, having tried to cure you of that by fair means in vain, cure you of it by a blow beneath the belt. Where did you get that attitude? IN THE SHOP. At the New Reform Club, when your knuckles touched the cloth, you said unconsciously, by reflex action, "Anything else today, madam," and later on "What's the next article?" Fortunately, you were inaudible, thanks to the attitude. Now I swear that the next time you take that attitude in my presence I will ask you for a farthing paper of pins. I will make a decent public man of you yet, and an effective public speaker, if I have to break your heart in the process.

Though they had a common faith in socialism (Wells spoke of socialism as "the form and substance of my ideal life, and all the religion I possess"), Shaw and Wells took opposing positions on other fraught questions of the period. Shaw was a Marxist and a Stalinist, while Wells deplored both creeds. Wells was a disciple of Darwin and

Huxley, while Shaw, who believed that Darwin had banished intelligence from the universe, had concocted for himself a bizarre faith that he dubbed "Creative Evolution," ruled by a mysterious "Life Force." Shaw distrusted scientists and abhorred vivisection, while Wells was a trained biologist with an unshakable faith in scientific method.

Though Shaw was consistently the superior polemicist, many of his theories were clearly untenable or absurd, and Wells dealt with them accordingly. "These doctors all think that science is knowledge," wrote Shaw, "instead of being the very opposite of knowledge: to wit, speculation"; to which Wells answered shortly, "Science is neither knowledge nor speculation. It is criticism ending in wisdom." As to Shaw's claims to be qualified to make scientific judgments, Wells was openly scornful. He accused Shaw of talking about biology "like a bright girl at a dinner party." "Your phrase . . . of the 'Life Force' embodies an almost encyclopaedic philosophical and biological ignorance."

In the interests of socialist solidarity the two men agreed to disagree on subjects from the Third International to votes for women to the conduct of World Wars I and II; relations remained more or less cordial, and in a half-admiring, half-annoyed note to Shaw, Wells described him as a "mixture of inspiration, deliberate wisdom and a kind of amiable quackery." It is as good a thumbnail sketch of Shaw as any that has been attempted. But the hostile feelings that had been aroused during the Fabian days had never died. When Wells's long-suffering but beloved wife, Jane, was diagnosed as having incurable cancer, Shaw jumped into the abyss with a bouncing, abrasive optimism and a barrage of pseudo-medical nonsense that Wells, trying to cope with his bitter grief, was not able to forgive.

Charlotte Shaw attempted to intervene with all the tact her husband so sorely lacked. "Please H.G. don't be angry with him. You know he is like that—he must sometimes let himself go in this aggravating way—& he means it all so more than well! He is very fond of you & Jane." But for Wells it amounted to the final straw. The two men continued to be cordial until Wells's own death eighteen years later, but any real warmth, at least on Wells's part, was gone.

In their letters to each other Shaw and Wells, for all their differences, were mutually generous and appreciative. The obituaries they wrote for one another at the behest of enterprising newspaper editors—documents that each could be sure the other would not read—tell a different story. Shaw wrote about Wells for *The New Statesman* immediately after Wells died in August 1946; it was breezy and charming but not entirely friendly, claiming, among other things, that Wells was "the most completely spoiled child I have ever known," his youth a story of "early promotion from the foot of the ladder to the top without a single failure or check"—a patently untrue statement. A private letter in which Shaw responded to the proposal of a memorial fellowship to promote Wells's ideas went further.

> What were his specific ideas? Those which took any practical form, the division of our absurd local government areas into planned regions, the tank, the radio-active bomb, need no promotion. His declaration of Human Rights was not a step in advance of Jefferson and Tom Paine 175 years ago, and left him in despair. He chalked up many ideas, but ran away from them when anyone proposed to put them into practice. He attacked his best friends at home and abroad furiously, denouncing Fabianism and Marxism, the Webbs and Stalin, recklessly. Finally his spleen made him, though once the most readable and inspiring of authors, almost unreadable and very discouraging.

Wells had written an obituary of Shaw in 1945, and it appeared in *The Daily Express* upon Shaw's death five years later. Though the essay begins genially, it quickly develops into a document of rage, exposing all the fury that Shaw with his "exasperating patience" had in life managed to deflect. Shaw, he wrote, was ruled by a naked, unqualified, ego-centered, devouring vanity, such as one rarely meets in life. . . . Apparently he could not think of any other human being, and particularly any outstanding and famous human being, without immediately referring it directly to himself. . . .

One method of his self-assertion was portraiture. The number of pictures, busts and portraits that encumbered Shaw's establishment was extraordinary. I used to imagine some great convulsion of nature making a new Herculaneum of London. As one art treasure was disinterred after another, the world would come to believe that for a time London was populated entirely by a race of men with a strong physical likeness to the Etruscans—men with potato noses and a flamboyant bearing.

That was one method of self-assertion peculiar to Shaw. Another, more general, has been practised since Homo sapiens began his career, and that is to inflict pain.

Wells had long discerned that Shaw used a theatrical mock vanity to conceal a vanity that was only too real. It is one of the more serious indictments against Shaw, and it is unarguable. But if the truth be told, neither Shaw nor Wells, for all their great qualities and their immeasurable contributions to the cause of intellectual liberty, will go down in history as a model of humility.

[*1995*]

Edith Wharton and the Rejection of Tradition

Edith Wharton counted her friendship with Henry James as the crown jewel of her career, but it just might have been a curse. During her lifetime she was labeled, inaccurately, as a disciple of James, an apprentice who inevitably fell short of the Master. After her death she has continued to be compared with him, never to her own advantage. Like her contemporary Georges Braque, she always comes in a poor second.

Wharton idolized James, to be sure, but she had a real sense of her own power as an author and of her artistic strengths, which were not his, and she chafed at the persistent coupling of her name with her friend's. "The continued cry that I am an echo of Mr. James (whose books of the last ten years I can't read, much as I delight in the man) . . . makes me feel rather hopeless," she complained in 1904. It is true that the two writers had some obvious points in common: they were both upper-crust, East Coast Americans who tended to write about their own kind; they both transplanted themselves to Europe in middle age but continued to be obsessed with their native country, despising its narrow culture but never ceasing to be haunted by its crude beauties.

Still, the differences between Wharton and James were more marked than the similarities. Many of James's tics and foibles, attractive to some readers and alienating to others, displeased his "disciple" and were avoided by her. Unlike James, Wharton was never precious or arch, and she usually preferred the straight route to the circuitous one. Her style is more decided, more "masculine," perhaps, than his. And she instinctively rejected his obsession with fictional structure, which she felt was too often achieved at the expense of truth and life.

> His latest novels, for all their profound moral beauty, seemed to me more and more lacking an atmosphere, more and more severed from that thick nourishing human air in which we all live and move. . . . [H]is stage was cleared like that of the Theatre Français in the good old days when no chair or table was introduced that was not *relevant to the action.*

No one could accuse Wharton of isolating her characters in such a rarefied atmosphere. She was expert, by nature and by training, at sensing the exact significance of every external detail. Each of her characters has his place within an intricate social web; each is circumscribed within a physical setting that tells us a great deal about who he is—or, just as often, who he is not. Here, for instance, is a woman who has just discovered that her second marriage, like her first, is failing:

> Her eyes wandered about the familiar drawing-room which had been the scene of so many of their evening confidences. The shaded lamps, the quiet-colored walls hung with mezzotints, the pale spring flowers scattered here and there in Venice glasses and bowls of old Sèvres, recalled, she hardly knew why, the apartment in which the evenings of her first marriage had been passed—a wilderness of rosewood and upholstery, with a picture of a Roman peasant above the mantelpiece, and a Greek slave in "statuary marble" between the folding-doors of the back drawing-room. It was a room with which she had never been

able to establish any closer relation than that between a traveler and a railway station; and now, as she looked about at the surroundings which stood for her deepest affinities—the room for which she had left that other room—she was startled by the same sense of strangeness and unfamiliarity. The prints, the flowers, the subdued tones of the old porcelains, seemed to typify a superficial refinement which had no relation to the deeper significance of life.

This is an exquisite example of emotional shorthand. So is a moment in Wharton's story "The Other Two" (1904), where a man meeting his wife's first husband is struck not so much by his person as by one particular garment: "It was grotesquely uppermost in Waythorn's mind that Haskett had worn a made-up tie attached with an elastic. Why should that ridiculous detail symbolize the whole man? Waythorn was exasperated by his own paltriness, but the fact of the tie expanded, forced itself on him, became as it were the key to Alice's past."

The very skill with which Wharton could give a garment or an object psychological meaning has to some extent told against her: for some readers, she is the supreme poet of decor, a second-rate art if indeed it qualifies as art at all. To this type of reader, the fact that she was a worldly woman—more than worldly: a grande dame, a châtelaine, the author of a perennially popular book on interior decoration—make her automatically suspect. What's more, she was a fluent, facile writer, the author of numerous best-sellers. Again the contrast with James, the prototypical ivory-tower, temple-of-art man, is unavoidable.

But the fact is that Wharton was one of the most important American writers, and she was important "during a period," as Edmund Wilson pointed out after her death, "say, 1905–1917—when there were few American writers worth reading." What is more, her books do not date. That fact is hard to account for, since her two best novels,

The House of Mirth and *The Age of Innocence*, deal largely with codes of manners that were already dead or dying when she wrote about them. Indeed, by the beginning of World War I, "what had seemed unalterable rules of conduct" in Wharton's nineteenth-century youth had already become, as she put it, "as quaintly arbitrary as the domestic rites of the Pharaohs." But even now, when all rules of conduct have apparently been thrown to the winds, the books work: they have an interior logic and an emotional coherence that utterly convince.

Yet it is true that Wharton never became a "great" writer on the level of James. It was not her intelligence that fell short, nor her descriptive powers, her humor, her command of the language. Perhaps her limitations lay essentially in the darkness of her vision; she showed life's tragedy and its deadening compromises but very seldom its corresponding and essential beauty. There is humor and a healthy respect for sensual pleasure in her work but no joy, no sublimity, no God, not even anything that could qualify as a God-substitute.

Not that beauty is not present in Wharton's fiction: it is everywhere, it positively palpitates; but Wharton mistrusts it. No one who has read *The Age of Innocence*, for example, can forget the description of May Welland and the other Newport *belles* pulling back their bows in the annual archery competition. May's iridescence, though, is a negative quality, her purity a blankness that deflects rather than absorbs love and life. It is uncompromised ignorance rather than compromised knowledge. Thus the tarnished Ellen Olenska is capable of moral beauty, while the untarnished May is not.

When we look beneath the high surface gloss of Wharton's world, we see a marketplace, pure and simple. Hers is an almost purely economic conception of life: every good thing has its price, and the greater the good, the higher the price. The vast majority of us are unwilling to pay for our happiness and must make do with the unappetizing leftovers that are all we feel we can afford. "Life is not a matter of abstract principles," she wrote in her 1907 novel *The Fruit of the Tree*, "but a succession of pitiful compromises with fate, of concessions to old traditions, old beliefs, old tragedies, old failures." It is a hopeless creed, some might say a cynical one.

There is a good reason why Wharton's great subject turned out to be the world of her youth, the rigidly stratified society of "old New York" and its invasion by the new industrial fortunes of the late nineteenth and early twentieth centuries. Its complicated social code provided a series of rules which were both inflexible and, as Wharton noted, perfectly arbitrary; to break them, in other words, was a matter not only of moral strength but of being able to make the imaginative leap—to conceive of American society and its code as what it was, a small and rather absurd corner of a large and infinitely interesting world. The tragedy does not lie in the fact that a Newland Archer or a Lily Bart gives up a chance of love and freedom, but in the worthlessness and futility of what they choose instead: in Archer's case, an enveloping nullity that is personal as well as social; in Lily's, a luxurious, degrading servitude. (Although in the end Lily, of course, proved herself a little too good for that life by passively rejecting it.)

The consensus seems to be that Wharton mellowed as she aged, and that by the time she wrote *The Age of Innocence* (1920) and her memoir, *A Backward Glance* (1934), she had come to regret the lost world of her youth. The citation that is usually trotted out in support of this theory is from *A Backward Glance:* "When I was young it used to seem to me that the group in which I grew up was like an empty vessel into which no new wine would ever again be poured. Now I see that one of its uses lay in preserving a few drops of an old vintage too rare to be savored by a youthful palate; and I should like to atone for my unappreciativeness by trying to revive that faint fragrance."

If nostalgia there was, however, it was about one part nostalgia to ten parts rage and disgust. Looked at carefully, *The Age of Innocence* is hard to see as anything but a blistering indictment of a repressive and mediocre society whose denizens sacrificed their young to the same ossified standards that had blighted their own lives: a world where "'bad manners' were the supreme offense"; literature was avoided out of "an awe-struck dread of the intellectual effort that might be required" in its perusal; there was "a blind dread of innovation, an instinctive shrinking from responsibility"; and "even the acquiring of money had ceased to interest." Ellen Olenska, who is strong, leaves New York for Paris (as Wharton herself had done); Newland Archer, who is weak, stays, and over the years dwindles into a sad sort of half-person. In reading Wharton's description of her father, who died when she was twenty, it is impossible not to recognize one source for Archer: "I have wondered . . . what cravings had once germinated in him, and what manner of man he was really meant to be. That he was a lonely one, haunted by something always unexpressed and unattained, I am sure."

Despite an extramarital affair and her divorce, after nearly thirty years of marriage, from her manic-depressive husband, Wharton remained a relatively conventional woman throughout her life and even, by some standards, a conservative one. Still, it is important to remember that she was probably, as Irving Howe noted, "the American novelist least merciful in her treatment of the rich," and in her fiction she is always, always on the side of the individual who rebels, however feebly, against imprisoning social norms.

Wharton produced some forty volumes of fiction, poetry, and nonfiction during her long career, but most readers today are familiar only with *The House of Mirth, The Age of Innocence, Ethan Frome,* and possibly *The Custom of the Country* and *Summer.* The Library of America has published Wharton's sixty-seven short stories in two volumes. This is a marvelous and very important project, for Wharton's better short fiction is every bit as rewarding as her best novels: its general quality is remarkably high, her range in both manner and subject is broad, and her taut, epigrammatic style seems especially suited to the short form.

Wharton wrote her stories for magazines, and collections of them were published in a series of individual volumes between 1899 and 1936. They show a remarkable technical skill combined with a freedom and playfulness, a willingness to experiment with styles and genres, that will delight readers who are familiar only with the major novels. Wharton's work ranged from stories like the famous "Roman Fever" (1934), a model of the well-made, tightly controlled, classic tale as practiced by writers like O. Henry, to long, episodic, and more complex pieces like "The Touchstone" (1900) and "Bunner Sisters" (begun in the early 1890s but not published until 1916). She made use of male and female points of view with equal ease; she was at home writing grimly realistic pieces, light social comedy, even ghost stories. Only her occasional attempts at historical fiction were an unqualified flop.

Much has recently been made of the autobiographical elements in Wharton's short stories. Wharton's emotional life was not a particularly happy one, but with characteristic energy and resolve she made the best of a rather bad bargain. Eager to escape the enveloping aura of her cold, fashionable mother, Wharton married at the age of twenty-three without ever having had the facts of life explained to her. She turned out to be both sexually and intellectually incompatible with Teddy Wharton, a kind man, typical of his class, whose interests extended to horses, dogs, and sailboats but not much further.

In 1907 she fell in love with Morton Fullerton, an American then working as the Paris correspondent for the London *Times*. Fullerton, three years her junior, had already enjoyed a colorful love life: he had many admirers of both sexes, including Henry James. Wharton and Fullerton had an affair which lasted until 1910, a fact not known to the public until the publication of R. W. B. Lewis's biography of Wharton in 1975. The other love of her life was her intimate friend Walter Berry, an American lawyer and aesthete: her feelings for him were more durable than they were for Fullerton, but were not reciprocated. It seems fairly certain that the ascetic, intellectual Berry was a homosexual (though not perhaps a practicing one); he has been proposed, all too convincingly, as the inspiration for such vacillating, unsatisfactory Wharton men as Lawrence Selden and Newland Archer. Wharton, a woman who seldom deviated from the conventions of her caste (except in the rather basic act of having become a writer in the first place), stuck with her unloved husband for years, until his recurring bouts of mania and depression made a life in common all but impossible: they divorced in 1913, and after that Wharton lived primarily in France.

Echoes of this drama certainly reverberate in Wharton's short fiction, as they do in her novels. The imprisonment of an unsatisfactory marriage is a frequent theme, and often that imprisonment reflects the larger and more diffuse imprisonment of a repressive society. It is an interesting fact that the prisoner is not always, or even usually, a woman; Wharton is at least as comfortable with the masculine as with the feminine point of view. Edmund Wilson, in fact, has proposed that, though "there are no first-rate men in these novels," her men are nonetheless more sympathetic than her women: "the typical masculine figure in Edith Wharton's fiction is a man set apart from his neighbors by education, intellect, and feeling, but lacking the force or the courage to impose himself or to get away. . . . [T]hese men are usually captured and dominated by women of conventional morals and middle-class ideals."

This scenario, clearly, resembles the marriage of Wharton's parents rather than her own. But there are examples, especially in the short stories, of the opposite case, the sensitive and imaginative female trapped in a fatal relationship with an emotionally crude man. There is Nora Fenway, for example, in "Atrophy," whose husband means nothing to her and her lover, Christopher, everything: she rushes to Christopher's house in the country when she hears he is dying, but she has been too long enslaved by good breeding and social convention to do what she longs to do, which is to force her way past his watchdog of a sister and go to his side. There is Christine Ansley in "Joy in the House," an errant wife who returns to her forgiving husband and finds him—well, a little too forgiving. And there is Margaret Ransom, the faded wife of a pompous New England college professor who falls in love with a young Englishman in the beautiful, ambiguous story "The Pretext" (1908).

Finally, there is the dead but very present Margaret Aubyn in "The Touchstone," one of Wharton's most complex and interesting stories if not, in the end, a wholly successful one. Mrs. Aubyn, a great writer, loved for many years Stephen Glennard, a perfectly ordinary young man. He was not in love with her and was clearly unworthy of her love, as even he was compelled to admit: "To have been loved by the most brilliant woman of her day, and to have been incapable of loving her, seemed to him, in looking back, derisive evidence of his limitations."

Wharton is at her best and most subtle in tracing, through the inconstant Glennard's memories, the course of their uneasy affair, if affair it can be called. Glennard tried to return her love, but it was a feeble effort: "It was not that she bored him; she did what was infinitely worse—she made him feel his inferiority." His vanity in his conquest, however, made him unwilling to sever the tie, and they drifted along unhappily, with Mrs. Aubyn frustrated at having her deepest thoughts deflected by his unreceptive intelligence, and Glennard oppressed and even humiliated by "her persistence in forcing her superabundance of thought and emotion into the shallow receptacle of his sympathy."

After Mrs. Aubyn's death Glennard falls in love with Alexa Trent, a person as different from the dead woman as anyone could possibly be: she is beautiful, placid, unintellectual, and above all, silent. They don't have enough money to marry, until Glennard realizes that he possesses a potential diamond mine in the form of Mrs. Aubyn's love letters. He sells them to a publisher, then marries and sets up house on the proceeds.

Before long, though, things begin to go wrong. All of society, and most significantly his wife, reads the hugely popular letters, praises the author, and condemns the anonymous and clearly second-rate man to whom they were addressed. Worse, Glennard begins to suspect his wife of being a beautiful blank, and to mourn Mrs. Aubyn after the fact, even to fall in love with her, or to think he has done so. Wharton deftly conveys the ironies of the situation, the psychological shifts, the poignant, abject inadequacy of Glennard's character—and then, nearly on the last page, she fails: the story's ending is discordant, sentimental, totally sham. What a disappointment! Still, in spite of the final gaffe, "The Touchstone" is one of the most interesting of all Wharton's stories.

Wharton tended to construct her tales around unhappy marriages, but the nature of the unhappy marriage, its constraints and possibilities, changed radically during the course of her career, and she had to adjust her themes accordingly. During her youth divorce was unthinkable; as she entered middle age it began to be possible, even among the diehards of her own caste; in her old age it was quite common. The stories reflect the changing standards with humor and, for those born too soon to benefit from society's steadily loosening grip, with an almost passionate pity.

The early "Souls Belated" (published in 1899) provides a darkly humorous glimpse of a young couple who have left their spouses and run away together: their plight shows how very unfit most people are to live outside conventional society. Lydia Tillotson and Ralph Gannett fetch up at an Italian resort hotel with its predictable little Anglo-American circle of guests. The young couple, who have thought themselves ready to give up the world for each other and to live as romantic renegades, find themselves clinging to this banal group, humiliatingly eager to appear respectable in its eyes.

A mere twelve years later, things had changed drastically, and Wharton's story "Autres Temps" (1911) illustrates the layers of accommodation and rationalization that accompanied the shift. Her heroine, Mrs. Lidcote, is a middle-aged woman whose divorce, some twenty years earlier, had closed New York society to her and sent her into permanent exile in Florence. Now her daughter Leila is divorcing and remarrying. Mrs. Lidcote boards an ocean liner and rushes back to America, determined to stand by Leila as she braves New York's ostracism. To her bafflement, she discovers that the fashionable, charming Leila and her new husband are as popular as ever. Times have changed: as an old friend remarks, "It would take an arbitration commission a good many sittings to define the boundaries of society nowadays." She is deeply relieved for her daughter. "It's as if an angel has gone about lifting gravestones, and the buried people walked again, and the living didn't shrink from them."

Mrs. Lidcote allows herself a tiny bit of hope. Might this mean that her own sins have now become insignificant? Might she be able to return to New York and resume her old life? But she is quickly disabused of the idea as Leila's elderly dinner guests pointedly cut her, just as they did so many years ago. "It's simply," she muses, "that society is much too busy to revise its own judgments. Probably no one in the house with me stopped to consider that my case and Leila's were identical. They only remembered that I'd done something which, at the time I did it, was condemned by society. My case has been passed on and classified." Chastened, she returns to Italy.

This is Wharton in a serious mode; but she was quick, too, to see the funny side, and in "The Other Two"—one of her most perfect and most delightful stories—we are shown the ridiculous aspect of the new moral code, and even the comforts that might be derived from it by those with a pragmatic bent.

Waythorn's wife, Alice, has been married twice before: first, in her youth, to a dowdy provincial businessman named Haskett, then to a rich man about New York, Gus Varick. Varick was morally rather lax, as Waythorn, who is slightly acquainted with him, is aware, and Alice has allowed her new husband to think—more by hints than by anything she actually says—that Haskett was a brute. Now, for one reason and another, Waythorn finds himself having to meet and deal with both of his predecessors, and he discovers to his surprise that he rather likes them. Alice, he notices, handles the embarrassing fact of their propinquity smoothly and with singular aplomb: "Even Waythorn could not but admit that she had discovered the solution of the newest social problem."

As the weeks go by, though, he begins to find Alice's social grace somewhat disturbing. "Her pliancy was beginning to sicken him. Had she really no will of her own—no theory about her relationship to these men? . . . She was 'as easy as an old shoe'—a shoe that too many feet had worn. Her elasticity was the result of tension in too many different directions. . . . Waythorn compared himself to a member of a syndicate."

In the final scene both Haskett and Varick drop in unexpectedly, and Waythorn finds himself presiding at a very awkward, uncomfortable tea table. While they sit trying to make conversation, Alice unexpectedly comes in from shopping.

> She stood drawing off her gloves, propitiatory and graceful, diffusing about her a sense of ease and familiarity in which the situation lost its grotesqueness. "But before talking business," she said brightly, "I'm sure every one wants a cup of tea."
>
> She dropped into her low chair by the tea-table, and the two visitors, as if drawn by her smile, advanced to receive the cups she held out.
>
> She glanced about for Waythorn, and he took the third cup with a laugh.

Here Wharton's humor is indulgent; elsewhere it could be merciless. While she had a certain sympathy for the lax and easygoing, like the Waythorns, and even for the social parasite—of which Lily Bart is the supreme example—she held the truly rapacious in horror. Undine Spragg in *The Custom of the Country* ("the prototype of the international cocktail bitch," Edmund Wilson called her) is the most fully realized character of this type; the stories contain a few equally extreme versions. The short-story form, which does not allow the author to build up a character slowly by a series of actions, demands a quick precision of characterization, and Wharton achieves this masterfully. The essence of the appalling Chrissie Brown in "Her Son" (1932), for example, is made vividly apparent to the reader at her very first entrance upon the scene: "She was a very pretty woman, with the alert cosmopolitan air of one who had acquired her elegance in places where the very best counterfeits are found. . . . I noticed that her long oval nails were freshly lacquered with the latest new shade of coral and that the forefinger was darkly yellowed with nicotine. This familiar color-scheme struck me at the moment as peculiarly distasteful."

Chrissie is a wonderfully low creation. Even better—in fact, one of Wharton's very best—is the dreadful Mrs. Sam Newell in "The Last Asset" (1904). Mrs. Newell is a greedy, bullying, piratical American woman who has cadged her way through Europe over the course of some twenty years. Now, at long last, her social resources are beginning to run dry, as her compatriot and sometime friend Garnett reflects: "Mrs. Newell really moved too fast: her position was as perilous as that of an invading army without a base of supplies. She used up everything too quickly—friends, credit, influence, forbearance. . . . He himself, for instance—the most insignificant of her acquisitions— was beginning to feel like a squeezed sponge at the mere thought of her."

Yes, Mrs. Newell has certainly begun her inevitable downhill journey. Then, suddenly, her quiet, overlooked daughter falls in love with an exceedingly eligible French nobleman. His family agrees to accept this déclassée little American bride, but only on the condition that her father, long since discarded by his wife, attend the ceremony.

It turns out that the Newells were never divorced. ("Mercy no!" cries Mrs. Newell. "Divorce is stupid. They don't like it in Europe.") Garnett is dispatched to search out the rejected husband, by now Mrs. Newell's "last asset." Garnett despises himself for dragging the poor man back into the family maelstrom, yet at the end dares to hope that he has acted for the best. "After all, neither Mrs. Newell's schemes nor his own share in them could ever unsanctify Hermione's marriage. It was one more testimony to life's indefatigable renewals, to nature's secret of drawing fragrance from corruption."

Several of Wharton's stories are shamelessly lightweight; she took her art seriously but not, like James, religiously. She worked hard and was, surprisingly for someone who possessed a private fortune, the consummate professional, with a real respect for commercial success and the effort and skill it requires. In one of her stories, "The Recovery" (1901), she gently mocks a painter named Keniston, who was "that favorite figure of imaginative youth, the artist who would rather starve than paint a pot-boiler. It is known to comparatively few," she points out, "that the production of successful pot-boilers is an art in itself, and that such heroic abstentions as Keniston's are not always purely voluntary." Some of Wharton's stories are potboilers pure and simple, but the great majority are not: they are full-bodied, mature pieces of work written by a powerful and sophisticated artist.

Edith Wharton had without doubt a forceful personality: many of her friends, especially Henry James and Percy Lubbock, liked to pretend to cower in terror when she swooped down upon them in her large motorcar, ready to whisk them off to parts unknown. The forcefulness was real: she had needed every ounce of it to escape the constraints of her early life and become the artist that she did. All art, all intellectual effort was deeply mistrusted by her society; these activities were considered subversive and, when all was said and done, distasteful. "None of my relations," she writes astoundingly, "ever spoke to me of my books either to praise or blame—they simply ignored them; . . . the subject was avoided as though it were a kind of family disgrace, which might be condoned but could not be forgotten."

Wharton's world seems as unlikely a one for a major artist to emerge from as the poverty and dirt that failed to suppress young artists like Henri Matisse or Charles Dickens. Wharton herself found it something of a puzzle. "I have often wondered, in looking back at the slow stammering beginning of my literary life, whether or not it is a good thing for the creative artist to grow up in an atmosphere where the arts are simply nonexistent. Violent opposition might be a stimulus—but was it helpful or the reverse to have every aspiration ignored, or looked at askance?"

I suspect that in cases like Wharton's—or Matisse's or Dickens's, for that matter—where the will is so vigorous, the intelligence so confident, the urge to create and to express oneself so strong, no amount of opposition can make much of a difference in the end. A lack of encouragement or a lack of means has doubtless destroyed many a talent and formed many a mute inglorious Milton, but when it comes to a force of nature like Wharton, mere class shibboleths cannot hold up.

In exposing those shibboleths and the moral nullity they were created to hide, Wharton proved that her family had had every reason to mistrust her scribblings. In her way she was as much a traitor to her class as Franklin Roosevelt. Her glory was that she was not afraid to betray it. Her tragedy was that she never, in either her life or her work, finally escaped its clutches: her characters can never forget the prisonhouse and the abyss, and neither could she.

[*2001*]

The Cult of Victimhood:
Virginia Woolf and
Modern Feminism

*W*riting the life of Percy Bysshe Shelley in 1927, Virginia Woolf observed that "there are some stories which have to be retold by each generation, not that we have anything new to add to them, but because of some queer quality in them which makes them not only Shelley's story but our own." This has proved true for the lives of any number of great men and women over the past few centuries; it has been true for no one, perhaps, so much as for Virginia Woolf herself.

In the opening of her comprehensive biography of Woolf, the British scholar Hermione Lee lists a few first sentences of other Woolf biographies: " 'Virginia Woolf was a Miss Stephen'; 'Virginia Woolf was a sexually abused child: she was an incest survivor'; 'Was Virginia Woolf "insane"?'; 'Was Virginia Woolf mad?' " Etcetera, etcetera. "What no longer seems possible," Lee comments, "is to start: 'Adeline Virginia Stephen was born on 25 January 1882.' "

Why not? Evidently because her life has come to stand for a great deal; it has become a heavily loaded symbol in the current dialogues over gender, class, madness, and marriage. The famously gifted, original, neurotic, courageous, difficult, and very imperfect human being she once was has disappeared, and in its place is a secular saint.

Ms. Lee points out that "all readers of Virginia Woolf's diaries (even those who have decided to dislike her) will feel an extraordinary sense of intimacy with the voice that is talking there. They will want to call her Virginia, and speak proprietorially about her life." This has proven to be so, to an extent that would have appalled the fastidious and publicity-shy novelist. Woolf's literary style, and the chatty, confidential skill with which she charmingly feminized the belletrist tradition of the previous generation, has long made readers feel they know her, while her beauty and vulnerability have made them feel protective toward her. It is possible to see similarities between the apotheosis of Woolf and the canonization that is currently taking place with Princess Diana, another beautiful and vulnerable, but not exactly saintly, woman.

Feminist critics and readers—and the cult of St. Virginia is due, above all, to the feminist revolution—have chosen to see in Woolf the kind of martyr-heroine that substantiates present-day dogmas about male and female relations. This version of Woolf portrays her as a frail woman who invited domination. She was a victim of sexual abuse—incest, even; she was oppressed by a patriarchal system personified by a devouring and controlling father; her unfortunate mental illness caused her to be further oppressed by "male" medicine and by a husband who jealously guarded her every move. To add insult to injury, this version has it, she continued to be victimized even after her death by her nephew and biographer, Quentin Bell.

There are such layers of nonsense in this picture that it is difficult to know how to begin to scrape them away. First of all, to see Woolf as having been victimized by these men is to deny her the very considerable triumphs, both material and psychological, that her life represents. Woolf proved herself to be no victim but a tough and resourceful person who overcame the handicaps of her sex and her mental illness to a remarkable degree and carved out for herself a life of freedom, work, and friendship which would hardly have been conceivable to women a generation earlier. The sexual abuse so lovingly dwelt upon by today's critics, a shameful catalogue of offensive groping and fondling by her older half-brother, George Duckworth, was an unsavory fact which she confronted with honesty; she was even able to joke about it with her sister Vanessa (also an object of George's ungoverned lust). The "male" medical treatment Woolf received during her bipolar episodes was a failure not, surely, because of its gender but because the miracle of lithium had yet to be discovered. Yet the picture of Woolf as a defenseless woman imprisoned by a cabal of wicked, conniving, and incurably masculine doctors—Mariana in her moated grange—has appealed to those who seek metaphors for male domination and female oppression. That Woolf herself did not see the situation in this light its testified to by the fact that when she fictionalized her experience in *Mrs. Dalloway* she made the sufferer a man.

The aspersions that have been cast by a generation of Woolf critics on Sir Leslie Stephen, Leonard Woolf, and Quentin Bell would have surprised and horrified Virginia Woolf, and rightly so. At their most extreme and destructive, commentators have agreed with Louise de Salvo's position, in *Virginia Woolf: The Impact of Childhood Sexual Abuse on Her Life and Work,* that "Virginia Stephen was raised in a household in which incest, sexual violence, and abusive behavior were a common, rather than a singular or rare occurrence, a family in which there is evidence that virtually all were involved in incest or violence or both." Others, while not expressing themselves quite so forcefully, have deplored the influence on the delicate Virginia of possessive and repressive men in her life.

It is true that Woolf was repelled by heterosexual sex and frequently preferred women to men as companions. Vita Sackville-West described her, interestingly, as "curiously feminist: she dislikes possessiveness and love of domination in men. In fact she dislikes the quality of masculinity." Yet she was deeply attached to the men in her life: attached to them and in many ways—whether her worshipers like it or not—dependent upon them.

There can be no doubt that Sir Leslie Stephen was a difficult father, but he was also a loving one. His relationship with his daughter—like the relationships of most parents and most children, it should be emphasized—was simultaneously destructive and enriching, and Virginia Woolf responded to his egotism with a combination of love and rage. As Hermione Lee intelligently observes, "Virginia wrote and rewrote her father all her life. She was in love with him, she was furious with him, she was like him, she never stopped arguing with him; and when she finally read Freud in 1939 she recognized exactly what he meant by 'ambivalence.'"

Stephen was emotionally voracious, demanding the attention, adoration, and servitude of all the women in his household: first his wife Julia, and then, after Julia's death, his stepdaughter Stella Duckworth and, to a rather lesser degree, his young daughters Vanessa and Virginia. If he had lived to ninety-six, Virginia Woolf wrote, "like other people one has known," she felt that "his life would have entirely ended mine. . . . No writing, no books;—inconceivable." This projection is probably true: not because her father wished her ill or begrudged her success, but because an ego so powerful tends to allow room for no other such in its immediate vicinity. Had he lived longer, Stephen would probably have been very happy for his talented youngest daughter to have had a nice literary career in his style and in his shadow, ending up, ideally, as his biographer.

A bossy paterfamilias, no better or worse than most. Yet Stephen has been portrayed in recent years as a veritable Mr. Barrett of Wimpole Street, a pattern of oppressive Victorian patriarchy. His detached and rather unsympathetic treatment of Virginia's retarded half-sister, Laura Stephen—the normal treatment, alas, for the period and never challenged by Virginia, either during her childhood or later—is used to add color and menace to the devilish picture. Even Hermione Lee, a fine critic and meticulous biographer, feels compelled to apologize for his excesses of "patriarchal" behavior. Indeed, one grows thoroughly sick of the word "patriarchy" before many pages of her *Virginia Woolf* have gone by: Lee is by no means immune to the glamour of academic jargon, even resorting to the disgusting affectation of using parentheses within words, as in "(en)treaties."

To reduce Stephen to a catalogue of oppressive and patriarchal values is to paint a figure that would have been unrecognizable to his contemporaries or even to his family. Although he had settled into a crusty and pessimistic middle age by the time his youngest daughter knew him, he had been in his time a highly influential radical, a supporter of Irish independence, church disestablishment, and parliamentary reform. "For some young men," writes Lee, "he paved the way (like his beloved Meredith, like Gissing or Samuel Butler . . .) for the intellectual revolution of the next century."

Perhaps if we are to settle on any definitive portrait of Sir Leslie Stephen, at least insofar as he figures in the life of his daughter Virginia, it should be Virginia's own portrait of him as Mr. Ramsay in *To the Lighthouse*. Only the most unresponsive reader could feel the self-indulgence and bombast of Mr. Ramsay without also feeling the softness and the dependence, could respond to the anger in the portrait without divining the helpless love. Mr. Ramsay is a critical and mocking comment on Sir Leslie Stephen, but he is also a deeply affectionate one, and anyone who fails to recognize the fact must be so patently dense that he, or she, should not be allowed to claim the title of literary critic.

The late Quentin Bell, Virginia Woolf's much-loved nephew, enjoyed a privileged relationship with his aunt throughout his youth; after Leonard Woolf's death he probably remembered her better than any person still living. His *Virginia Woolf* (1972), intelligent and humane, affectionate but unsparing, is one of the masterpieces of the genre; it was also considered the definitive Woolf biography until the appearance of Ms. Lee's. As such it has inevitably come under fire as a phallocentric document from feminist critics who seek to deliver their heroine from male hands. Hostile critics like Jane Marcus have railed against Bell, the obsolete sexist who, they contend, misrepresented "their" Virginia. Bell was attacked for every even slightly unflattering thing he wrote about his aunt. He was brought to task merely for being a man and daring to write about a woman. He committed the ultimate sin, though, when he stated that Virginia Woolf was not a feminist.

Well, of course, that depends upon what your definition of feminism is. Bell, coming from a generation with very different points of reference and standards of behavior from his younger, largely American critics, probably adhered to the rather narrow notion that feminists are overtly political, strident, often mannish. Virginia Woolf did not attach her name to political causes; she was ambivalent about votes for women and did not join the suffragist struggle; she was, in spite of her unconventional sex life, an intensely feminine person. A more catholic definition of feminism, one that would accept as both "feminist" and beneficial the great revolution that over the course of the last hundred and fifty years has allowed women the fundamental right to control their own lives and income, would have to classify Virginia Woolf not only as a feminist but as one of the most important feminists of our era: as the author of *A Room of One's Own* alone, she has exerted an unparalleled imaginative influence on feminist thought.

It is all a question of definition, and if the question were put to him, Quentin Bell would surely have agreed that if his aunt were not the first sort of feminist, she was most undoubtedly the second. However he might define "feminist," Bell wrote of his aunt with extraordinary grace and insight. He wrote with love, yet accepted that his aunt did not always behave in a lovable fashion. He included every wart while painting a comprehensive portrait in which the overwhelming impression was one of singular beauty. Yet Woolf's self-proclaimed defenders cannot forgive Bell for having included any unattractive features at all. What could he know about her, anyway? How dare he claim to define, to "own," to criticize, their exalted Virginia? Even Hermione Lee goes along with this way of thinking.

> As they grew up, the [Bell] children conspired with their parents to create a family image of Virginia Woolf as the batty, playful, malicious, untrustworthy, eccentric genius. The letters between the children about Virginia always strike this note; it lingers on into Quentin Bell's biography, and has greatly influenced the British reading of her life.

There is a great deal of truth in this image, however, and nowhere in her 760-page biography does Lee really succeed in dislodging it. Virginia Woolf *was* playful, untrustworthy, and eccentric; it is what makes her impossible to define and pin down, as current feminist critics would so much like to do. She was also, beyond any doubt, snobbish and malicious. Were she by some magic able to come back to life, there can be no doubt that among the first victims of her snobbery and malice would be the earnest political academics who have claimed her for their own.

The third perceived maleficent male in Virginia Woolf's life was the one she cared for the most: her husband. It is my opinion after reading both Bell and Lee that Leonard Woolf was one of the most devoted and long-suffering husbands in history. Romantically in love with his wife, he gave in, shortly after marriage, to her decision that they forgo sexual relations, which were intolerable to her. His assiduous care undoubtedly kept her out of mental institutions and allowed her to have a productive and creative life. He took pride in her talent and intellect and encouraged her to exercise them to the utmost; he suppressed his own ego, judging her work to be more important than his own. It is true that he pushed for a quiet life in the country when she would have preferred the excitement of London, and that he made clear his opinion that they had better not have children. But on balance Leonard must be seen as having been tremendously beneficial to his wife, a fact that her final letter to him bears out: "I want to tell you that you have given me complete happiness. . . . No one could have been so good as you have been."

Of course, it is possible to go overboard in praising this unconventional marriage. Lee pooh-poohs the idea that the Woolfs' marriage might have been lacking an important element, blaming "standard assumptions about what a full-blooded sexual life needed to consist of." Are these "standard assumptions" so very wrong, then? I don't think so. And as a reader I feel no need to know about the Woolfs' pseudo-sexual fantasy life, in which they took on the personae of cuddly animals. ("In their secret play Leonard was often the little stringy creature, the mongoose, the 'Servant,' and she was the big mandril, goddess or mistress." Ugh! These, like so many revelations about the sex lives of the Bloomsberries, are details that posterity could well have lived without.)

Still, whatever their initial motivations might have been, Leonard and Virginia chose each other and stood by their choice unwaveringly. They tried, as Lee points out, to reshape the possibilities of marriage, and to a large extent they succeeded. For Leonard to be calumniated as a parasite feeding on his wife's genius, a domestic tyrant who controlled her every move and kept her in an emotional prison, is a libelous disgrace.

The truth is that critics like Jane Marcus and Elaine Showalter seem unable to accept the fact that Virginia Woolf decided to marry and to place herself in a position of dependency upon a man. The fact that a woman so passionately sought independence on one level while shrinking from it on another seems too difficult for the literal-minded, who expect their heroes never to behave unheroically, to stretch their imaginations around.

The canonization of St. Virginia has turned Woolf into an untouchable figure she was not and could never be, and has obscured the imperfect and vastly more interesting reality. She was a powerful, important, and revolutionary writer but possibly not one of the very greatest. Her dislike for the vulgarity she perceived on first reading the manuscript of *Ulysses* indicates her own great failing, for an artist who is afraid of being vulgar will always be handicapped. Her avoidance of vulgarity led her too often to vulgarity's opposite, and far more serious, sins: preciosity and fancy. Her recognition, however, of Joyce's "show-offishness" indicates one of her own strengths: she did not use her work for ostentation; she undertook her literary experiments with a sincere desire to achieve new effects, to translate the immediacy of experience to the page more exactly than had ever been done before. She was the author of a masterpiece of art, *To the Lighthouse*, and a masterpiece of polemic, *A Room of One's Own;* an excellent but not wholly successful novel, *Mrs. Dalloway;* and a number of interesting but not immortal experimental novels. She was also indisputably one of the greatest literary critics of the last two centuries. Her essays are as fresh and pertinent now as they were when she wrote them, although some of her judgments—as, for example, those on Arnold Bennett and H. G. Wells—are accepted too religiously. As a critic, she was always far wiser than her critics have been about her.

IT IS FOR HER BEAUTY, her psychic pain, and the odd and tragic circumstances of her life as much as for the quality of her work that Virginia Woolf has attracted a certain type of critical attention; as one sharp commentator noted, she is the Marilyn Monroe of the intellectual world, "genius transformed into icon and industry." While Woolf's diaries and letters demonstrate that she could be cruel and vulnerable in equal parts, her popular image has come to elevate the vulnerabilities to the point of obscuring the tough, self-protective streak that sustained her and kept her alive and productive for a lifetime of nearly sixty years. An idealized and essentially misleading picture of Woolf as female victim of patriarchal oppression has become the dominant one, and countless stupid and condescending books and articles have supported it, the newest and stupidest being *Who's Afraid of Leonard Woolf?*, by the Australian author Irene Coates.

Although Coates presents herself as a bold individualist who daringly trespasses on hallowed ground by suggesting that the Woolfs' marriage was less than idyllic and that Virginia was not really "mad" at all, it's merely the last in a long and not very distinguished line of psychostudies of the perennially fascinating writer. As long ago as 1977, Jean Love, in *Virginia Woolf: Sources of Madness and Art,* was referring to Woolf's "so-called madness," a tag Coates uses repeatedly. In 1978 Roger Poole's widely read book *The Unknown Virginia Woolf* established an entire school of anti-Leonard critical studies and advanced exactly the same theses Coates insists upon: Leonard was a reductive, left-brained rationalist, constitutionally incapable of understanding or handling the sensitive artist he married, and Virginia's madness was no madness at all but an avenue of escape and creative independence. (Coates blithely ignores Poole's book, presumably because its existence negates her own right to be considered an original thinker: his name appears in neither her text nor its bibliography.) Finally, in 1981 Stephen Trombley published *All That Summer She Was Mad: Virginia Woolf, Female Victim of Male Medicine,* another serious claim—and taken seriously by the academic community—that Virginia Woolf was sane.

Now there is some (very slight) excuse for Love, Poole, and Trombley: they wrote their studies before the publication of the plethora of information on manic-depressive illness that has recently become available to the general reader. In light of current knowledge it has been widely accepted that Virginia Woolf, like many writers and creative artists, suffered from manic-depression, or bipolar disorder as it is also called. Hers was an almost textbook case, with onset occurring early in life and proceeding in periodic bouts broken by long stretches of sanity and good health. Bipolar disorder is a hereditary condition, and several members of Woolf's family, the Stephens, also suffered from affective disorders. Virginia's father, Sir Leslie Stephen, and her brother Adrian both had a mild form of manic-depression bearing the clinical name of cyclothymia, while her other full siblings, Thoby and Vanessa, underwent periodic episodes of depression; one of their first cousins was a manic-depressive, and their half-sister Laura Stephen (granddaughter of William Makepeace Thackeray) was either retarded or disturbed in some undiagnosed way—possibly she was autistic—and spent most of her life in an asylum.

To posthumously diagnose Virginia Woolf as a manic-depressive is not to go very far out on a limb. Yet many of Woolf's academic worshipers have passionately resisted the diagnosis, especially feminist scholars who have a great deal invested in the image of Woolf as a victim of patriarchal oppression, and who have fashioned an up-to-date Foucaultian model of Woolf's madness and femaleness as a form of transgression and "otherness." Another and more reasonable objection was the persistent use of the terms "mad" and "madness"—words used by Woolf herself—which are not at all useful in describing manic-depressive illness. Unlike, for example, schizophrenics, manic-depressives suffer from their disease only periodically and are normal for the rest of the time; literal-minded scholars—and so many Woolf scholars have been painfully literal—cannot accept that a woman who was clearly sane for much of the time can have had anything much the matter with her.

Other scholars and Woolf fans have resisted the idea of manic-depression because they find it reductive to boil Woolf's genius down to pathology, as though it were the disease writing and not the woman. This is simply to misunderstand the nature of the illness, which does not flatten out the personality of the sufferer but if anything makes it more distinctly his or her own, intensifying and crystallizing the individual vision. Woolf, like Byron, Shelley, Gerard Manley Hopkins, Robert Lowell, and other sufferers from bipolar disorder, found rich material for art in her periods of illness. "As an experience," Woolf wrote, "madness is terrific I can assure you, and not to be sniffed at; and in its lava I still find most of the things I write about. It shoots out of one everything shaped, final, not in mere driblets, as sanity does. And the six months . . . that I lay in bed taught me a good deal about what is called oneself." It cannot be a coincidence that such a high proportion of writers have been manic-depressives: medical studies have indicated that creative artists suffer from eight to ten times the rate of major depressive illness, ten to forty times the rate of manic-depressive illness, and up to eighteen times the rate of suicide of the general population.

If Irene Coates had spent a tiny fraction of the time reading about manic-depressive illness that she devoted to wallowing in Bloomsburiana, she might have sensed the thinness of her theory. (To take an example at random: she characterizes mania as "uncontrollable rage," when it is nothing of the sort.) There is not a single book on mental illness included in her bibliography, and this in spite of the fact that recent years have seen several first-class popularizations of the subject, notably Dr. Kay Redfield Jamison's *Touched by Fire: Manic Depressive Illness and the Artistic Temperament,* which contains a chapter on Virginia Woolf and the Stephen family. Also strangely absent from Coates's bibliography is Thomas Caramagno's prizewinning *The Flight of the Mind: Virginia Woolf's Art and Manic-Depressive Illness* (1992), one of the few truly respectable and revealing books on Woolf's psychological history and its relation to her work to appear.

But Coates's argument for Woolf's sanity is only half of her agenda. The other half is her contention that Leonard Woolf was a sadistic, oppressive, scheming husband who married Virginia Woolf for her money and position, promoted his own interests above hers throughout her life, was consistently unfaithful to her, and finally drove her to suicide.

I myself have always thought Leonard deserved the Purple Heart for keeping his wife safe, cared for, and out of the nuthouse for three decades, but I am always prepared to listen to nasty gossip: Leonard has always sounded too good to be true, and, as Regina Marler pointed out in *Bloomsbury Pie,* her amusing study of the evolving public passion for Bloomsbury and everything to do with it, the "saintly characterization of Leonard" in Quentin Bell's official biography of Virginia "invited reaction. . . . In later writings, Leonard would increasingly be portrayed as controlling, small-minded, tightfisted, and dogmatic, first as a husband, then as a literary executor."

Coates has a special axe to grind when it comes to Leonard. Author also of a pseudo-scientific tract called *The Seed Bearers: Role of the Female in Biology and Genetics,* she subscribes to a cockeyed creed of male "left-brain" rationality and rigidity and female "right-brain" fluidity and flexibility, and ruthlessly presses these templates onto her two elusive subjects. Leonard had a "black and white, rigid left-brain," a "limited rationalist attitude"; he personified "the alienated and alienating male egocentricity that drives a man to attempt to make the world in his image." Virginia, as a right-brained woman with the additional advantage of having been spared the male-oriented classical education that stunted men like Leonard, was free to explore "the depth and precision of her perceptions."

> Throughout their partnership he embodied the heavy rock walls that were never able to confine her spirit. That free spirit was able to descend down the column of upward energy when the walls he erected around her loomed too ominously over her head; in this way Virginia escaped from him to find enrichment in the darkness below.

Woe betide the critic or biographer who sets herself the task of writing about, and sitting in judgment upon, people vastly more intelligent, subtle, humorous, and educated than she: this is the job Coates has taken on, and she is pathetically unequal to it. When Leonard characterizes his kindergarten teacher, for example, a Mrs. Mole, as "incompetent," Coates chastises him for expressing "male contempt for women's intellectual capabilities." When he describes how he and his brother managed as school captains to change the atmosphere of their prep school, "as we were both strict disciplinarians . . . from that of a sordid brothel to that more appropriate to fifty fairly happy small boys under the age of fourteen," she leaps to the titillating conclusion that Leonard thus "learnt to wield power at an early age and taste the pleasures of being a 'strict disciplinarian.' " And of course that pleasure would inevitably lead, according to a mind soaked in late-twentieth-century intellectual clichés, to further exercises in misogyny and imperialism. Leonard, serving with the Colonial Civil Service in Ceylon, came to "personify the belligerent, autocratic imperialist administrator and was able to indulge to the full the strict disciplinarian side of his nature," claims Coates, not troubling to provide any evidence for this statement; he also had an "appalling attitude towards women, who are objectified." As if all men don't objectify women! In any event Coates herself isn't above a little objectification: you can hardly get through a paragraph of her prose without stumbling over the ubiquitous word "patriarchy."

Simplification to the point of fatuity is at work throughout Coates's book. For instance, "Virginia, unlike Leonard, was open and straight in all her relationships." What??! That touchy, mercurial, malicious and masochistic woman—open and straight? Or Virginia "became a lesbian with Vita because she was starved of the essential water of love." *Became* a lesbian, when by her own admission she had never been physically attracted to any man, including her husband? Or—and this is my favorite for sheer unanswerable fatuity—"We cannot apply conventional standards to members of the Bloomsbury Group, since they were rebelling against Victorian constraints." In the tradition of recent Woolf scholarship, Coates takes dangerous liberties with facts, cheerfully reading Woolf's fiction as literal autobiography. (In an outrageous aside, she asserts that "It is admissible in [Woolf's] case to read much of her creative writing as autobiographical, at least as something remembered because it was felt intensely at the time.") Worse, she invents scenes between her key players, Leonard, Virginia, Vanessa Bell, and others, and presents them as though they actually happened.

But it is pointless to enumerate the hundreds or even thousands of false conclusions, clueless comments, and missed points in this book. Embarking on her researches with a firm conviction of her own righteousness, Coates found no reason to adjust her theories as she proceeded: "Whether anyone else agrees with me," she writes in conclusion, "I neither know nor, deeply, care." She presents Virginia's last year or so as high melodrama, with Leonard in a sinister role: he keeps Virginia isolated; forces her down on her hands and knees to scrub floors; gets involved in a shady conspiracy with their neighbor, Dr. Octavia Wilberforce (in reality a kind and generous friend to both the Woolfs); fornicates with the maid; and in the end stage-manages Virginia's suicide and dictates her final notes to himself and to her sister. Coates, like Roger Poole before her, quotes only the sources that might, when sufficiently removed from their contexts, serve to bolster her ridiculous notions and ignores Virginia's many letters and diary entries that speak of her love for Leonard, her dependence upon him, and her sense of peace when they are together. She also ignores all references to the real reasons behind Virginia's eventual decision to die: the worries that her psychotic episodes were becoming more frequent and her rising sense, as World War II progressed, that she was losing both her readership and her gift.

"I have come to believe," Coates says officiously, "that the Woolfs were inimical." Well, so are most married couples, at least up to a point. Coates would have done well to read the play whose title she ripped off to make her own, Edward Albee's *Who's Afraid of Virginia Woolf?* At one point in the play George, enraged by Martha's drunken accusations, shouts out "I can't stand it!"—to which Martha shoots back something to the effect of "You can stand it! You married me for it!" Now there is a little of George and Martha in nearly every couple, and the Woolfs were no exception. If Virginia decided to share her life with a perhaps excessively rationalistic man, it was because she, with her overdeveloped sensibility and fragile emotional defenses, needed that quality; similarly, however much Leonard might have chafed under the constraints of being an on-again, off-again nursemaid, he was eminently suited to the task and must have found a certain fulfillment in it, or he would never have stuck it out for thirty years.

There is something weird and wonderful in every long-term marriage, and the Woolfs' was more complicated than most. For Irene Coates, who would be hard put to make sense of anything more subtle than *Thomas the Tank Engine*, to try to analyze a partnership that has puzzled some of the finest critics of the century is an absurdity that doesn't, in the end, merit the slightest notice—not even a dismissive review like this one. Not that the hubris of contentious ideologues like Coates will be punctured by adverse criticism. As Quentin Bell wrote to Olwyn Hughes, sister-in-law of Sylvia Plath, commiserating about her struggles with legions of Plath scholars, "It is in fact amazing how closely these creatures seem to resemble each other: the leaden prose, the persistent lying, the equivocations, the crude feminism. I know them all from personal experience. And the worst part is that they teach." And, he might have added, they keep coming—with no apparent end in sight.

[*2000*]

The Elusive Henry Green

Henry Green is one of the literary enigmas of the twentieth century. Twenty years after his death, posterity seems still to be groping for an evaluation of his slim *oeuvre*—nine novels and a memoir,* all produced between 1926 and 1952, when he stopped writing at the age of forty-seven. "I find it so exhausting now I simply can't do it any more," he told an interviewer, though he lived on for more than twenty years, increasingly eccentric and reclusive. He refused even to leave his London house for the last seven years of his life, nor would he consent to being photographed except from the rear. In 1973 he died, a very old sixty-eight.

He achieved neither commercial success nor wholehearted enthusiasm from the literary pundits, though he commanded, then and now, excitement amounting to passion from certain readers, an oddly assorted group including W. H. Auden, Elizabeth Bowen, Terry Southern, Eudora Welty, and John Updike. About his readership he exposed the ambivalence that characterized every attitude he ever held. "I write for about six people (including myself) whom I respect and for no one else," he claimed, though he never gave up the vain, one might even say deluded, hope that his work would one day bring in a com-

---

Blindness (1926); *Living* (1929); *Party Going* (1939); *Pack My Bag* (the memoir, published in 1940); *Caught* (1943); *Loving* (1945); *Back* (1946); *Concluding* (1948); *Nothing* (1950); and *Doting* (1952).

62

fortable income. So oblique and subtle is Green's style that, as Terry Southern pointed out, he has been called not merely a writer's writer but a writer's writer's writer; yet he himself criticized Joyce and the later Henry James for allowing the excesses of their styles to hinder communication between author and reader.

If Green's working aesthetic was delicate, allusive, and cryptic, it was in mysterious contrast to the anti-intellectualism he otherwise affected. He despised literary conversation, preferring flirtation and gossip. Though he read about eight books a week, according to his son, Sebastian Yorke,

> the standard of the novels never seemed to matter. . . . He rarely praised a book; there were some American authors he would admit to liking, but he seemed to admire no contemporary English writers. He never re-read a book or selected one from his small library of "classics" collected in his Oxford days. Nor can I recall him reading anything by his professed idols: Gogol, Turgenev, [C. M.] Doughty [the author of *Travels in Arabia Deserta*], Céline or Faulkner. He only liked novels—he would not read poetry or biography. He loved thrillers and magazines, particularly *Time* magazine.

This most artful and self-conscious of writers was very clearly uncomfortable in the role of artist. The discomfort was perhaps inevitable when one takes into consideration the fact that Green never rejected his decidedly philistine background.

It seems fitting to follow Green's own careful differentiation between his literary and nonliterary selves and to call him by his pseudonym when speaking of his work and by his real name, Henry Yorke, when speaking of his life. Henry Vincent Yorke was born in 1905. His father was the owner of a large Gloucestershire estate and the chairman of the Birmingham engineering works of which Henry was to become managing director, H. Pontifex & Sons. (With his usual love of the grotesque, Henry liked to claim that the firm manufactured toilets, though its principal products were in fact beer-bottling machines.) His mother was a daughter of the second Baron Leconfield. Henry Yorke was thus not only an aristocrat but an industrialist as well. Anthony Powell, a lifelong friend, remarked that "if one side of Yorke found the silver spoon a handicap to respiration, another accepted it as understandably welcome; and coming to terms with opposed inner feelings about his family circumstances, his writing, his business, his social life, was something he never quite managed to achieve to his own satisfaction."

Apart from his writing, Yorke led a fairly conventional life. He was not academically brilliant like his father and older brothers; though he was a published novelist while still an undergraduate, he left Oxford without a degree. He then began working for Pontifex, spending his first year on the shop floor with the men before joining the management in London. He passed the rest of his working life with the firm, living in a comfortable house with his wife, Dig (Adelaide), and their son. Though Yorke was not a successful industrialist, he was a dedicated one, and he never let his writing take precedence over his business responsibilities. His books were written in his spare time, and his habits were those of any upper-middle-class businessman; he abhorred all things bohemian. It has become customary to refer to him, in his youth, as a Bright Young Thing, but the cliché is misleading: Diana Mosley, writing that "The Bright Young People [was] an expression that always made us laugh," says that she and her circle used it "of our particularly serious friends, Bright Young Roy Harrod or Bright Young Henry Yorke."

Green's unwillingness to pontificate about aesthetics has resulted in a general critical uncertainty about his actual importance as a writer. His books are rarely in print and, though he receives a few passing glances from the academy, an enthusiasm for Green is now seen as evidence of specialized, even arcane tastes. When speaking of his work, people hesitate to commit themselves, usually saying that he is an *interesting* writer, but. . . . For if it is difficult completely to swallow Green's demanding, often precious prose style, it is also impossible to write him off. And the extraordinary range of his gifts is indicated in the fact that, among the nine novels, there is virtually no repeat material; each novel attempts something wholly different from the last. Green was not one to develop a style or theme over the years, building onto it with every new book. Rather, with reckless confidence he attacked each novel as though it were his first.

Nor did Green ever attempt to take the easy route in his writing. He always reached for extremes, sometimes becoming labored in his efforts to avoid the elegant and the Augustan. His own literary tastes were for the strenuous, the magnificent, the muscular: Carlyle and Doughty were lifelong passions, and his admiration for James and Woolf is unsurprising. In *Blindness,* his first novel, begun and mostly written while he was still at Eton, Green had already begun seeking the limits of the possibilities of English syntax, and in his second novel, *Living,* he found those limits and began to stretch them.

A certain degree of failure, of course, was inevitable, and the diversity of Green's achievements is matched by a corresponding variety in quality. In one paragraph he will hit the bull's-eye with a magnificent felicity of phrasing, in the next he will overreach himself and produce a piece of prose that is very bad indeed. He could create a vivid image with the minimum of words, and he was always strongest when handling the concrete, either in descriptive prose or in dialogue. In *Nothing,* for example, a young couple enters a French restaurant without having reserved a table: "They were standing before Pascal, close together in an attitude of humility while Gaspard sneered in their faces. It was plain they were not known." By the same token, Green's stylistic exertions can be disastrous. His omission of the definite article in many of his early stories and in *Living* is a case in point. "I wanted to make [my prose] as taut and spare as possible," he later said, "to fit the proletarian life I was then leading." Intermittently the trick is effective, producing scenes of great beauty, as in this passage from *Living:*

> Mr Craigan smoked pipe, already room was blurred by smoke from it and by steam from hot water in the sink. She swilled water over the plates and electric light caught in shining waves of water which rushed off plates as she held them, and then light caught on wet plates in moons. She dried these. One by one then she put them up into the rack on wall above her, and as she stretched up so her movements pulled all ways at his heart, so beautiful she seemed to him.

In 1958 Green said that he would not employ this technique again, giving as his reason that "it may seem, I'm afraid, affected." And so it does, especially when he insisted upon the principle too dogmatically:

> Sang birds. They lay, arms round each other. Waved ferns in the wind and they were among them, lying silently. Above trees hung a cloud against blue sky and leaves clustering from branch above and tall ferns hid these two deep in the wood from anyone and the sky. Soft the air.

The conceit is audacious, and in order for it to succeed each sentence must be perfect; even a slight bungling is enough to make an entire passage ridiculous. Green's style thus often descends into pure mannerism, and it is certain that he has antagonized many readers who ought otherwise to be favorably disposed to his work. Both Southern and Updike describe Green's "tendency toward authorial invisibility," but in fact precisely the opposite is true, for there is never a moment, even during Green's smoothest displays of ventriloquism, when the reader could possibly mistake his work for that of any other author. *Concluding,* a case in point, establishes atmosphere with such oppressive detail that it becomes a book about atmosphere to the exclusion of everything else. *Caught* is another novel in which style takes center stage; Green focuses so single-mindedly upon recreating nuances of voice and dialect that the central psychological situation is finally consumed within the showy display of fine characterization. Orville Prescott complained of Green's "excessive concentration on method rather than matter," and Philip Toynbee called him a "terrorist of language"; " 'the,' " he wrote, "is both an innocent and a useful word and to concentrate so heavy a gun against it seems a curious misdirection of this writer's fire-power."

These censures are too often merited. But in a masterpiece like *Loving*, where Green was able so exquisitely to modulate his idiom to suit his glorious and trivial subject, the reader forgets all of Green's sins in pure admiration of his virtuosity.

> "Oh Edie," he gasped moving forward. The room had grown immeasurably dark from the storm massed outside. Their two bodies flowed into one as he put his arms about her. The shape they made was crowned with his head, on top of a white sharp curved neck, dominating and cruel over the blur that was her mass of hair through which her lips sucked at him warm and heady.
>
> "Edie," he muttered breaking away only to drive his face down into hers once more. But he was pressing her back into a bow shape. "Edie," he called again.

This novel about the goings-on among a group of servants in a great country house in Ireland during the owners' absence is perhaps the best known and best loved of Green's novels. It is characteristic, too, of one of the features that has made Green such an anomaly among English writers of this century: his apparent classlessness. Though Green could describe his own milieu, and brilliantly (*Blindness, Party Going, Nothing, Doting*), he seems equally at home among the petty bourgeoisie (*Back, Caught*) and the working classes (*Loving, Living*). In fact he is perceived by many readers to be a writer specifically proletarian in sympathy and focus. But the fact that these same readers all tend themselves to come from the upper and upper-middle classes should put us on the alert. Though *Living* has been called the "best proletarian novel ever written," Green himself was quick to point out that "the workers in my factory thought it rotten. It was my very good friend Christopher Isherwood used that phrase . . . and I don't know that he ever worked in a factory." Green's year on the works floor in Birmingham gave him a lifelong respect for the proletariat, and it is possible that *Living* celebrated that world with just a touch of romanticism. Though Green himself believed the proletarian inspiration to be central to his aesthetic, he led (except for the Birmingham period and his time in the Auxiliary Fire Service during the war) an unexceptionably upper-middle-class life.

And while Green was a member of the so-called Auden generation, he was entirely out of step with that group's philosophy of political commitment and activism. Throughout the thirties (the decade in which Auden, Day Lewis, Orwell, and Edward Upward, all Green's contemporaries and social coequals, were producing literature of passionately left-wing inspiration) Green was engaged in the painstaking composition of *Party Going*, a novel that dwells almost exclusively upon the fatuous doings of a group of rich and aimless young people.

In reality Green was concerned less with any one social group than with the entire spectrum of human grace and folly. Rather than being divided by socioeconomic factors, his characters, finally, are united by the vanity, greed, and generosity common to the species as a whole. It is not that Green was uninterested in the minutiae of social distinction; indeed, he liked to point out that there exist not three, or five, but hundreds of clearly demarcated social classes in England, and he spoke scornfully of "the English novelist's worst restriction— ignorance of life in all social classes but his own." Social distinction, however, manifested itself for him not as a monolithic or necessarily desirable aspect of culture but as yet another facet of the human race's ever-imperfectible nature. Inverse snobbery has caused critics of the last novels, *Nothing* and *Doting*, to belittle their "significance" because of the impenetrable frivolity of their upper-class characters. But these characters are not so very different in essence from the lower-class ones in *Loving* and *Living*, and the books' libidinous middle-aged men and scheming women are every bit as deserving of their happy endings as are *Loving*'s scoundrelly butler and less-than-honest maid. It is difficult to see where *Nothing* and *Doting* are more "trivial" (an insult often aimed at them) than any of the other novels. The pursuit of self-interest is to Green both natural and acceptable; Green, wrote V. S. Pritchett, is "inside the human zoo, preoccupied with it, and occasionally giving a sad startled look at the bars he had momentarily forgotten."

Hence the apparent moral vacuum that mystifies or repels those readers who demand from literature the affirmation of a system of values. Green's refusal to judge his unregenerate characters is absolute, as is his refusal to endow them with any of the redeeming features most authors allow. All of his creatures are commonplace in the truest sense of the word: they are without intellectual or spiritual interests, without philosophy, wholly lacking in curiosity about the rest of the world and even in self-knowledge. But they are comic rather than tragic, and their very humanity is ultimately a force for redemption.

Surviving: The Uncollected Writings of Henry Green is a valuable volume, adding substantially to the little we possess of Green's output. As well as stories, articles, and reviews by Green himself, it contains an introduction by John Updike, an interview from the *Paris Review: Writers at Work* series, and a superb memoir by Sebastian Yorke, who has clearly inherited his father's love of the macabre and the absurd. The contents of this collection, according to the editor, Green's grandson Matthew Yorke, represent three-quarters of the material in the slender Green archive. Arranged chronologically, the pieces begin with a schoolboy story dated 1923, and wind up with a short, eccentric self-portrait published in *The Spectator* in 1963. Fiction predominates in the twenties and thirties, essays and reviews from the forties on.

The collection is interestingly named. *Surviving* suggests that the quality of the work continues to stand on its own merits—but does it? The question is a difficult one, for in the end these pieces will probably be of interest only to the confirmed Green enthusiast. Green's reputation still must rest on his nine novels, and not on the material in this volume, which varies wildly in quality.

The short stories are of interest mostly for the light they throw upon the developing sophistication of Green's touch. Unlike so many novelists, Green did *not* produce his best work early in his career, for his particular vision—dark, morbid and with a powerful sense of the ridiculous—is one that comes naturally with middle age rather than youth. In 1958 he stated, as though it were a generally accepted fact, that "the whole of life is now of course absurd," and said that "most of us walk crabwise to meals and everything else. The oblique approach in middle age is the safest thing." It is this instinct for absurdity and obliquity—which he did not begin to develop fully until his thirties while writing *Party Going*—that is fatally lacking in the early stories of *Surviving.* Most of these are experiments in the use of language. They proliferate in the kind of syntactical excess that Green largely succeeded in purging from his novels, but they nevertheless contain strokes of brilliant originality.

The most considerable story from this early period is "Mood" (1926), the beginning of what was to have been Green's second novel, abandoned after twenty pages. It is a subjective narrative from the point of view of a young girl, Constance Igtham, upper class, unmarried, somewhere in the no-man's-land between childhood and adulthood. As she wanders through London the reader is made privy to her mixed impressions and memories. One hesitates to call this narrative "stream-of-consciousness," for there are occasional, sometimes ironic, comments from the narrator (". . . she went everywhere and was everyone's bridesmaid. Constance was utterly charming. This book is about Constance. When you have read it you too will say how charming Constance is"). "Mood" is in fact remarkably close in technique to *Mrs. Dalloway,* which had been published only a year before, and it confirms one's instinctive feeling that Green, in his visual power, his irony, and his insistence upon the caught impression, was a close artistic ally of Virginia Woolf. (Green admired Woolf, calling her "one of the great women of our time," but he suspected that she was less enthusiastic about his own books and had taken him on as a Hogarth Press author purely as a favor to John Lehmann.)

"Mood," for all its beauties, is not wholly successful. Later in life Green was embarrassed by his youthful self's innocent use, in the fragment, of the most obvious Freudian symbolism, and he wrote that "to establish a girl . . . in a static situation where nothing is happening to her except her thoughts and feelings, is an impossible project for the novelist and one which only a young man, as I was then, would try for." Of course, other novelists have tried and succeeded in this venture; what Green really meant was that it was an impossible project for the kind of artist *he* was. For Green's most successful technique is the vivid presentation of significant surfaces: in his best work he never presumes to trespass upon his characters' thoughts or pasts. "Do we know, in life, what other people are really like?" he wrote. "I very much doubt it. . . . How then can the novelist be so sure?" Green's characters, as his work developed, communicate only by accident, as it were; they expose their real motives and passions not through straightforward thoughts and deeds but through chance actions and vacuous asides.

The quantity of the fiction thins out as Green ages, but its quality improves immeasurably. While the rhapsodic nature of the early work wanes, the cool, restrained tones that suited Green so well now make their appearance, and one very short story, "The Great I Eye" (1947), is as good a piece of fiction as Green ever wrote, a combination of macabre fantasy and bland realism. A hungover husband wakes on the morning after a party, trying to remember what exactly went on the evening before: it is a masterly, surrealistic story that grazes the mysterious and obscure origin of marital guilt, a subject to which the later Green returned again and again.

> We go about our daily lives, in great cities, thinking entirely about our personal affairs; perhaps every now and then sparing a thought for our partners, that is, the person we live with, and of course with even greater guilt, of our children. After a time, in married life, it becomes the other partner's fault that they have married one, but the only child, or as chance may have it, the many children, have had no choice, they are ours, and this is what fixed the guilt on us.

This, from a 1954 essay called "Impenetrability," represents for Green not a passing mood but a deeply felt conviction. Another excellent and disturbing exploration of this theme is "Journey Out of Spain," a short, never-produced play that Green wrote for television. Ostensibly a variation on the hackneyed subject of the travel nightmare, in this case the apparent inability of an English couple to escape from the vile Spanish backwater they are visiting as unsuspecting tourists, the play is also a disturbing and sinister vision of the guilt, demands, and devouring selfishness behind the façade of a very conventional marriage. The sincere and almost religious conviction of the primacy of guilt in human relations is one of Green's most fruitful sources of inspiration, and he forcefully develops it in *Doting* and *Nothing*, his last, great, and dismally underrated novels.

Surviving shows the line of development in Green's fiction to be straight and strong, but his nonfiction, particularly his criticism, tends to be weak throughout his career. For while certain advantages accrue to an artist who remains purely an artist as opposed to a critic, he will tend to be shown up rather badly when he does turn to criticism. And

Green's anti-intellectualism, worn like a badge of honor, finally turned into a terrible handicap. His thought processes were finely adjusted to every nuance of observed behavior, but when he tackled the abstract they became convoluted and clumsy, his usually delicate prose fumbling. In his only attempt at art criticism, for example, a 1953 essay on the painter Matthew Smith, he is tentative in every statement, as though fearful of sounding either foolish or pedantic. He obviously recognized the problem, for he said at the time: "I have never written about painting before and never shall again. It has given me hell." Some of his attempts at expository writing show just how bad things could get when he lost control:

> Now that we are at war, is not the advantage for writers, and for those who read them, that they will be forced, by the need they have to fight, to go out into territories, it may well be at home, which they would never otherwise have visited, and that they will be forced, by way of their own selves, towards a style which, by the impact of a life strange to them and by their honest acceptance of this, will be as pure as Doughty's was, so that they will reach each one his own style that shall be his monument?

What a tangle! One can only fear that Green's style, too, will be his monument—worse, his mausoleum. As H. G. Wells said of the later Henry James, "his great sentences sweat and strain," and the more desperately he reaches for precision the further it retreats from his grasp. Green's essays on fictional technique also suffer from want of a frame of reference. In the fifties he wrote several remarkably naive pieces on narrative theory. Here, for example, is his case against the omniscient narrator:

> Writing in this sort of way the novelist speaks directly to his readers. The kind of action which dialogue is, is held up while the writer, who has no business with the story he is writing, intrudes like a Greek

chorus to underline his meaning. It is as if husband and wife were alone in the living room, and a voice came out of a corner of the ceiling to tell them what both were like, or what the other felt. . . . What he tries to do is to set himself up as a demi-god, a know-all. That life has been so created in novels, in the past, is not for me to argue for or against.

It might be 1870 and Green inveighing against the despotism of Dickens and Thackeray, rather than 1950 with Proust, Joyce, and Woolf (to name just a few) already in their graves; one would think the author didn't control what his creatures *say* as well as what they *think*, and that the novel had a life of its own independent from that of the author. The violence of his reaction to what he seemed to perceive as unquestioned literary convention is bizarre in view of the preceding century's achievements.

But fortunately Green the novelist never paid undue attention to the dicta of Green the theorist. His art was both too delicate and too ambitious to yield to formulae, and indeed the reader who still turns to Green does so as much for his mysteries and illogic as for the frequent beauty of his style.

A man falls in love because there is something wrong with him. It is not so much a matter of his health as it is of his mental climate; as, in winter one longs for the spring. He gets so that he can't stand being alone. He may imagine he wants children, but he doesn't, at least not as women do. Because once married and with children of his own, he longs to be alone again.

A man who falls in love is a sick man, he has a kind of what used to be called green sickness. Before he's in love he's in a weak condition, for which the only prognosis, and he is only too aware of this, is that he will go on living. And, in his invalidism he doesn't feel he can go on living alone. It is not until after his marriage that he really knows how wrong or sick he has been. . . .

The love one feels is not made for one but made by one. It comes from a lack in oneself. It is a deficiency, and therefore, a certifiable disease. We are all animals, and therefore, we are continually being attracted. That this attraction should extend to what is called love is a human misfortune cultivated by novelists. It is the horror we feel of ourselves, which draws us to love, but this love should happen only once, and never be repeated, if we have, as we should, learnt our lesson, which is that we are, all and each one of us, always and always alone.

That this magnificent and uncompromising declaration is sincere there can be no doubt. But neither can we doubt that Green was also sincere in agreeing, at about the same time, that all of his books are love stories, "inspired by the belief that love is the most absorbing human experience of all and therefore the most hopeful." Green himself ardently mixed darkness and light, and his work must always appeal to those readers who, like him, do not fear life's inevitable contradictions.

[*1993*]

Evelyn Waugh—with
All the Warts

With the completion of his two-volume biography of Evelyn Waugh, Martin Stannard has made a valuable contribution to English letters. Biographical material on Waugh is plentiful—memoirs by his family members, army acquaintances, country neighbors, and Oxford contemporaries deal with Waugh to a greater or lesser extent, and his friend Christopher Sykes published a full-length study in 1975—but until Stannard's there has been no first-rate and inclusive biography. Sykes's book, *Evelyn Waugh: A Biography,* is, though serious and well documented, too evidently the work of a coreligionist and a sycophant to make a convincing portrayal. It is also painfully dull, a fault inexcusable in the biography of an artist whose interest to posterity lies above all in his outrageous, often offensive, humor.

The virtue of Stannard's biography is the author's apparent detachment, difficult to maintain when dealing with a subject who has, both during his life and beyond the grave, consistently provoked both ire and adulation. Stannard displays no partisanship; he ventures little in the way of artistic judgment on Waugh's work, and his treatment of his subject's religion is so balanced that it is impossible to tell whether Stannard is himself a Catholic.

All this being said, however, it must also be admitted that the second volume is on occasion dull, in sad contrast with the delightful first volume. This is not entirely the author's fault, for this volume, unlike the first, tells an often dreary story. Until his death Waugh maintained a vigorous public bluster, manifested in irate letters to the newspaper, libel suits against the Beaverbrook press, and spirited attacks upon Picasso, Vatican II, and other specimens of modern degeneracy. The bluster, though, masked the deep unhappiness of his later years, now revealed by Stannard. The story of Waugh's last two decades is an almost unrelieved chronicle of failure, depression, financial difficulties, and, saddest of all, declining artistic powers.

At the age of thirty-six (where the second volume begins), Waugh had already completed the bulk of his best work, enjoyed the last of his "adventurous" travels, and begun the long descent into *accidie* that was to characterize the rest of his life. At forty-six he was an old man, physically feeble, intermittently tortured by persecution mania and by white-hot flashes of rage against the rest of the world. During the war, he said, he had stopped thinking people were funny, and the loss of this greatest of life's consolations marked also the beginning of his loss of talent.

The last of Waugh's fully lighthearted books, *Put Out More Flags,* was written during the early part of the war. It is generally considered rather lightweight, but even if it is not Waugh at his very best, it contains a great deal of top-notch comic material. It is significant that at the time of writing Waugh considered the book a potboiler, investing much more labor and hope in *Work Suspended,* an autobiographical novel (never completed) in a new, more serious, "richer" style. *Work Suspended* is the first of Waugh's attempts to escape from his comic typecasting into the role of serious novelist. Stannard, as always deferential to Waugh's often wrongheaded appraisals of his own work, calls the fragment one of "extraordinary literary power"; it is in fact a slight, frail thing, elegantly written (like all of Waugh's work) but self-conscious and affectedly elegiac. His had always been a two-dimensional art, suitable to comedy; and, as E. M. Forster knew, "a serious or tragic flat character is apt to be a bore." Both in style and substance, unfortunately, *Work Suspended* indicated the direction his work was now to take.

Brideshead Revisited's faults, especially its sentimentality, are by now legendary; they were obvious even to Waugh when he reread the novel in 1950. *Edmund Campion*, his life of the Jesuit martyr, is a mediocre work of apologetics. *The Ordeal of Gilbert Pinfold* is interesting principally as biographical material and as a chronicle of mental illness; the *Sword of Honour* trilogy a fine series of novels, though "good-tempered Waugh," as one critic wrote, "and therefore Waugh at his second best"; *A Tourist in Africa* a feeble follow-up to the exuberant prewar travel books; *Helena* intolerably twee. Of all his postwar work, only *The Loved One* shows Waugh once again at the height of his powers, and after that, as Stannard points out, "he never wrote another 'cruel' book. From this point his work represented a form of *pietas*."

For Waugh was painfully aware of each one of his faults: his sinfulness, his lack of charity, his never-diminishing distance from grace. His life represented an attempt to conquer his failings, and if he found it impossible to be himself the pattern of a Christian gentleman—"it was difficult to promote asceticism with a cigar in one hand and a glass of champagne in the other"—he could at least celebrate simplicity, asceticism, and humility in others. "Dimness" was to become, bizarrely, an ideal, and his new protagonists—St. Helena, Crouchback, Scott-King—reflected the dimness he valued but could never emulate. Dimness, of course, makes unnourishing literary fodder, and Waugh's artistic failures grew from his unsuccessful attempt to create for himself a specifically Christian literature. Graham Greene tried to dissuade him from this object, quoting Newman: "I say, . . . if Literature is to be made a study of human nature, you cannot have a Christian literature. It is a contradiction in terms to attempt the sinless literature of sinful man." Waugh, always far more idealistic than Greene, disagreed.

Combined with this abstract literary agenda was Waugh's deliberate withdrawal from the outer world. From early middle age he retreated into his own home and saw few people other than family and close friends. This was fatal to his art: he had always drawn directly on experience rather than on reflection. Fantastic as his work often seems, he was essentially a realistic artist. "His characters are drawn from life," wrote Gore Vidal, "sometimes still struggling as he pins them to the page." As his circle of acquaintance contracted, he lost access to the rich material he had crammed with such profligacy into his early novels.

During the last twenty years of his life Waugh was only too aware that his imagination and talents were burning out. He was desperately worried, not so much for the sake of his professional vanity as out of fear that he would not be able to continue supporting his large and expensive family. As his marketability continued to plummet, he accepted every offer, however demeaning, that his agent proposed: anything for quick cash. Widely considered a has-been, a relic of the past, Waugh feared bankruptcy throughout the latter part of his life, and this fear was not unfounded. With his reputation at its lowest, Waugh's fame was temporarily eclipsed by that of his son Auberon, still in his early twenties and already a rising novelist, and even by the success of his long-scorned brother Alec, who surprised everyone by suddenly writing his first best-seller in more than forty years, *Island in the Sun.* Added to this was Waugh's humiliation at being offered a mere C.B.E. instead of the knighthood he coveted: "the death-blow," Stannard comments, "to a lifetime's social climbing."

All this makes painful reading, the more so since Waugh brought so many of his troubles upon himself. The list of those who had much to endure from him is legion: his brother, his accountant, his agent, his publisher—not to mention his wife and children. It is interesting, though, that they did continue to endure, and to endure with affection; Waugh had the gift of inspiring loyalty and the wish to please in those around him. Certain of his friends—Cyril Connolly, Lady Diana Cooper, Randolph Churchill—continued to love him in spite of behavior that would have been unforgivable in anyone else. Waugh also retained their respect. Connolly, though cruelly lampooned in *Sword of Honour* as the frowsy editor Everard Spruce, later rose above his hurt feelings to call the trilogy "unquestionably the finest novel to come out of the war." Alec Waugh, after suffering countless insults and rebuffs from his brother, gently admonished their mother when she complained about Evelyn's high-handedness: Evelyn had brought great honor to the name of Waugh, he wrote. "The world is full of agreeably mannered people, but lamentably short of men of genius. We ought, I think, to be grateful and proud that he is what he is." Graham Greene, one of the few of Waugh's friends not to receive the vicious edge of his wit, thought Waugh the greatest novelist of their generation; Spender and Auden, who had suffered vitriolic public abuse from Waugh for decades, "admired him immensely," Spender wrote, "as a writer of genius."

There is nothing Waugh would have wished more than to be able to return the affection he continued to receive, in spite of everything, from those around him. But he was possessed by a devil of perversity, an instinct to hurt—was even, Stannard posits, a little mad. Though he lavished love on his daughter Margaret, he was seemingly unable to express any for Auberon, refusing to visit the boy as he lay on the brink of death for weeks following an army accident with a machine gun. He was not even able to give himself fully to his chosen faith, for "every attempt at loyal service had been stained by his egotism. The talents which distinguished him corrupted his spiritual exercises. His art was a theatre of cruelty; his temperament instinctively uncharitable." He longed for the consolation of group loyalties, but he despised group mentalities of every kind. Stannard puts it succinctly: "Waugh was always a solitary in search of a club."

Stannard omits (perhaps wisely since this has been done so often elsewhere) to offer final opinions on the relative merits of Waugh's books. He gives Waugh's own opinions, quotes the critics, and leaves the reader to draw his own conclusions, generally assuming a familiarity with the entire *oeuvre*. He thus sidesteps the unresolved argument that has been carried on for some forty years as to what, exactly, is Waugh's place in literary history. Are his later, serious works to be taken as more important than the early ones? Is he even to be taken seriously as an artist at all? The *TLS* review of *Pinfold* made a bold case:

> It is time people stopped treating Mr. Waugh as a failed Mauriac. He is a lightweight who has suffered from being bracketed with completely different writers like ... Greene. ... Like Sheridan or Fitzgerald or Max Beerbohm, [Waugh] has a freak talent and is entitled to be judged on what he writes without any attempt to relate him to trends or other writers or anything else.

Stannard takes exception to this evaluation, but there is much justice in it, and read without bias it is hardly insulting to Waugh himself. He did indeed have a freak talent, if by that one means that he had an extraordinary style quite unlike anything that has appeared before or since, and a brilliant, unprecedented gift for black comedy. Nor would Waugh scorn a place in the immortal company of Sheridan and Beerbohm, or see their work as in any way inferior to that of their heavier-hitting contemporaries. The writing (and all art) for which Waugh had always expressed the loudest admiration was unabashedly "minor," often patently artificial, decorative rather than "high." Among his own contemporaries he was most lavish in praise of writers who, like Ivy Compton-Burnett and Christopher Isherwood, kept their subject matter relatively narrow, the better to perfect their special techniques. When writing about Swift, Dickens, or James, Waugh was judicious and measured in his praise: but when he used the word "master," it was of Beerbohm and Wodehouse that he spoke.

This is not to say that Waugh did not take his role as artist seriously. In fact he was throughout his career obsessively concerned with the nature of artistic creation, and many of his literary protagonists are artists of one sort or another, all in some way extensions of Waugh himself: Charles Ryder, the architectural painter; John Plant, the skillful detective-story writer; his father, the out-of-date Academic painter; John Boot, the fashionable novelist; William Boot, the florid nature writer; Adam Fenwick-Symes, the gossip columnist; Mr. Joyboy, the inspired embalmer; Gilbert Pinfold, the meticulous craftsman; Dennis Barlow, the Eliotic poet. Waugh was passionate about his vocation as an artist, though, refreshingly, he did not overestimate his own work.

Sad this biography certainly is; irritating too in that so many of Waugh's fantasies and bugbears soon become overwhelmingly tiresome; also tragic, in that so much of his career was wasted on preoccupations unworthy of his mental powers. His criticisms of Connolly apply in equal measure to himself: ". . . a pagan addressing theological problems; a dandy hedonist turned eccentric don; a fat man with a thin man inside, struggling to get out; a skilful writer whose style unaccountably rotted with cheap sentiment." Finally, however, Waugh had a triumphant life. The very painfulness of his spiritual struggle makes his efforts toward grace the more important. His was a great and idiosyncratic talent, which bore fruit in a handful of masterpieces. Like his idol P. G. Wodehouse, he created a unique world which will continue to bring pleasure to many future generations. He did as much to define the *Stimmung* of his era as anyone in this century. Stannard's biography, though often giving more details about Waugh's life than would interest anyone but a specialist, fully transmits this sense of triumph.

YET ANOTHER Waugh biography, this time more than six hundred pages, would not seem to be a strict necessity. Yet Stannard's work was a bit too voluminous, Sykes's a bit too fawning; the idea, then, of an accessible new version for the general reader is alluring, especially since this biographer is Selena Hastings, the author of a really first-rate life of Waugh's longtime friend and partner in wit, Nancy Mitford. As an added attraction, the Waugh family has allowed Hastings access to many family papers to which previous biographers were not privy. She has been able to draw extensively upon family documents, particularly the letters and diaries of Waugh's father, the publisher Arthur Waugh, and of his brother Alec, a popular novelist in his own right.

Also, in spite of all the attention given to Waugh, there have remained a number of unanswered questions about his life. His extravagant public persona is by now the stuff of legend, probably better-known than the novels themselves, and he has become a key figure in the English national mythology: his notorious rudeness continues to shock and titillate his compatriots, many of whom would like to behave the same way, as well as Americans, who get a masochistic *frisson* from being sneered at by Brits. But while he went to pains to cultivate a public persona—mad, bad, and dangerous to know in youth, in middle age "a combination of eccentric don and testy colonel"—he guarded his family's privacy, and his real feelings, fiercely. The true nature, for example, of his short first marriage to the fickle Evelyn Gardner has always been a mystery, and his second wife, Laura Herbert, was so slippery and impassive as to elude biographers and even gossipy acquaintances entirely: in spite of her having been for twenty-nine years Waugh's wife and the mother of his six children, to the outsider she remains a cipher, a gigantic blank spot at the very center of his life.

Hastings's strongest point as a biographer is that she understands her subject's sense of humor without sharing his prejudices, or his awe of the dashing and the aristocratic, and that, like Waugh himself, she has a fine nose for gossip. She doesn't scruple to give her own, biting assessments of characters usually treated with reverence. For example she reveals Katherine Asquith, often depicted by contemporaries as a saint, to be a humorless prude; Harold Acton, she claims, was sexually attracted to Waugh and perpetually jealous of his wives and lovers, not to mention his superior literary gifts. The beautiful Diana Cooper was possessed of "devouring vanity, richly nourished by a permanent and doting chorus of sycophantic admirers. . . . [She] was physically cold, voracious for admiration, indifferent to sexual love."

In narrating Waugh's life—the happy Hampstead childhood, the arcadian Oxford years, the frantic social life in twenties and thirties London, the long middle age and decline in the West Country—Hastings is going over well-trodden ground, and she compensates, happily, by focusing on personalities rather than events, probing Waugh's more complicated relationships with considerable insight. Arthur Waugh is a case in point. Evelyn himself had given an affectionate and factually accurate account of his father in *A Little Learning*, but Hastings reveals the essential hostility into which his thin supply of filial piety soon degenerated. A contented suburbanite, an extrovert with a taste for amateur theatricals, Arthur affected a Pickwickian pose while bearing a marked resemblance to Mr. Pooter in *Diary of a Nobody*, an affinity which is the more striking in his amiable, fatuous autobiography, *One Man's Road*. Arthur, Hastings writes, "had the fatal facility of the second-rate, a facility inherited by his elder son Alec, and regarded with contempt by his younger son Evelyn." Evelyn being Evelyn, he found it impossible to disguise his contempt. Many of his school and Oxford friends found his rudeness to his father so disturbing that they avoided visiting the Waughs.

Though Arthur's ridiculous aspects are not downplayed, Hastings's depiction of this long-suffering father is remarkably moving. Hidden behind his compulsive histrionics was a more decent and a far more intelligent man than his son cared to admit. Arthur longed to be allowed to love Evelyn and his family but had finally to confess that they had successfully baffled his every attempt. Of Laura Waugh he wrote in frustration, "I don't know whether she has a very strong character, & is able to keep all her feelings to herself; or whether she is a case of arrested development, soothed by Papal dope." When Evelyn and Laura's third, unwanted child died twenty-four hours after her birth, Arthur was by this time bitterly resigned to the parents' impassivity, writing, "there seems to me something quite pathetic in this little star of life, which just flickered and went out. She wasn't wanted, and she did not stay. Evelyn announced her coming as 'to the regret of all and the consternation of some.' Well, she didn't trouble them for long, and she is spared a great deal."

Like Arthur, Laura Waugh gains some dimension from Selena Hastings's treatment. If she fails yet again to come alive for the reader, it is due to her almost neurotic shyness and reclusiveness, and to a fear of displaying emotion, which her intolerant husband can have done nothing to ease. As one of her daughters later said, "Mummy had a very strong character, but very suppressed. Everything was very suppressed with Mummy." Laura Herbert, the third child of an ancient family recently converted to Catholicism, was brought up in the country and exclusively interested in country pursuits; when she married the thirty-four-year-old Waugh at the age of nineteen she had virtually no experience of life outside her own protective, eccentric family circle (the chaotic Herbert house is the model for Boot Magna in *Scoop*). Married women of her class usually had some life of their own, some circle of friends independent of their husbands, but, as Hastings writes, for Laura "there was never to be much chance of that." Evelyn's tremendous, violent, lowering personality used up most of the available oxygen, and Laura found her defense in withdrawal. She avoided Evelyn's smart London friends, refused to accompany him on his junkets to the city, and became a passionate farmer on a small scale, lavishing affection on her little herd of cows. She loved them, as her son Auberon wrote, "extravagantly, as other women love their dogs or, so I have been told, their children." Though Laura certainly possessed a steely quality of self-preservation—"She could be surprisingly judgmental, and to some observers there was a quiet arrogance about her, often a slight curl to her lip"—Hastings's account gives occasional, harrowing glimpses of deep unhappiness.

Laura might have been wooed and won expressly for her utter unlikeness to Waugh's first wife, Evelyn Gardner (who, incidentally, was Laura's cousin). She-Evelyn, as everyone called her, was brutally represented by Waugh as the adulterous Brenda Last in *A Handful of Dust,* and though certainly She-Evelyn herself was by all accounts flighty and immature, it was not hard to believe that Waugh had cruelly exaggerated her shallowness in the novel. Hastings, however, leaves one not so sure. It appears that She-Evelyn had been engaged to eight different men before she finally made it to the altar with Waugh, that she married him purely to get away from her mother, that she was addicted to pleasure, hated and feared even an evening of solitude, and possessed only the feeblest moral principles. In any case the marriage, whose breakdown was precipitated by She-Evelyn's adultery within a year of the wedding, would never have stood a chance in the face of She-Evelyn's silliness, which was outstanding even in the context of twenties fashion: the mind boggles at the thought of the self-conscious, fastidious Waugh yoked in marriage to a woman who referred to Proust as "Prousty-Wousty" and declared her new father-in-law to be "a complete Pinkle-Wonk."

What does this new biography really achieve? We learn many new details but nothing that will alter the image of Waugh already so firmly impressed upon the collective mind. The well-known portrait remains essentially the same, though Hastings paints the fine details with a skillful brush. The multitudinous warts do not diminish in number— Waugh was not a nice man, and Hastings does not pretend that he was—though the point of view is, on the whole, a sympathetic one. A good many of the fresh revelations are to do with Waugh's sex life. Two homosexual affairs at Oxford, with Richard Pares and Alastair Graham, seem to have been the most intense romantic experiences of his life, and are clearly the models for the relationship between Sebastian and Charles in *Brideshead Revisited*. It should be emphasized, though, that this narrative finally puts paid to the notion, often advanced, that Waugh was homosexual by nature and repressed his true inclinations in adulthood: the fact is that Waugh's homosexual love affairs were intense because they were adolescent; when he left Oxford and entered the larger world he transferred his attentions avidly, and permanently, to women, and could never be tempted to return to his old ways. It was Waugh's misfortune that many people found him sexually unattractive, including his first female love, Olivia Plunkett-Greene, his first wife, and the woman he ardently pursued after his divorce, Baby Jungman. Yet in other women Waugh could arouse not only passion but the most intense loyalty and friendship.

But with all the gossipy tidbits Hastings tosses in, finally somehow the book is not gossipy *enough*. Honest, well researched, lucidly written, it nevertheless smacks of the "authorized" biography, and there is an obvious hands-off principle in operation when it comes to Waugh's domestic life, perhaps in deference to the Waugh family's cooperation with the endeavor. Yet it is possible that Hastings's tact, her deadening and rather unconvincing pose of respect for Waugh, results from a subtle failure of author and subject to connect. Hastings appears to find less enjoyment in Waugh than she did in Nancy Mitford—he is to her less exhilarating, less infuriating. She feels admiration (though not much passion) for Waugh the writer, and a palpable distaste for the man himself. Understandable: a lot of people felt distaste for Waugh. But a biographer should ideally experience some sort of intense engagement, positive or negative, with his subject.

And Hastings's comments upon Waugh's novels betray an indifferent appreciation of his gifts. She deferentially parrots his own, so often wrong, judgments on his work. "*Brideshead* is undoubtedly a great novel with a fair claim to be Waugh's finest achievement"; the *Sword of Honour* trilogy "showed him to be at the height of his powers"—although those who appreciate Waugh at his most distinctive must surely acknowledge that *Brideshead* is so deeply flawed that it cannot be considered anything but a second-tier effort, and that *Sword of Honour* is fatally lacking in the rude energy, amounting really to brutality, that was Waugh's greatest strength. And it is likely that posterity will come to judge Waugh's masterpiece to be not *Brideshead,* or even *A Handful of Dust,* powerful though it is, or the brilliant *The Loved One,* but *Decline and Fall,* his first, most characteristic, and most vital novel.

Selena Hastings's *Evelyn Waugh* fails to give a new view of the man; fair enough, since in fact there remains probably very little to be learned on that front. But it also fails to reassess Waugh's importance as a writer, and that is a more necessary undertaking. Though Waugh is perhaps too offensive a figure ever to be elevated to our canon of "great" writers, there is a case to be made for him as such. Perhaps as the political passions of the twentieth century disappear into history the contentious Waugh will emerge from his frame and be seen simply as a writer, and not as an invidious snob stranded in the Century of the Common Man. To the twentieth century he appeared as a gifted oddity; out of his own time he may assume his proper level, that, one might venture, of a Jonathan Swift.

[*1992, 1995*]

The Mitford Girls

I. NANCY

Great gossip is as rare as great literature—rarer. As an art form it requires a fine balance between delicacy and vulgarity and a naked joy in the foibles of others that is not always given to even the most exquisite literary minds. Thus though the twentieth century has produced "major writers" aplenty, few of them can claim to be first-rate gossips. Sometimes, though, this gift is possessed by so-called minor writers, such as Nancy Mitford, a truly original light novelist and a world-class practitioner of the art of tittle-tattle.

One of the most important requisites for fine gossip is a like-minded recipient, and these Mitford possessed in spades. She numbered among her most frequent correspondents Raymond Mortimer, Evelyn Waugh, Anthony Powell, Cecil Beaton, and Robert Byron, not to mention her famous and infamous sisters—Diana, a dedicated fascist and the wife of Sir Oswald Mosley; Unity, a Nazi and friend of Hitler; Jessica, a communist transplanted to America; and Deborah, now the Duchess of Devonshire. (Of the family, only the retiring Pamela and Tom, who was killed in the Burma campaign of 1945, kept out of the limelight.) These were people whose wit and relish for farce matched Nancy's own, and her correspondence—teasing, intimate, full of private jokes and public scandal—is one of the most enjoyable of the century. It is beautifully edited by her niece Charlotte

Mosley and is now published as *Love from Nancy*, twenty years after the author's death.

There are inevitable disappointments. Only one letter to Nancy's husband, Peter Rodd, has survived, and very few to her publisher, Hamish Hamilton. There is almost no correspondence with her father, the second Lord Redesdale, the most attractive and eccentric member of her family and the inspiration for her greatest comic creation, the ferocious Uncle Matthew of *The Pursuit of Love*. But fortunately most of Nancy's friends treasured her letters, and some of the correspondences are little masterpieces in their own right: that with Evelyn Waugh merits separate publication in a book of its own.

These letters are long overdue. The 1975 memoir of Mitford by Harold Acton, himself a famous gossip, was surprisingly dull: a model of opaque discretion, it was the work of a friend rather than a biographer. It stressed what we already knew—that Mitford was beautiful, gifted, amusing, and aristocratic—while skating over less happy topics. Though Acton allowed that her wit could be mordant, even cruel, he chose not to examine the bitterness that underlay it.

A number of books catered to the British public's seemingly insatiable obsession with all things Mitford, and in these Nancy appeared only obliquely, often attacking with caustic barbs but keeping her deeper feelings—how unlike the rest of her family!—under wraps. It was not until 1985 that Selena Hastings, in her excellent *Nancy Mitford: A Biography,* revealed a sadder, more pathetic, and unexpectedly valiant figure behind the sparkling self-presentation. The letters—a selection of five hundred out of the surviving eight thousand—help complete the picture.

The Mitford childhood has been amply recorded, most memorably in Nancy's own *The Pursuit of Love*. In its literary version it seems idyllic; in reality, we find, Nancy was a lonely and unhappy child, ignored by her mother, snubbed even by a much-loved nanny. The vague, distant Aunt Sadie of the novel is a benign figure; her model,

Nancy's mother, was less so. "I had the greatest possible respect for her; I liked her company; but I never loved her, for the evident reason that she never loved me. I was never hugged & kissed by her as a small child—indeed I saw very little of her." As an adult Nancy claimed to have few feelings even for her father; but it is impossible to see the portrait of Uncle Matthew as anything but affectionate, and the truth is probably that Nancy cultivated her indifference to her parents in response to a certain coolness she felt from them. Her letter to Jessica after their father's funeral describes the futile sadness of incomplete relationships.

> I've just got back from England. Three funeral services—such tear jerkers . . . with the old hymns (Holy Holy Holy) & the awful words, I was in *fountains each time.* Then the ashes were done up in the sort of parcel *he* used to bring back from London, rich thick brown paper & incredibly neat knots & [Pamela] & I & Aunt Iris took it down to Burford & it was buried at Swinbrook. Alas one's life.

The funniness of *The Pursuit of Love* and *Love in a Cold Climate* masks the desperation with which Nancy fought her cloistered life at home. She was the eldest child, and her parents seemed not to realize that the Victorian age had passed and the 1920s were in full swing. She defied their vigilance by joining forces with a group of rather younger men from Oxford, friends of her brother, almost all homosexual: Mark Ogilvie-Grant, Robert Byron, Brian Howard, Harold Acton. The contrast between these colorful aesthetes and Nancy's philistine family was titillating to her, and she saw only their attractions. Almost inconceivably innocent, she fell in love with the most outrageous member of the group, Hamish St. Clair-Erskine. Amoral, flamboyant, a heavy drinker, the narcissistic Hamish was incapable of returning any affection, particularly that offered by a woman. (There is much of Hamish in the character of Albert Memorial Gates in Nancy's first novel, *Highland Fling*.) Nancy tried to laugh off his bad behavior.

"The other day H. said to me in tones of the deepest satisfaction 'you haven't known a single happy moment since we met have you.' Very true as a matter of fact; what he would really like would be for me to die & a few others & then he'd be able to say 'I bring death on all who love me.'" In vain her friends warned her against him, including Evelyn Waugh, who was to remain perhaps her best friend until his death in 1966. "I'm making such a lot of money with articles," she wrote in 1930—"£22 since Christmas & more owing to me so I'm saving it up to be married but Evelyn says don't save it, dress better & catch a better man. Evelyn is so full of sound common sense. The family have read *Vile Bodies* & I'm not allowed to know him, so right I think."

This doomed love set the pattern for Nancy's entire life. The saddest paradox in the story of this contradictory woman was the fact that while she glorified romantic love above all other emotions, she was able to give her own love only to men who were patently incapable of returning it. There were two great loves in her life—three if one counts her husband—and she could hardly have found three unworthier objects of the unswerving devotion it was in her nature to lavish. Her misery over the affair with Hamish, and later over the more serious one with Gaston Palewski, was real enough; but her knee-jerk habit was always to make a joke of her own unhappiness. After a temporary split with Hamish:

> I tried to commit suicide by gas, it is a lovely sensation just like taking anaesthetic so I shan't be sorry any more for schoolmistresses who are found dead in that way, but just in the middle I thought that Romie who I was staying with might have a miscarriage which would be disappointing for her so I got back to bed & was sick. Then next day I thought it would be silly because as we love each other so much everything will probably be all right in the end.

The affair ended definitively in 1933. Nancy was approaching thirty, eager for marriage and independence, and when Peter Rodd proposed, almost jokingly, soon after Hamish jilted her, she took him up on it. Rodd was rather a well-known character in his day—he was the inspiration for Waugh's dreadful Basil Seal—but though his exploits were amusing from a distance, he was an appalling bore in person, posing as an expert on every conceivable subject. (His friend Edward Stanley parodied him: "I know, I know, I *am* a displaced person/painter/journalist/financier/poet/Italian pimp.") In spite of his undoubted gifts, "his only genuine success," Peter Quennell said, "was having married Nancy Mitford." There are aspects of Peter, or Prod as he was usually called, in both of Linda's husbands in *The Pursuit of Love.* Like Tony Kroesig, he was boring and had a pompous family; like Christian Talbot, he was indifferent to his wife's unhappiness but selfless when it came to the suffering masses. Like Christian, too, Peter took his wife to Perpignan to help refugees from the Spanish Civil War.

In Perpignan, Nancy unexpectedly discovered that she had a political conscience. She had always been understandably wary of political enthusiasm, seeing the terrible rifts it had caused in her own family. The teenaged Jessica's doctrinaire communism she considered something of a joke, but Unity and Diana's fascism was more sinister, and her mother's enthusiasm for Hitler was to bring an end to the Redesdales' marriage. In 1935 Nancy had mocked both Unity and Sir Oswald Mosley in *Wigs on the Green,* and though she instantly regretted having hurt her sister ("Oh dear how I wish I had called it mine un comf now because uncomf is what I feel when ever I think about it"), in early days she seldom lost an opportunity to poke fun at fascism:

> I hear that Unity & Diana are going to stand outside the Polls next polling day & twist people's arms to prevent their voting, so I have invented (& patented at Gamages) a sham arm which can be screwed on & which makes a noise like Hitler making a speech when twisted so that, mesmerised they will drop it & automatically spring to salute.

But Nancy ceased to find anything to joke about after her experiences with the refugees. "If you could have a look," she wrote to her mother, "as I have, at some of the less agreeable results of fascism in a country I think you would be less anxious for the swastika to become a flag on which the sun never sets. . . . Personally I would join hands with the devil himself to stop any further extension of the disease." But Nancy had a more conciliatory character than her sisters and managed to remain on good terms with all her family—though, surprisingly, in 1940 she volunteered to the authorities her opinion that Diana was a dangerous person and should join her husband in prison for the duration of the war. The disasters of the 1930s turned her into a lifelong socialist, and she proudly called herself pink, an adjective Diana qualified as "synthetic cochineal."

Nancy held several jobs during the war, as an ambulance driver, canteen assistant, and First Aid worker ("Well my job is writing on the foreheads of dead & dying in indelible pencil. *What* I write I haven't yet discovered. . . . Meanwhile I sit twiddling my indelible pencil & *aching* for a forehead to write on"). From 1942 she worked as an assistant in Heywood Hill's bookshop, which she turned into a salon for the most interesting people in wartime London, but which Americans, because of her rudeness to them, called "The Ministry of Fear." A brief affair with an officer in the Free French Forces caused an ectopic pregnancy which left her, tragically, unable to have children.

It was during the war that Nancy's life changed course dramatically. She fell in love with Gaston Palewski, then head of de Gaulle's *cabinet* in exile. Her passion would endure for the rest of her life. He was forever her *beau idéal*, and inspired all the romantic characters of her postwar books: Fabrice de Sauveterre in *The Pursuit of Love* and *Love in a Cold Climate*, Charles-Edouard de Valhubert in *The Blessing*, even the character of Louis XIV in her historical work *The Sun King*. As for Palewski, or "the Colonel" as she called him, he was amused by her, enjoyed her company, but was never in love. Aware of this, she tried hard to make the best of it ("I suppose the next best thing to having one's sentiments returned is to have them *appreciés*").

She moved to Paris to be near the Colonel, and from that moment on France came to represent to her warmth, romance, and beauty, England ugliness, cold, and her unhappy youth. "Oh my passion for the French. I see all though rose coloured spectacles!"

Her one idea was to be available for Palewski during the rare moments he could spare from his political obligations and his myriad amours. Prod, in any case long unfaithful to Nancy, now got short shrift. Her infatuation with him had been brief; she soon saw how he bored her friends, "like Raymond Mortimer & Willie Maugham who like the sound of their own voices punctuated with my giggle, but who hate being told about the origin of toll-gates by Rodd." Once the Colonel entered her life he always took priority.

> I am really fond of Peter you know but the whole thing is complicated, & the person I live for is the Col & if he can't run in & out of my house at all times I know in the end he will feel lonely & his thoughts will turn to marriage. Also I *can't* see what poor Pete gets out of it as I'm not really very nice to him—surely he'd much better marry again & produce an heir to the lands & titles.

Whatever the miseries of Nancy's affair with Palewski, there is no doubt that with his appearance the quality of her writing reached its height. Largely inspired by her love for him, she wrote *The Pursuit of Love* with unprecedented ease in 1945, following it with *Love in a Cold Climate* (1949) and *The Blessing* (1951). These are widely agreed to be her best novels, far surpassing the extremely lightweight prewar books. During these years she also wrote her popular historical works, *Madame de Pompadour* (1954), *Voltaire in Love* (1957), *The Sun King* (1966), and *Frederick the Great* (1970).

For those who love Nancy Mitford's books, the most interesting of the letters will be those discussing their gestation, particularly the correspondence with Waugh, her chief professional adviser. She quizzed him at length on the plot and technique of the superbly funny *Love in a Cold Climate*, though she followed his advice only selectively, since she was nothing if not realistic about the nature of her gifts.

> What I wonder is whether I can (am capable of) doing better. You speak of Henry James but he was a *man* of intellect, you must remember that I am an *uneducated woman* (viz punctuation). . . . You see I'm afraid that what you really criticize are my own inherent limitations. . . . I can't do more really than skate over surfaces, for one thing I am rather insensitive as you know, & for another *not* very *clever.*

She enjoyed baiting Waugh—"I do think Catholic writers have that advantage, the story is always there to hand, will he won't he will he won't he save his soul? Now don't be cross"—and he her: "The punctuation is pitiable but it never becomes unintelligible so I just shouldn't try. It is clearly not your subject—like theology." He was also helpful when it came to her finding a voice and a readership, a critical problem with the historical works. "To be enjoyed by [Diana Cooper] and Pam Berry," Waugh wrote about *Madame de Pompadour;* "Write for the sort of reader who knows Louis XV furniture when she sees it but thinks Louis XV was the son of Louis XIV and had his head cut off."

In 1967 Nancy moved from Paris to Versailles, and in 1968 she contracted a rare form of Hodgkin's disease that was rooted in the spine. She spent the last years of her life in indescribable pain, a pain intensified by the long-dreaded marriage of the Colonel. Her bravery, her continued wit and high spirits as she slowly died can only be described as heroic. There were a few bright spots: she was made Chevalier of the Légion d'Honneur in 1972, "the only honour I ever coveted," and shortly thereafter awarded a C.B.E. "A book I've got called *Titles* . . . says never on an envelope & of course never on a card. In other words ONE knows & nobody else."

The funniness of the letters, right up to the end, is wonderful; it is also sad, for it shows the extent to which Nancy had trained herself to hide pain and depression. The Colonel was bored by sadness, and Nancy had for years only managed to keep his friendship by amusing him. She did so, valiantly, until the day of her death. Hence the paradox of these wonderful letters: full of jokes, they describe a painful life.

II. DIANA

IT IS LUCKY FOR ENGLAND that her homegrown would-be führer finally turned out to be little more than a weird historical footnote. Sir Oswald Mosley, leader of the British Union of Fascists (BUF) and its "Defense Force" of thuggish Blackshirts, was a sinister character, to be sure, but he was also something of a buffoon. Mosley's onetime associate Harold Nicolson saw the perils inherent in his chosen role early on, and warned him that

> fascism is not suitable to England. In Italy there was a long history of secret societies. In Germany there was a long tradition of militarism. Neither had a sense of humour. In England anything on these lines is doomed to failure and ridicule.

Whether it was really because of the national sense of humor (a self-flattering notion) or because of the country's long and largely successful parliamentary tradition, or in fact because of fatal flaws in Mosley's own character—underneath everything he was, as Beatrice Webb intuited early in his career, a cynic—England was to prove infertile soil for his movement, and Mosley, after a brief flirtation with power, spent the last forty years of his life a pariah.

It is possible—and to be hoped—that Mosley will be best known to future generations as the original for P. G. Wodehouse's immortal character Sir Roderick Spode, leader of a fascist organization called the Black Shorts. In *The Code of the Woosters,* the usually timorous Bertie Wooster musters his courage and faces down the bullying leader:

> Just because you have succeeded in inducing a handful of half-wits to disfigure the London scene by going about in black shorts, you think you're someone. You hear them shouting "Heil Spode!" and you imaging it is the Voice of the People. That is where you make your bloomer. What the Voice of the People is saying is: "Look at that frightful ass Spode swanking about in footer bags! Did you ever in your puff see such a perfect perisher?"

Mosley was also lampooned, and even more ruthlessly, considering the source, by his sister-in-law Nancy Mitford in her farcical novel *Wigs on the Green,* a silly soufflé of a book that would seem the height of absurdity if one didn't know the facts of the Mitfords' lives: in fact it was not far short of kitchen-sink realism.

Mosley's notoriety was heightened by his marriage to Diana, the most beautiful of the beautiful Mitford sisters. Diana Mosley, today nearly ninety and residing in Paris, wrote a memoir—*A Life of Contrasts* (1977)—but has never been the subject of a biography; now Jan Dalley, literary editor of the *Financial Times* and the wife of the poet Andrew Motion, has produced a readable life of this surpassingly strange woman. It couldn't have been an easy task. Diana Mosley's character is in essence a negative one: her life, her gestures, her opinions were quite conscious reflections of those of her man. She deliberately allowed herself to be obscured by her husband's gaudier personality, as she had been obscured during childhood and adolescence by her powerful older siblings, Nancy and Tom. Diana Mosley has always been a cipher, and, despite Dalley's efforts, she remains one.

The various members of the Mitford family were full of passionate, violently expressed convictions, and at first the self-contained Diana seemed out of place among them. Her political awakening came during the General Strike of 1926: she was shaken by the poverty and unemployment she saw as though for the first time, and turned away from her parents' dearly held conservatism to become a Lloyd George liberal.

Lord and Lady Redesdale did not believe in sending girls to school, and Diana's formal education was limited to instruction from a motley series of governesses and a few months at the Cours Fénélon in Paris at the age of sixteen. She read widely under the guidance of her older siblings and became very well informed; later she expressed her belief that "it really depends, ultimately, on oneself whether one is educated or not." The Mitfords' lives were hermetic by modern standards, but for a curious and impressionable girl there were potent outside influences to be soaked up: the gregarious Nancy, six years older than Diana, brought home many of her friends, aesthetic and homosexual "butterflies" who tended to enrage the conventionally masculine Lord Redesdale. It was the high noon of the Bright Young Things, and Nancy's friends, who included John Betjeman, Robert Byron, and Evelyn Waugh, eventually became Diana's as well. Diana found frequent refuge, too, with the Churchills at Chartwell; Clementine Churchill was a cousin of Lady Redesdale. (Dalley points out that Diana had the odd distinction of being one of the few people who knew both Hitler and Churchill well.)

Diana's time in Paris, where she stayed with the painter Paul-César Helleu and his family, was her first real journey outside the family orbit, and it came as a revelation of freedom and sophistication. Sadly, Helleu fell ill and died that year, and Diana returned to England. The hiatus was supposed to be only temporary, but disaster struck: Muv (Lady Redesdale) discovered and read Diana's Paris diary, with its descriptions of her very mild amorous escapades. "Even by the standard of Mitford family storms," Dalley writes, "the ensuing argument was a big one." Neither of Diana's parents would speak to her for days; she was forbidden to return to Paris and banished to the seaside with her three little sisters and their governess. Bored and furious, smarting under the ignominy, Diana vowed to get away from home once and for all, and as quickly as possible.

With this goal in mind, she became engaged only months after her official debut, choosing a young man who was kind, rich, intelligent, spectacularly eligible, and deeply antipathetic to her own personality. Bryan Guinness was twenty-two years old when they met, a popular member of her social circle, and heir to the fabulous Guinness Brewery fortune. They had known each other only three months when he proposed, and it seems clear that they misread one another from the start: Bryan "loved in [her] the fresh country girl he took her to be" while Diana, desperate for independence, persuaded herself that she really cared for this pleasant, undemanding man who offered it to her.

They were married in January 1929 at a huge society wedding, honeymooned in Paris, and returned to a pretty house in Westminster. Less than two years earlier, Diana had been considered too young to come downstairs for a dinner party; now she had a rich husband and a large establishment, and she quickly became one of the leading younger hostesses, entertaining constantly both in London and at their country house. She had plenty of avid admirers—Waugh, depressed at the breakup of his first marriage, fell in love with her during her first pregnancy, a situation he described in his aborted novel *Work Suspended*—but she was not, nor would she ever be, interested in casual affairs. It was not until she met the mesmeric Mosley that she turned away from Bryan.

It was the spring of 1932: her new lover was thirty-five, she not yet twenty-two, with two baby sons. Sir Oswald Ernald Mosley, sixth baronet, was a member of the old aristocracy. Expelled from Sandhurst in 1914 for the kind of violent altercation that would later make him notorious, he was hurriedly recalled two months later with the outbreak of World War I, in which he served until invalided out in 1916. Back in London for the last two years of the war, he launched himself into a social and political life, eventually gaining a seat as Unionist MP for Harrow, supporting Lloyd George's coalition and advocating a sort of "socialistic imperialism." "The beginning of Mosley's parliamentary career contained, in embryo, all its later characteristics," Dalley writes. "From the start, he hardly seemed to care which party he chose . . . his own views were what mattered."

Mosley fell out with Lloyd George over the latter's Irish policies, specifically the use of the hated "Black and Tans," and he was instrumental in bringing about the negotiations with Sinn Fein that led to the declaration of the Irish Free State. "For the next few years Mosley was the darling of the liberal press . . . and of progressive thinkers and the growing Labour movement." In 1922 he won a seat in parliament as an independent, and two years later he was recruited by Ramsay Macdonald for the new Labour Party.

In 1920 Mosley had married the middle daughter of Lord Curzon, Lady Cynthia—always called Cimmie. Aside from being an heiress, Cimmie was a tremendous political asset, for she possessed all the warmth and genuineness the hard, glittering Mosley so conspicuously lacked. Many Labour members taunted the couple for their ostentatious wealth and lifestyle, but that worked two ways: as Dalley points out, Mosley's "rousing speeches, and the sight of Lady Cynthia swathed in her furs, drew working-class supporters in their thousands." In 1927 Mosley was elected to a Labour seat, and two years later Cimmie joined him in parliament.

Although he truly loved Cimmie, Mosley's prodigious energy was never satisfied unless he was carrying on one or more extramarital affairs, mostly with bored young married women of his own set. (His motto: "Vote Labour, Sleep Tory.") He was, as he would continue to be during the years with Diana, quite straightforward about his goings-on, even procuring a bachelor pad just a few hundred yards from the family home, complete with a large bed on a raised dais in a curtained alcove.

Mosley had entered the cabinet in 1929 as chancellor of the Duchy of Lancaster, with a special responsibility for unemployment. The depression was under way, and like many others Mosley felt that the slow give-and-take of parliamentary democracy was not equal to the challenge. He issued a memorandum proposing a series of short-term emergency schemes. Many of them were sensible, the same sort of ideas that Keynes was advocating and that the Roosevelt administration in America would later adopt, but others smacked to Mosley's opponents of dictatorship, and the memorandum was rejected.

Mosley resigned from the cabinet and gathered around him a group of disaffected MPs and thinkers, including the all-powerful press lords Rothermere and Beaverbrook. In December he issued a proposed policy called the "Mosley Manifesto," and three months later he launched his "New Party." Some of the New Party members were pure socialists, while some, like Mosley himself, were moving toward fascism. The movement was soon rent apart from within and formally disbanded in 1932. Mosley's parliamentary career was over; his life as a fascist now began in earnest.

It was at this point that he and Diana met. For her it was, as her son Jonathan Guinness later wrote, "the passion of Juliet and . . . the conversion of St. Paul; emotion and conviction were inseparable." "In politics, as in everything else, Diana had a taste for the extreme," Dalley comments, and Mosley—whom most people called Tom but whom Diana dubbed Kit—satisfied that taste, both on the personal and political levels. Mosley had no intention of losing Cimmie; if Diana wanted him, she had to accept him on his terms. She accepted them, and in an extraordinarily risky and, for the era, outrageous move she left Bryan and set up on her own, living openly as Mosley's mistress, with small hope of marriage.

Mosley possessed an enviable gift for eating his cake and having it too. He squired Diana about with little care for the effect their romance was having on Cimmie; he continued to sleep with other women too, including Cimmie's younger sister Baba (who was married to a man with the wonderfully Wodehousian name of Fruity Metcalfe). Then in 1933, very unexpectedly, Cimmie Mosley died.

This was a stroke of luck for Diana, but at the time she was afraid to interpret it as such; Mosley was devastated, and Diana "realized straight away that Cimmie's death, with all its ramifications of guilt and grief and family concerns, might spell trouble for her relationship." Cimmie's sisters, Baba Metcalfe and Lady Irene Ravensdale, rallied round Mosley and did their best to expel Diana from his life.

It was agreed that Baba and Mosley should spend the summer motoring through France together, while Irene took the children away on a cruise: Fruity Metcalfe, Baba's husband, was given a talking-to by Irene and told he must quell his jealousy and allow Baba to comfort Mosley, "for Cimmie's sake."

Now Mosley began to toy with Baba and Diana as he had once toyed with Diana and Cimmie, and Diana knew that she would have to play her own hand with restraint. With Mosley and Baba off to France and her Guinness children on holiday with their father, she made what was to be a fateful plan: she and her sister Unity, by now an awkward and unpopular debutante, would pay a visit to Germany at the invitation of Putzi Hanfstaengl, Hitler's foreign press secretary, whom Diana had met at a London party.

The two soon-to-be-infamous sisters set off for Munich, arriving just in time for the 1933 Parteitag, the first Nuremberg rally of the Nazi era. Diana's later contention that her trip had nothing to do with the BUF is dubious; so is her claim that "We heard the speeches Hitler made, most of them very short, and we understood not a single word." That's as may be, but since these speeches formally launched Hitler's campaign for racial purity, it seems odd that she heard or comprehended no talk about *Kultur, Rasse,* and *Volk* on this German trip. She was deeply admiring of everything she witnessed there.

Unity was more than admiring; she was besotted, and from the spring of 1934 she spent most of her time in Germany, providing Diana and Tom Mitford, also a budding fascist, with a convenient home away from home. (David Pryce-Jones's *Unity Mitford* [1976] provides a vivid chronicle of these prewar years.) Unity, who seems to have been emotionally if not mentally retarded, developed a whopping crush on the führer and was an assiduous stalker, sitting in his favorite Munich restaurant for hours and gaping at Hitler until he eventually befriended this big, blond Aryan goddess. Unity introduced Diana to Hitler in 1935, and for the next four years the sisters were regularly seen in his company, by his side at every Parteitag, at every Bayreuth Festival, and at the 1936 Olympic Games. Hitler was even a guest—one of the very few—at the Mosleys' wedding.

Diana thought her ties with the German regime would be helpful to Mosley. In the end they merely added extra tarnish to the violence, the racist oratory, and the contempt for democracy that fatally discredited the BUF. Mosley had many gifts, but good judgment in choosing his associates was not one of them, and from the beginning he entrusted vital duties within the BUF to the unstable extremists in his camp, for example handing over the movement's official organ, *The Blackshirt,* to the crazed anti-Semite William Joyce (who would be executed in 1946 for his seditious wartime broadcasts as "Lord Haw-Haw"). The famous BUF roughhouses—the Olympia rally of 1934, the Battle of Cable Street—continued to attract the worst sort of riffraff to the BUF and to drive the more thoughtful and respectable elements away from the party. As early as 1937 Goebbels privately dismissed Mosley as a "busted flush" and was on the lookout for new and more powerful allies in England.

Mosley and Diana were secretly married in 1936 at the Goebbels home in Berlin. Three years had passed since Cimmie's death, during which time Diana and Baba (now known to her friends as Baba Blackshirt) had continued to enjoy Mosley's company on a time-share basis. Thanks to its own excesses, the BUF was on its way to bankruptcy and disgrace; the wearing of Blackshirt regalia was outlawed, and the BBC placed a ban on appearances by Mosley that was not lifted until 1968. Mosley devoted his waning influence to a doomed campaign for peace, which he carried on right up to the outbreak of hostilities in 1939. In May 1940 he was arrested under Defense Regulation 18b, a wartime suspension of habeas corpus, and sent to Brixton Prison.

For the time being Diana, who had a newborn baby, was left alone, but there was a growing movement to have this sinister character put behind bars as well: among those who insisted that she was dangerous and urged the government to lock her up were Diana's sister Nancy and her former father-in-law, Lord Moyne. She was eventually arrested in late June and taken to Holloway.

Her privations, at least at first, were real enough, though it is hard to feel much sympathy for this privileged woman who happily condoned murder and concentration camps. At the end of 1941 she and Mosley, at Churchill's personal request, were granted permission to be together, moving to the preventive detention block at Holloway where they lived with four other couples. Sex offenders ("because they are so clean and honest") were sent to do their housework, and Diana befriended a pretty bigamist. The prisoners were allowed to grow produce in the sooty soil; Diana, in her inimitably Marie Antoinette-ish tone, remarked that she "never grew such *fraises de bois* again."

Mosley's health began to deteriorate in prison, and in November 1943 he and Diana were released by order of the home secretary, Herbert Morrison, who told parliament that there was "no undue risk to national security" and that he had no wish to "make martyrs of persons undeserving of the honour." They spent the rest of the war under house arrest, getting reacquainted with their various children, including the two new little boys who hardly knew them.

Diana was thirty-three when she was released from prison. The greater part of her life was still in front of her, but, as Dalley remarks, "what she and Mosley had lived for—their political dreams and ideals, their guiding sense of purpose—was already over." She exercised her considerable energies in decorating and running their various houses in England, Ireland, and France, and in making life comfortable and pleasant for Mosley. He continued rather halfheartedly in politics, founding the Union Movement whose main platform was a campaign against nonwhite immigration. Diana became a parttime writer and editor, launching *The European,* the organ for the Union Movement, writing a book about the Duchess of Windsor and a group portrait of some of her interesting friends, *Loved Ones,* and editing Mosley's "surprisingly readable" and successful autobiography, *My Life* (1968). Mosley died in 1980. In 1982 his son Nicholas published *Rules of the Game,* the first volume of a searching and honest biography of his father. It was a little *too* honest for Diana, who never spoke to Nicholas again.

Mosley and Diana remained defiant and unapologetic for the rest of their lives. The Holocaust was regrettable, but it was none of their doing: Diana professed a belief that "it was all part of the appalling price innocent people pay for a misguided war, and . . . it never would have happened if Britain and France had not declared war on Hitler"—a position, as Dalley comments, of "breathtaking illogic." They simply "never," as Diana herself wrote, "considered that Hitler's excesses were anything to do with [them]."

It must be admitted that fascism, whatever subsequent high line Diana has chosen to take, destroyed the Mitford family. Lady Redesdale, under the influence of Unity, Diana, and Tom, became an enthusiastic convert to the creed. Lord Redesdale, who unconditionally loved and admired Tom, went along for the ride at first, but was soon repelled by events in Germany. His relationship with his wife never recovered, and from the early days of the war they lived apart. Unity was irreparably brain damaged by her attempted suicide in 1939 and lived with the bullet lodged in her head until she died from aftereffects of the wound in 1948. Tom, the golden boy, was killed in Hitler's war; Jessica, who despised her sisters' politics, became an exile and to some extent an outcast from the family.

Lady Gladwyn (formerly Mrs. Gladwyn Jebb) remarked in her diary in 1947 that "Both Diana and Oswald Mosley are evil characters, Lucifer fallen from heaven and he in particular has a sinister and almost hypnotic power." Jan Dalley has valiantly tried to muster some sympathy for Diana, but in vain. Diana didn't have the excuse of stupidity, like Unity; she was intelligent, cultivated, and intimately connected with some of the most brilliant and admirable people in England. Just as some people are mentally handicapped, she seems to have been morally so, and if, for a short, ugly time, she became a visible symbol of the rottenness at the heart of Western civilization, she has no one to blame but herself.

[*1994, 2000*]

Sylvia Townsend Warner

*T*he urge to escape is probably as universal, and as intellectually inexplicable, as the urge to procreate. Even the richest, the most beloved, the most successful, the most powerful must occasionally long to get away from their lives. It's not really glamour or adventure one wants; it's anonymity. Driving through the further reaches of Queens, for example, it often strikes me that I could change my name, rent one of these identical little houses or rooms, and disappear forever. What do we want to run away from? Habit; routine; soul-deadening daily tasks; obligatory but meaningless social engagements; mind-rotting small talk; the tyranny of family; the arbitrary jollity of holidays; the exhausting responsibilities of love itself.

It is not a subject that is treated often in fiction. One who has done it brilliantly is Sylvia Townsend Warner, the British writer who died in 1978 and was the author of seven novels and countless short stories, 153 of which were published in *The New Yorker*. Beginning with her first novel, *Lolly Willowes* (1926), she treated the instinct for escape with a level of delicacy, humor, and respect that exposed it for what it really is: the defense of one's very soul.

Throughout her long career, Sylvia Townsend Warner enjoyed early success and renown, if not fame. Since her death, her work has found a home under the feminist umbrella: feminist because many of her characters were women in search of some variety of independence and also because she was a lesbian who lived openly with her longtime lover, the poet Valentine Ackland, and published their love letters after Valentine's death. But while she could fairly be called a feminist, her fiction is not, I would say, feminist so much as a plea for the freedom and integrity of every person, regardless of sex, and if she can be said to be the heir of any particular writer it would be Samuel Butler, one of the great misogynists of all time. She admitted to "reprobating" both church and family and managed to be consistently subversive to the received values of both institutions while at the same time practicing, in her own life, strict monogamy, a wide range of domestic skills, and admirable industry. In short, she excelled in the bourgeois virtues while despising most bourgeois values.

Lolly Willowes, Warner's first novel, remains her best known and has recently been reissued. Laura Willowes is what the young Sylvia Townsend Warner might, under slightly different circumstances, have become. An upper-middle-class country girl, Laura sees no reason to marry: she and her father are everything to one another, and she takes no interest in young men. When her father unexpectedly dies, the world as she knows it comes to an end, and, being an old-fashioned girl and not in the habit of questioning plans made for her, she falls in with the standard scenario for women of her class and type.

> Even in 1902 there were some forward spirits who wondered why that Miss Willowes, who was quite well off, and not likely to marry, did not make a home for herself and take up something artistic or emancipated. Such possibilities did not occur to any of Laura's relations. Her father being dead, they took it for granted that she should be absorbed into the household of one brother or the other. And Laura, feeling rather as if she were a piece of property forgotten in the will, was ready to be disposed of as they should think best.

Laura's beloved childhood home goes to a brother who doesn't care about it, and she goes to the other brother in London, who cares not much more about her. She spends more than twenty years in what amounts to comfortable and well-upholstered servitude to her spoiled brother, his capable cipher of a wife, and their uninteresting children. On the surface, she is everyone's familiar, predictable Aunt Lolly, confirmed in "the habit of useless activity."

Her inner life is rather different.

But while her body sat before the first fires and was cosy with Henry and Caroline, her mind walked by lonely seaboards, in marshes and fens, or came at nightfall to the edge of a wood. She never imagined herself in these places by daylight. She never thought of them as being in any way beautiful. It was not beauty at all that she wanted. . . . Her mind was groping after something that eluded her experience, a something that was shadowy and menacing, and yet in some way congenial.

Finally, awakened from her spiritual slumber by the sight of an armful of beech leaves in a flower shop, Laura decides to leave her brother's house and move to a village in the Chilterns called Great Mop, a wild place where she has no ties and no acquaintance. Her brother, it turns out, has speculated with her capital, and she has very little money left, but it is enough to purchase freedom. Little by little she begins to feel at home in Great Mop, to shake off her chains and respond to the place's hard, elusive spirit.

But then her charming and self-involved nephew Titus comes for a visit, likes the place, and decides that he will move there too. Laura is appalled, "shaken and sick with the grinding anger of the slave." In despair she calls for help and is answered not by God but by Satan. She makes a pact with him and becomes a witch; discovers, in fact, that nearly everyone in Great Mop is a witch or warlock. The unsuspecting Titus is driven off by a series of harmless spells, Laura happily joins her new community, and the story ends satisfactorily for everyone.

Lolly Willowes, Warner's first book, is the only one that could be described as explicitly feminist.

> "When I think of witches [Laura remarks to Satan], I seem to see all over England, all over Europe, women living and growing old, as common as blackberries, and as unregarded. If they could be passive and unnoticed, it wouldn't matter. But they must be active, and still not noticed. Doing, doing, doing, till mere habit scolds at them like a housewife, and rouses them up—when they might sit in their door-ways and think—to be doing still!"

Her later novels and stories would still condone the breaching of social and family constraints but would venture well beyond the purely feminist zone.

Sylvia Townsend Warner's life is chronicled in Claire Harman's fine 1989 biography, now sadly out of print. She was born in 1893, into a conventional late-Victorian society that was soon to change forever. Her father, George Townsend Warner, was a legendary history master at Harrow, the great public school, and Sylvia was his best friend and, intellectually, his creation; as an only child she received the full force of his love and his very considerably educative zeal. (One former pupil, the novelist L. P. Hartley, recalled him as "a teacher of the first order [who] got more out of his pupils than it seemed in their power to give. He was a genius.") After an unsuccessful year at a local kindergarten, where Sylvia behaved so obstreperously that her parents were asked to remove her, she was educated entirely at home. She more than repaid the attention, being, according to an aunt, "an abnormally intelligent child, even at an early age."

A ferocious, frizzy-haired bluestocking who took no interest in parties or young men, Sylvia was a disappointment to her mother, Nora, but was her father's pride. Her first love was music; she studied piano and organ, music theory and history under the tutelage of the well-known musicologist Percy Buck, another Harrow master who was to be not only her mentor but her longtime lover as well. By 1911 she was composing regularly; in 1914 she was planning to go to the continent to study with Arnold Schoenberg when the war intervened.

In 1917 George Townsend Warner, who had been engaged in secret war work, suddenly died, possibly of a burst stomach ulcer. Sylvia was, as she recalled many years later, "mutilated." "It was as though I had been crippled and at the same moment realized that I must make my journey alone," she wrote. With a tiny income of a hundred pounds a year, Sylvia felt unable to launch out on a life of her own, as she would have liked, especially since her mother's devouring grief and dependence held her in a death grip. She might have gone the unfortunate way of Laura Willowes had an extraordinarily convenient offer not come her way in the form of a project, funded by the Carnegie Trust in England, to collect, edit, and publish the entire corpus of Elizabethan and Henrician music. Sylvia was to be one of five editors. The project was expected to last for about five years; in the end it took twelve.

Sylvia was much younger and less experienced than the other editors, and one can only go along with Harman's assumption that Percy Buck, also on the committee, arranged the job to provide her with an independence. With her new salary of three pounds a week, she moved to London, alone for the first time and delighted to be so.

Young and tender she may have been, but she possessed a powerful personality of a peculiarly English sort: she had enough of the Victorian *pukka memsahib* in her background and character not to mind making an impression or to be easily embarrassed. Sylvia had "this extraordinary, this very cultured voice," said her friend Bea Howe, "but she never altered her talk when she was speaking either to her daily or a roadmender, or anybody she wanted to have a talk with."

Looking back on his first meeting with her in 1922, David Garnett remembered

> an alarming lady with a clear and minatory voice, dark, dripping with tassels—like a black and slender Barb caparisoned for war—with jingling ear-rings, swinging fox-tails, black silk acorn hanging from umbrella, black tasseled gloves, dog chains, key rings, tripped lightly in and speaking to me in sentences like scissors . . . it was you, dearest Sylvia.

With the passing years, she toned down the sartorial flourishes but never softened her approach.

Aware that she was not quite talented enough for a career as a composer, Sylvia turned to writing. She had always written poetry for her own pleasure, and in 1925 she published the first of her many volumes of verse, *The Espalier*. It was well reviewed and earned her influential admirers. *Lolly Willowes* appeared a year later. It proved both a fashionable and a critical success, the "smart" thing to read that season, and played into a current vogue for so-called fantasy novels. A best-seller in England—the only one of Sylvia's books to attain this status—it was also a success in the United States and was the first choice of the newly launched Book-of-the-Month Club.

A second novel, the charming *Mr. Fortune's Maggot*, appeared in 1927. Each of Sylvia's novels was to be entirely different from one another in setting and theme, and in *Mr. Fortune's Maggot* she forsook the contemporary England of *Lolly Willowes* for a South Sea island in the late-Victorian era. Timothy Fortune is a naive, well-meaning man whose career as a bank clerk has been interrupted by a dissatisfied yearning he interprets as a vocation for the church. He travels to the remote island of Fanua as a missionary and begins an attempt to convert the happy-go-lucky islanders. In three years he makes only one convert, the beautiful boy Lueli who has attached himself to him from the very beginning. Eventually, however, Mr. Fortune discovers that Lueli still worships, in secret, the fetish that represents his god and goes along with Christian rituals only out of politeness. Although the fetish is destroyed, it is Mr. Fortune, and not Lueli, who loses his god, and in a fever of remorse he banishes himself from Fanua's paradise of beauty and innocence.

Her next novel, published in 1929, was *The True Heart,* a retelling of the Cupid and Psyche tale, set in the Essex Marshes in the late nineteenth century. It is a beautifully told story but puzzling to many readers in that it deals with a heroine who is simple almost to the point of simplemindedness. It met with polite but not very enthusiastic reviews, though it has always had its share of admirers.

By 1929 Sylvia's own true heart was wavering a bit: her long affair with the married Percy Buck was winding down after seventeen years. She was in any case beginning to feel middle-aged and unattractive; when a French friend, after boasting of her own lovers, asked about Sylvia's, she replied that she "should require a little notice in order to beat the moth out of them." Not long after putting an end to her relationship with Buck she met Valentine Ackland, a solitary, thoughtful woman twelve years her junior.

The "marriage" of Sylvia and Valentine, which lasted, despite a couple of serious glitches in the late 1940s, until Valentine's death in 1969, was one of those strange love stories in which chemistry inexplicably triumphs over character. Sylvia was a strong and at times overpowering woman, confident, industrious, happy by nature, cheerfully irreligious, mentally and physically healthy. Valentine was depressive, intelligent but uncertain of herself (she suffered, as we would say now, from "low self-esteem"), physically vulnerable though tall and handsome, alcoholic, and guilt-ridden. Sylvia was gregarious; Valentine, painfully shy. Sylvia was from the very beginning a successful author, and once her relationship with *The New Yorker*—she called the magazine her "gentleman friend"—was established in the late thirties she earned a very respectable living; Valentine never made more than a pittance from her writing and suffered from a crushing sense of professional failure.

Sylvia, Valentine later wrote, "has a character that does not doubt itself: when she makes a mistake she does not doubt for a moment that it is *not* a mistake, and when she discovers beyond doubt that it *is* one, she feels no despair. I wish I had that kind of courage but as I have not I must study to endure instead." Sylvia, however, thought that Valentine "has more heart. My heart is passionate, but it has a rind on it, a pomegranate heart. Hers has a fine skin, a fig heart." Nevertheless the two were happy together. They quickly settled into the country life that was congenial to both of them, moving several times before finding Frome Vauchurch in Maiden Newton, Dorset.

In 1935 the two women, disturbed by the ominous events in Europe, joined the Communist Party. It was the closest thing to a religious faith Sylvia ever possessed, and she retained her admiration for Stalin and his works long after more sensitive souls, including Valentine, had turned from the Soviet example in revulsion. Throughout the rest of the thirties, party activities occupied a substantial portion of Valentine's and Sylvia's energies: among other duties they spent two weeks in Spain during the civil war as delegates to the second International Congress of Writers in Defense of Culture. Sylvia was slyly observed on this trip by a rather unsympathetic fellow delegate, the young Stephen Spender, who was to put her into his memoir *World Within World* as "the Communist lady writer" who

> looked like, and behaved like, a vicar's wife presiding over a tea party given on a vicarage lawn as large as the whole of Republican Spain. Her extensory smiling mouth and her secretly superior eyes under her shovel hat made her graciously forbidding. She insisted—rather cruelly, I thought—on calling everyone "comrade," and to me her

sentences usually began, "Wouldn't it be less selfish, comrade," which she followed by recommending some course of action highly desirable from her point of view.

Summer Will Show (1936), written under the spell of her new political faith, is Sylvia's only really bad novel; as with almost all doctrinaire fiction, its message eats away at its essence. It describes the adventures of Sophia Willoughby, an early-Victorian Englishwoman who, having lost her two children to smallpox, comes to Paris to try to snare her shallow, insubstantial husband into giving her a third. Once there she falls under the spell of his revolutionary lover, a Lithuanian Jew named Minna Lemuel, and takes part in the 1848 revolution. The first part of the book, dealing with Sophia, her two children, and their deaths, is powerful and at times hair-raising, but then it was written before Sylvia had developed a political agenda. The French portion of the story is nothing but bad, and misguided, political fiction.

In 1938 she published *After the Death of Don Juan,* a novel that begins where the libretto of *Don Giovanni* leaves off. It was, as she wrote, "a parable, or an allegory, or what you will, of the political chemistry of the Spanish War, with the Don Juan—more of Molière than of Mozart—developing as the Fascist of the piece."

World War II changed the world Sylvia and Valentine had been born into almost beyond recognition. As the postwar years progressed Sylvia stubbornly held on to her Communist faith, but Valentine, by now uncomfortably aware of Stalin's iniquities, moved away from her earlier allegiances. A woman who strongly felt the need for faith of some description, she turned to Christianity, eventually being accepted into the Catholic church (though later, in the wake of Vatican II, she rejected Catholicism in favor of Quakerism). This was territory onto which Sylvia was unable to venture, for she vehemently disliked Christian mysticism. When Valentine wrote in her diary, for example, that "Only the eternal Creator could conceivably forgive what I have done," Sylvia replied brilliantly, in a characteristically bracing vein:

> You are aligning yourself with the great majority of Xian thinkers in thus expressing a latent dislike of God; for to draw this rigid line between what you can do and what God can do is, in effect, to assert that you and God have nothing in common, that though you may love him (*odi et amo*) you do not think that humankind can accept him as a fellow-citizen of the universe. This arbitrary quarantining of the creator is the odder in the sentence quoted because it is so plainly unjustified. It is ridiculous to assert that forgiveness is only possible to God. To err is human, and to forgive is human, too.

Sylvia's own spirituality, such as it was, was earthbound and pagan. In 1948 she published *The Corner That Held Them*, a novel set in an English convent between 1345 and 1382, the era of the Peasant Revolt and the Black Death. The concerns of Warner's nuns are almost exclusively practical and economic: a less spiritual group of women would be hard to find outside of a Wall Street brokerage house. *The Corner That Held Them* is experimental in an understated, unshowy way; there is no plot per se and no major character, and the action passes as smoothly and arbitrarily as life itself. Unfortunately the novel—though it was Sylvia's personal favorite—evokes the nuns' lives perhaps too well, in that it has a cumulatively soporific effect.

My own favorite among the novels is *The Flint Anchor* (1954), a devastating critique of Victorian ethics that focuses on an upper-middle-class Norfolk family. The historical novel tends for any number of reasons to be an unsatisfactory genre, but Sylvia had an uncanny ability to imagine her way into the mental environment of an era. *The Flint Anchor* is in effect a novel that Thackeray might have written if he had not had to abide by the pretensions and constraints of his day. Adultery, homosexuality, alcoholism, are all dealt with explicitly, in a way that the Victorians were never allowed to do: Samuel Butler, for example, chose not to publish *The Way of All Flesh*, whose blistering honesty would have created a scandal in the 1880s, and it saw the light of day only in 1903, when the world was ready.

Sylvia wholeheartedly shared Butler's view of conventional family life as a constraint and a prison. *The Flint Anchor*'s patriarch John Barnard, like Butler's Theobald Pontifex, has good intentions without good instincts. He follows, almost slavishly, the courses of action prescribed by his culture in his efforts to mold his wife and numerous children into acceptable shapes. The results are uniformly disastrous, and in old age he clearly sees his past life, "springing like some malformed tree from where he had planted it in a bad love. Every branch of it was twisted awry, and from the branches hung calamities like dismal fruit."

Sylvia's own old age was a time of great creative energy: she published a remarkable assortment of short stories, translated Proust for Chatto & Windus, and wrote a biography of T. H. White which proved greatly popular, as well received as anything she had written since *Lolly Willowes*. Valentine died of cancer in 1969; Sylvia's grief was intense, and she raged against the indignities of her own advancing years. But eventually her spirits rallied and she lived on, busily writing almost to the end, until her own death on May 1, 1978.

While Sylvia Townsend Warner left behind a fine group of novels, her short stories might well endure longer. She wrote a great many: there are fourteen published volumes of them, as well as an excellent *Selected Short Stories of Sylvia Townsend Warner* chosen by her literary executors, Susanna Pinney and William Maxwell. Michael Steinman has edited Maxwell and Warner's charming correspondence, published as *The Element of Lavishness*, also a group of previously uncollected short stories, *The Music at Long Verney*.

Both of these volumes are extremely welcome and even necessary, since Warner's books (with the exception of *Lolly Willowes*) are out of print, and she has for some time been in danger of being forgotten. *The Music at Long Verney*, in fact, comes as a real surprise: each story in it is first-rate, and some are among her very best; why were they not anthologized before?

"An Aging Head" is clearly drawn from the author's own character and, to some extent, her experience. Georgina is a sixtyish woman, strong and independent; she likes living alone but likes, too, the ever-reliable devotion of her rejected suitors, particularly the faithful George. After a bad flu, however, she finds that the scene has subtly shifted: she is no longer in command of every situation, and she watches grimly as George takes an unexpected interest in her despised niece, Antonia.

> She heard their diminishing voices, and their lingering farewells. She heard George cough, and Antonia deplore. She heard them start their cars and drive away. Presently they would set out on an entirely novel way of life, hyphenated into George-and-Antonia—one of those late marriages that at first seems so surprising and soon after seem so natural that one can't imagine why they did not happen earlier. And she would go on pretty much as usual—an aunt to Antonia, to George an old acquaintance, a headless phantom. They would always treat her with kindness, and Antonia would unfailingly remember her birthday and ask her to lunch.

Other stories, too, stand out. "Tebic" is an indescribably charming picture of a happy marriage and its feeble, benign little deceptions; "QWERTYUIOP" is a vivid memory of what it feels like to be a child, straining at the chains that bind one to one's unsatisfactory relations.

The Music at Long Verney also contains five stories about Mr. Edom, the canny antiques dealer who made several appearances in *The New Yorker* before William Shawn grew tired of the series and asked that it be suspended. The Edom stories are among Warner's more muted, less spectacular pieces of work, but in their lightly ironic way they give considerable pleasure. Valentine ran an antique business for several years, and Sylvia, like Mr. Edom, was well aware of the imaginative and emotional power an object can hold over a person. "A Brief Ownership" shows the happiest side of Warner. Its narrator, flipping through a gazetteer of Scotland, finds a town named Dull that inspires an extended fantasy. "In spirit," she says, "I had already struck root in Dull" and settled in a stone house called Dull Lodge. "I did no gardening, because I had gone to Dull Lodge in order to retire. I had furnished it with retirement in view. For once in my life, I had a sufficiency of bookshelves. I also had four black horsehair sofas." The narrator lies on a sofa for hours on end, reading about nineteenth-century Church of England bishops.

> Thus, moving from bishop to bishop, returning them to the London Library and unpacking new ones (it was extremely rare for a bishop to be unavailable), listening to the wind, watching the changing color of the fields, admiring the snowdrops, eating quantities of ripe figs, tapping the barometer, strolling out in the wistful autumnal dusk when the gardener would not be about to suspect my intentions and even staying out long enough to see the public lighting of Dull extinguished at 10:30 P.M., I lived in contentment and satisfaction at Dull Lodge.

A beautiful and eccentric fantasy, which at the end is rudely interrupted when the narrator discovers that the real Dull is something quite different, not at all what she had in mind.

"A love affair in letters" is one of literature's more tired clichés, but it might be used almost seriously of Warner's long correspondence with William Maxwell. As a junior editor at *The New Yorker*, he "inherited" Warner when her previous editor, Katharine White, left the magazine in 1938. They met for the first time the next year. "She was dressed in black," he later wrote. "Her voice had a slightly husky, intimate quality. Her conversation was so enchanting it made my head swim. I did not want to let her out of my sight."

In fact, Maxwell and Warner were seldom to meet over the course of their friendship, and perhaps this is what makes the correspondence so free and lighthearted. As Claire Harman has written, "Some of Sylvia's most highly valued friendships were founded and maintained by her transatlantic correspondences. She loved, and needed, the uncluttered intellectual intimacy which depended on distance and separateness and which such correspondence allowed." The fact that the two writers inhabited entirely different worlds is a mixed blessing for the reader. On the debit side, they had no friends in common, and therefore the letters contain no gossip and are astonishingly free of malice. Maxwell was a famously gentle and kind human being, but Sylvia possessed a healthily bitchy side; that side, however, was not in evidence when she wrote to Maxwell. In the credit column, though, the reader is not inundated with the usual footnotes explaining personal references, since there are none; all the "conversation" comprised by the letters is general, and very fine conversation it is too.

A significant portion of the correspondence is concerned with writing, as is to be expected between a writer and her editor, who was also a good novelist in his own right. Maxwell had a properly ambivalent attitude toward editorial work: "I'm glad you think I'm a good editor," he wrote to Warner in 1947, "even though a still small voice tells me that there is no such thing for writers of quality and that they should be left strictly to their own devices."

Following that principle, it seems to me that the only way to communicate a real sense of these lovely letters is to give a few appetizers, as it were. For instance, on their own and each other's work:

I sometimes think that I am alone in recognizing what a moral writer I am. I don't myself, while I am writing; but when I read myself afterwards I see my moral purpose shining out like a bad fish in a dark larder. (Warner to Maxwell, 9/16/62)

I am not so sure that you can be said to have a moral purpose at all. You have a moral tone. (Maxwell to Warner, 10/3/62)

What a grand (in the sense that Sir Joshua Reynolds used the word) bore. [Here Maxwell is referring to a character in Warner's story "An Act of Reparation."] I sometimes think people aren't as boring as they used to be when I was young, and you have renewed my faith in human nature. (Maxwell to Warner, 7/15/63)

On other writers:

I think you will come to Balzac yet. When one has disproved all one's theories, outgrown all of one's standards, discarded all one's criterions, and left off minding about one's appearance, one comes to Balzac. And there he is, waiting outside his canvas tent—with such a circus going on inside. (Warner to Maxwell, 1/28/61)

I so much don't envy myself the job of reviewing [Virginia Woolf's] letters that I haven't done it. One curious thing I noticed—that there are three people she shows off to, Strachey, Duncan Grant, and Vanessa, and usually it is by being harsh or cruel or unkind or unfeeling about somebody. As if it were a game they played. (Maxwell to Warner, 11/12/76)

On religion:

I find myself envying people who believe in the Management, but that isn't of course the same thing as believing in it. (Maxwell to Warner, 10/22/62)

I will keep my views on God the Father to myself, only remarking that he repented him that he made man—a common fatherly custom. (Warner to Maxwell, 6/11/76)

On politics:

I despair of my country. If there was a wilderness I would cry out in it, but that too we've disposed of. (Maxwell to Warner, 4/9/68)

For a writer, Sylvia Townsend Warner was unusually sane and clearheaded about her own talents. She had a healthy measure of professional self-respect while accepting that her work was not, perhaps, of the very highest rank. After having translated Proust's *Contre Saint-Beuve*, she confided to her diary that "even at my best, I could never write like that, for I have not got that stuff of genius, that steady furnace, only a few rockets and Catherine wheels." If she had a serious fault it was a very English tolerance for unnecessary whimsy and fancy, and at her worst the shadow of the vicar's wife—to use Spender's comparison—can fall over her fiction. She was at her best where her sensibilities and ideas diverged from those of her caste rather than reflecting them; at such moments she commanded a cool ruthlessness and an entirely individual lack of sentiment. She deserves to be far better known than she is.

[*2001*]

Brilliant Frivolity:
Christopher Isherwood's Diaries

*C*hristopher Isherwood's reputation has been tainted ever since he and W. H. Auden left Europe for the United States in 1939, on the eve of World War II. It was seen by many in England as abandonment, even flight, and ill-wishers scoffed as the two writers who had been the darlings of literary anti-fascism throughout the thirties turned tail for America the moment war seemed imminent.

There is a certain amount of justice in this interpretation of events, as Isherwood himself was only too aware, though he considered himself a committed pacifist and stated that, should war break out, he would be perfectly willing to return to England and do whatever work the government might require of conscientious objectors. In the event, he did not go back to England, but he did volunteer for wartime work with the Quakers in Pennsylvania, helping European refugees to get settled and launched in the United States. Yet he was never to be easy in his mind about his own motivations for emigrating. In 1944 he wrote to Cyril Connolly that

> our coming to America . . . was an altogether irresponsible act, prompted by circumstances—like our trip to China, and my wanderings about Europe after 1933. When the war broke out in 1939, it was a fifty-fifty chance what I'd do. I was a bit bewildered, a bit guilty, pulled by personal relationships to stay here, and pulled by others to

return. I delayed, because that is always easiest. Then came the press attacks, and cowardice and defiance hardened. Yes, I quite admit that there was cowardice—not of the Blitz . . . but chiefly because I knew that, if I returned to England, I would have to take the pacifist position and strike out on my own line—not yours.

In view of the sort of war it would turn out to be, with untold suffering inflicted on millions of defenseless people, Isherwood's rationalizations and his individual brand of pacifism now seem selfindulgent and unreasoned. He tended to confront issues of political or social principle by personalizing them, often in inappropriate ways, a fact of which he was conscious: "I have never been able to grasp any idea except through a person." His reluctance to go to war stemmed from affection for the friends of his Berlin days, particularly Heinz Neddemeyer, his former lover who had been forced into the Nazi army. "Suppose I have in my power an army of six million men," he proposed. "I can destroy it by pressing an electric button. The six millionth man is Heinz. Will I press the button? Of course not—even if the 5,999,999 others are hundred per cent Jew-baiting blood-mad fiends (which is absurd)."

There is a clear failure in logic here, as well as a lack of judgment. In quotations like the above, one hears distinct echoes of the writer who, in his work and in his life, influenced Isherwood more than any other: E. M. Forster. It was Forster who had declared the absolute primacy of personal relationships, and who had made the statement—felt by many at the time to herald a joyous liberation from the forces of mindless nationalism but in retrospect a deeply disturbing opinion—that if he were given a choice between betraying his friend and betraying his country, he hoped he should have the courage to betray his country. Forster's influence, for better and for worse, is everywhere evident in Isherwood's life and work.

Many people found it hard to forgive Isherwood, either for his initial defection or for the success that, as an American, he continued to enjoy. Several years ago, for example, David Pryce-Jones attacked him in an aggrieved tone:

> No other contemporary writer was so petted and indulged. Invariably his prose style was praised for making no demands upon the reader. . . . Born into a prosperous and well-connected family in Cheshire, Isherwood was numbered among those who had a stake in the country, as he liked to boast. The family manor house dated back to the seventeenth century. . . . Some rich uncle could be relied on to give him a private income; some influential friend was always ready to bail him out of trouble or to buy him a ticket for traveling.

This is a somewhat extreme view, and while it reflected a certain truth about the youthful Isherwood, it no longer applied to the older one. When Isherwood eventually inherited the seventeenth-century manor house and the rich uncle's estate, he signed the entire package over to his younger brother without a backward glance, readily resigning himself to an uncertain financial future as a screenwriter. The charge that Isherwood's writing makes "no demands upon the reader" is equally reductive: in fact his talent, if never fully realized in a "great" work, produced several exquisite and original minor ones, particularly *Mr. Norris Changes Trains, Goodbye to Berlin, Prater Violet,* and *A Single Man.* He was a master of English prose in whose hands the language achieved singular beauty and lucidity, modestly disguised as simplicity.

For all his faults, Isherwood was hardly the monster of selfishness his critics liked to depict, and the first volume of his diaries offers readers ample opportunity to make their own judgments about his character. This volume, which covers the period between Isherwood and Auden's departure for America in 1939 and 1960, with the author at work on *Down There on a Visit,* fills nine hundred pages; a second one, progressing from 1960 to the writer's death in 1986, will follow.

The decision of Isherwood's companion, Don Bachardy, to publish the diaries in full seems perverse. Isherwood looked on journal writing as a duty and forced himself to make frequent entries whether or not he had anything to say. As a result, at least half of the diaries consist of repetitive and uninteresting material: complaints about boyfriends and neighbors or injunctions upon himself to work harder, to straighten out his love life, to cut down on smoking and drinking, to diet, to spend more time in prayer and meditation.

About the last named: Isherwood had met the Indian swami Prabhavananda in 1939, soon after settling in Los Angeles, where he would spend the rest of his life. Auden, he wrote, "had his Anglo-Catholicism to fall back on. . . . I had nothing of this kind, and I didn't yet clearly realize how much I was going to need it." "Certainly, my own life badly needed some kind of discipline. I was still suspicious of the occult, however, and hated anything which sounded like 'religion.'" Nevertheless he converted to Hinduism soon after meeting the swami, and was to adhere to that faith until his death; he even spent an unsuccessful, faintly ludicrous year as a novice monk in the Vedanta Center on Ivar Avenue.

Only a genius, possibly, can give universal meaning to his own spiritual struggle. Isherwood was certainly no Augustine, and his efforts toward what he refers to as "ego-bashing" are at worst tedious, at best conducive only to a certain cynical, unedifying amusement. When the swami urges him to send thoughts of peace and goodwill toward people of all countries, he observes that it is "easy as long as I think of typical people in each country" but that "for some reason, it is most difficult to send goodwill toward the South Americans." He finds it painfully difficult to focus his mind on prayer:

> Arrived to find the shrine room empty. Tried to pray for my friends, but could feel absolutely no affection for anybody. . . . Then the usual bad feelings—vanity, because Swami came in late and saw that I was

already in the shrine; self-accusations, because I'm not in England. . . . Then satisfaction because, technically, I'm still keeping all the rules. Then sex thoughts. Then resentful feelings toward Chris and Gerald and Peggy and Paul Sorel.

To give him his due, he stuck with it over the years, but prayer was never to come naturally to him. "If I really desire God more than anything else," he wrote, "then I must desire my periods of prayer more than anything else. (I most certainly don't.)"

Isherwood never ceased to revere the swami, with whom he collaborated on a number of publications including a translation of the Bhagavad Gita, and who was the subject of his 1980 book, *My Guru and His Disciple.* But in the diaries the swami comes across as a charlatan: how seriously are we to take a Hollywood spiritual guide who happily admits his greatest heroes to be Greta Garbo and the Duke of Windsor? One can only smile at the swami's suggestion that Isherwood had the makings of a saint. (Even Isherwood, who in fact had a very shrewd estimate of just how far his own spiritual enlightenment reached, suspected that the swami was laying it on a bit thick because of his usefulness as a free translator, writer, and propagandist.) And the Ivar Avenue monastery, far from being the calm refuge Isherwood hoped to find, turned out not surprisingly to be a hotbed of jealousy and petty rivalries.

Isherwood was also, if not a disciple, at least an admirer of Gerald Heard, one of the foremost quacks of his day, apostle of spiritual growth through hallucinogenic drugs, electromagnetic radiation, UFOs, and other branches of pseudo-science and pseudo-religion—a New Ager before the New Age. Isherwood's tolerance for Heard and his claptrap is mystifying, considering his very real ability, always his stock in trade as a novelist, to skewer the phony and the inflated.

He certainly had no difficulty in doing so in his other friendships. On John van Druten, for example: "sententious . . . [saying] 'What have I ever suffered in comparison with what the Rosenbergs are feeling, waiting for execution?' I guess, when he talks like this, one is supposed to fall on one's ass with amazement at such charity and cosmic sensibility." Or on his sometime friend Peggy Kiskadden: "Peggy is much concerned with the change of life and anxious not to try to be attractive any more. (She will, though.) She is transferring her sexual vanity to her children, as bankers transfer money from a city which may be bombed."

Such telling little strokes are what make Isherwood's novels so persistently clever and attractive; they are also what make the diaries worth reading, in spite of all the excess baggage:

> Thomas Mann died last Friday—tidily, as he did everything. There was a greatness in his dry neatness. . . . He was somehow very supporting—not because of his great gestures, his "open letters" to world leaders, his public self-questionings. No, he was lovable in a tiny, cozy way—he was kind, he was genuinely interested in other people, he kept cheerful, he was gossipy, he was quite brave—he had the virtues of an admirable nursery governess.

More often the negative predominates. Bette Davis is an "arrogant and not overly talented parrot-faced bitch," Lee Strasberg an "unspeakable arch-ass." John Lehmann "watches himself with the greatest respect, to see what he'll do next—but alas no humor"; Lehmann's autobiography induces "doldrums. . . . All accounts of childhood are boring, except the very greatest, and his is not the very greatest or the greatest or even the very." Aldous Huxley is fastidious: "stupidity afflicts him like a nasty smell—and how eagerly he sucks at the dry teats of books! Every time I open my mouth he is obscurely pained and distressed. I am such a hopeless ignoramus, such a barbarian."

As is evident from the cast of characters here, Isherwood's circle of acquaintance was enormous. His feet were firmly planted in two Hollywood camps: the movie industry and the community of expatriate European intellectuals, which included Mann, Huxley, Heard, Berthold and Salka Viertel, Igor and Vera Stravinsky. He was also one of the prominent members of what could be described as a sort of international gay confraternity, along with Auden, Forster, Lincoln Kirstein, Tennessee Williams, Gore Vidal, Truman Capote, John Gielgud, and Somerset Maugham. The result is that the unlikeliest combinations of people turn up in these pages: Dylan Thomas at the Players Restaurant on Sunset Boulevard, pawing Shelley Winters's breasts over the dinner table; Bertrand Russell and Greta Garbo hobnobbing at a beach party. (Isherwood, incidentally, agreed with Peter Viertel's opinion that Garbo was "a dumb cluck.")

For all his intelligence Isherwood was a surprisingly unintellectual writer, brilliant at observation, less so at analysis. He was never a very serious thinker; his real gift was for comedy, often comedy of the silliest and most lightweight sort. But because of the circumstances of his life and the political attitudes he struck, he took on something of a symbolic role in the intellectual life of the century. Just what he was supposed to be symbolic of depended on the observer: he was variously seen as a romantic wanderer, a courageous anti-fascist, a parlor pink, a coward, a mystic, a pioneer of gay liberation. To cast Isherwood in any of these roles, however, is probably to take him more seriously than he should be taken—certainly more seriously than he took himself. There was always a goofy absurdity about him, which he exploited brilliantly in his fictional self-portraits, and which he seldom loses sight of in the diaries. Though he made an unremitting effort to impose a serious structure on his life, his strong suit, ultimately, was frivolity.

[*1997*]

The Many Worlds of
Angus Wilson

Angus Wilson's finest novel, *Anglo-Saxon Attitudes,* has been reissued by St. Martin's Press. Along with his other fiction, it has been out of print in this country since 1985. That one of the oddest and most fascinating bodies of work in postwar literature should have been so long ignored is shocking; so is the fact that its author, an elderly and respected knight, should have died penniless.

Throughout his life Wilson was fascinated by Dickens, with whom he was frequently compared. The similarities are obvious enough: lavish histrionic gifts; a genius for mimicry; a fascination with the intensity of childhood experience; an uncanny ability to cut across class boundaries based on rackety, déclassé beginnings. Yet Dickens was a great popular writer while Wilson's books were always rather esoteric. The most fundamental difference would seem to lie in sentiment, a condiment Dickens applied generously, Wilson sparingly and with a bleak honesty. The British, in the postwar years, "had been congratulating themselves smugly on having won the war, and Angus exposed them to themselves as a nation of beggars, snobs, bullies, black-marketeers and hypocrites, ill-dressed, plain, timid, and adventurous only in pursuit of selfish ends: it was not a flattering portrait."

So writes Margaret Drabble in her satisfying new biography of the writer who, she claims, strongly influenced her own work and that of a number of her contemporaries, including Ian McEwan and Martin Amis. It is to be welcomed for many reasons. For one thing, it is the first extensive biographical treatment of Wilson: the only directly autobiographical work he himself wrote was the extremely slim volume *The Wild Garden*, published in 1963 when Wilson was fifty, and covering only his childhood and youth.

Also, the fact is that Wilson led an unusual life. He threw himself enthusiastically into the spirit of his century, participating in all the social revolutions that took place during his lifetime (though at all times retaining his intelligent skepticism). A rather outspoken homosexual, he saw the world transformed for people like himself, and his story is, as Drabble emphasizes, "in part a history of what we now call gay liberation, and the decreasing need for discretion."

Finally, Wilson was obviously a man of considerable personal charm. Not that he was what anyone could call handsome. An old school-friend describes him in youth: "Retreating forehead, retreating hair, the back of the head, in silhouette, a wavy question mark; little round watery eyes sparkling with cultured joviality; a rather small white nose which tried hard to apologize for its presence on his face . . . a lightly receding chin, a high-pitched consequential voice." A distinctly camp manner completed the picture. As a young man he was said to resemble something out of the retinue of Marie Antoinette; as he aged, with his mane of prematurely white hair, he came to bear a striking resemblance to Dame Margaret Rutherford. One friend unkindly described him, in his dotage, as "half . . . Old King Cole, half Sugar Plum Fairy."

Vivacious, curious, cultivated, he consistently charmed and amused. His students (and he had many, not only at the University of East Anglia where he taught for years, but at numerous American universities where he did stints as a visiting professor) adored him. One pupil later said that he "made up in angelic sweetness for all we lacked in genius." He was known to be an easy touch for any good cause. He even enjoyed publicity tours, the bane of more timid authors' careers: "With me it's the old actress thing really," he explained to V. S. Pritchett. "There are all those lovely people out there: you reach out and make contact with them."

Angus Wilson was always an autobiographical novelist, and like Dickens he found the principal wellspring for his fiction in his own childhood, which was certainly bizarre enough to rival anything in Dickens's life or work.

Willie Johnstone-Wilson (his son Angus was to drop the Johnstone upon the publication of his first book) was a real-life Micawber. "If my father had ever known employment one might have spoken of him as in retirement," Wilson wrote in *The Wild Garden*. Except for a brief flirtation with the law, Willie trained for no career and never, apparently, did a day's work. Having come from a once distinguished Scottish family, he decided to live as a Gentleman of No Occupation on the income from the family's Dumfriesshire estate—a source that was never adequate and became, with the years, less and less so. He spent his days at the racetrack, the Gaity, the Trocadero, or his club, a small-scale *rentier* gambling his funds away and living well beyond his means.

Willie married Maud Ellen Caney, a good-looking young woman from a prosperous Durban family of whom, since she had social pretensions and they had made their money in trade, she was ashamed. The newlyweds settled in Richmond where their eldest son, Frederick (Fred), was born. They produced four more in fairly short order: Winn (1892), Clive (1894), Colin (1897), and Patrick (1900). They thought their family complete, and the arrival of Angus on August 11, 1913, when his closest brother was thirteen and his mother forty-five, was a surprise. Angus spent his first years in Bexhill-on-Sea on the South Coast. Spoiled and precocious, "he belonged," Drabble comments, "to no generation."

Amazingly, all of Angus's brothers survived World War I. The most

133

eccentric, and those with the most powerful influence on the young Angus, were Colin and Pat, a strange, interdependent pair who were to live together until their deaths as elderly men in cheap lodgings in Lisbon. From his earliest childhood Angus was aware that Pat and Colin were homosexual. They involved him, a very small boy, in their charades and dramatic tableaux (all of the Johnstone-Wilsons were enthusiastic play-actors) most of which revolved around stories of executed royalty, principally Marie Antoinette or Mary Queen of Scots; years later, Angus was to describe them in an *Observer* article as "queenly." As they grew up, they did not confine their activities to the histrionic but went to work as prostitutes, supplementing their extremely slender means by propositioning clients while dressed in ladies' underwear. Their experiences would reappear as those of the young Marcus Matthews in *No Laughing Matter*.

After a couple of years spent in South Africa unsuccessfully seeking greener pastures, Angus and his parents returned to England in 1924 and once more took up their by now hopelessly raffish existence—genteel poverty in a succession of seedy lodgings which "my mother enjoined us to call 'private hotels.'" As grim as this life must have been for the young Wilson, the sense of displacement and the weird assortment of human flotsam with which he came into contact was to prove a fruitful source for his fiction. One of his fictional alter-egos is Meg Eliot, the upper-middle-class heroine of *The Middle Age of Mrs. Eliot,* who has lost her husband and her money and avoids Kensington hotels as "emblems of the plucky reduced gentility she feared"; Willy and Maud reappear, in unflattering guise, as the improvident and narcissistic parents in *No Laughing Matter.* In *The Wild Garden,* Wilson observed that

> the very small scale *rentier* and professional group to which my family belonged had no place in Labour's England and was subsequently to prove the most expendable element of the Tory Party's supporters

when the Conservatives began to convert social-welfare England into an affluent opportunity society. My attitude to this social revolution was inevitably ambivalent, my affections often in conflict with my reason; this is reflected in my stories.

Fortunately brother Winn—the only respectable member of the Johnstone-Wilson clan—had founded a boys' school, Ashampstead, and Angus was a pupil there from 1924 to 1927. It was an unconventional and rather happy school, but a pall was cast over it by Winn's cadging family who, Wilson wrote, "made my poor headmaster brother's life nightmarish as [they] borrowed his livelihood away." Despite what appears to have been really good schoolmastering—Winn was a fine teacher and so, it seems, was the ladylike Pat—the Johnstone-Wilson ménage at Ashampstead was "a melancholy, Chekhovian house, for there my family sat about and talked the hours away like people waiting for a long overdue train."

For Angus alone of all her sons, Maud financed a real education. She found the money to send him to Westminster School, where he began in 1927, and provided in her will for the continuation of his education after her death in 1929. Westminster turned out to be an inspired choice: it was a school where intellect counted for much more than athletic prowess, and there was none of the bullying that went on at "heartier" schools. There were a number of first-rate teachers, of whom the most influential to Wilson was the energetic John Edward Bowle. Bowle not only had interesting friends, he made sure that his boys benefited from them; thus as a teenager Wilson met Bertrand Russell, Aldous Huxley, H. G. Wells, even Gandhi. "I nearly died of mental indigestion under the diet of Spengler, Croce, Roger Fry, Freud, Cole, Gerald Heard . . . and all that [Bowle] provided," wrote Wilson.

A great success at Westminster, Wilson nevertheless failed to get the expected Hinchcliffe scholarship to Christ Church; instead he went up to Merton, as a commoner, on the strength of his mother's legacy. His years at Oxford were happy but not very eventful. He was active in the Oxford University Dramatic Society, where his most memorable performance was in the role of Buggery in a tableau of the Seven Deadly Sins, "wearing flame-colored pajamas and carrying a Madonna lily" (Terence Rattigan appeared as Treachery in the same pageant). He took his degree in history—a Second—in 1935.

His prospects were not good. He now had sole care of Willie, who had become a frail and dependent old man. The economy was depressed and job prospects were poor, on top of which, as Drabble points out, "many professions were not open to someone who could not disguise a camp manner." After an absurd interlude as amanuensis to a dilettante lady who wanted to write her memoirs, Wilson applied for work at the British Museum, and in early 1937 he began his career there as a "temporary assistant cataloguer" in the Department of Printed Books.

A year later Willie Johnstone-Wilson died, and Angus began to emerge from his chrysalis. Having for years played the role of good daughter (as Colin spitefully observed), his development had been delayed: "Prematurely responsible in some ways, he had been mildly (and willingly) retarded in others, like many a dutiful spinster"—a situation Wilson would describe with special insight in his early "A Story of Historical Interest." His circle of friends widened, and he joined a political crowd, "very red" as one of its members recalls. He shifted his support from the Peace Pledge Union to Stafford Cripps's "United Front of the Working Class to Fight Fascism and War" and kept himself occupied with what he was later to describe as "that most satisfactorily escapist of all activities—busy political work."

The busy comradeship, the endless political talk of those years did in fact use up the blank time which might otherwise have driven me to think a little more deeply. In addition this left-wing work gave me a certain moral satisfaction which in turn delayed any serious self-analysis. . . . We generated with our lively political talk and coterie jokes a somewhat cozy warmth in which I, at any rate, was able to doze off while believing I was living an intense, engaged existence.

Wilson spent much of the war at Bletchley Park in Buckinghamshire, the wartime operational headquarters of the Government Code and Cypher School. His activities there remain secret—it is not even known whether his work was high or low level; more important to Wilson's own life, it was there that he suffered a rather severe breakdown. The details of this nervous collapse are vague both in Drabble's treatment and in *The Wild Garden*, but one of its elements, which Wilson would recreate dramatically in Bernard Sands's breakdown in *Hemlock and After*, was a shocking self-realization, specifically the discovery of a streak of cruelty—even sadism—in himself. "I had always thought of myself as a person of unusual gentleness and a natural liking for other human beings. I now learnt that I could hate intimately, if not for long periods, and that I was capable of cruelty, indeed addicted to it, particularly towards those who attracted me most strongly."

Whether or not this period of Wilson's life was the source, it is notable that in each of his novels it is self-knowledge, of all possible human achievements, that poses the ultimate hurdle and test. Gerald Middleton in *Anglo-Saxon Attitudes* is a prisoner of his own weak will until he faces up, not only to the part he unwillingly played in a scholarly hoax many decades earlier but to his many failures in human relationships; when he does, as an elderly man, he is given a new and undreamed-of measure of freedom. The sudden advent of self-knowledge to Bernard Sands in *Hemlock and After*, on the other hand, is so intense and appalling that it kills him. The same pattern, with differing results, is repeated in each novel.

Wilson's obsession with self-knowledge, with facing up to one's own truth, must also have sprung in large part from his disgust at his upbringing within his mother's Christian Science faith. He saw Mrs. Eddy's teachings as investing every human act with an aura of utterly false sweetness and love. "I know well," he wrote, "the unreal sweetness that hangs around that Church. It would be hard to choose a creed—and it was that of Lady Astor and Lord Lothian—better fitted to play into the hands of Hitler's gang. It is never, I suppose, very wise to deny the existence of evil, but it was particularly unwise from 1933 to 1939." In *The Middle Age of Mrs. Eliot,* Meg's vision of the empty, hostile desert stretched out in every direction beneath her airplane is interrupted by an absurd old lady opposite who spouts cozy Christian Science platitudes. And many of Wilson's most baneful characters— Ingeborg Middleton in *Anglo-Saxon Attitudes,* for instance, or the procuress Mrs. Curry in *Hemlock and After*—affect a grotesquely whimsical manner. Any Wilson character who uses the word "loving" is automatically suspect.

With the end of the war, Wilson's fortunes almost immediately looked up. He had moved to a cottage in the village of Little Hadham during the war and there he began—in an almost offhand manner— his career as a writer. "I never wrote anything—except for the school magazine—until November, 1946," he later told *The Paris Review.* "Then I wrote a short story every weekend for twelve weeks. I was then thirty-three. My writing started as a hobby." On a visit to Little Hadham, Wilson's friend Robin Ironside read the work and, impressed, showed it to Cyril Connolly, to whom Wilson, like so many authors of the period, was to owe his initial success: "Mother's Sense of Fun" appeared in Connolly's *Horizon* in November 1947, "Crazy Crowd" the following April. In March 1949, Secker & Warburg brought out the whole collection as *The Wrong Set and Other Stories,* to considerable acclaim. Sean O'Faolain wrote, "He has already written some of the best satirical stories of his generation . . . he is already completely *déniaisé*, though without, thank goodness, losing his pity or his feeling. It may be this rare combination of sharp wit and soft heart that makes one reader at least believe that this is a man marked out for fame." John Betjeman, Philip Toynbee, and Frank O'Connor agreed, and the book sold out in two weeks.

Wilson was moving up in the hierarchy of the British Museum, too. In 1950 he was made deputy superintendent of the Reading Room, an extremely congenial position to him. He quickly became a fixture, still remembered vividly by many readers. Drabble writes, "His elevation placed him conspicuously on a raised dais in the center of the Reading Room beneath Panizzi's beautiful dome, a colourful bird in a vast circular cage, bow-tied, blue-rinsed, chattering loudly to readers and staff and friends on the telephone. . . . He never ever said 'Shh!' "

In December 1945 Wilson had noticed a handsome young assistant at the museum. He was Anthony Garrett, an intelligent boy from a lower-middle-class background who had had to leave school at sixteen without the higher education he had hoped for. Wilson was involved elsewhere at the time, but he definitely took an interest. Their relationship gradually developed until, by around 1950, they had become an established couple. They were to remain so until Wilson's death forty years later.

Tony emerges from Drabble's narrative as an almost saintly character. For decades, with unfailing and impeccable manners, he played what Wilson described as "the difficult role that is seldom perfectly played—the celebrity's helpmate." It was often rough going. Though Tony acquired credentials in social work and launched himself into a career as probation officer in the Metropolitan Magistrates Court—a job he enjoyed and performed well—widespread gossip over his relationship with Wilson forced him, in 1960, to resign. From that moment he became Wilson's full-time secretary and chauffeur as well as his companion.

Gay helpmates of celebrities, of course, tended to get even shorter shrift with the public than celebrity wives. As Nancy Mitford wrote from Paris to a friend at about that time,

> There is a new problem for the hostesses here do you have it? which is this. Chaps ring up and say can they bring their homosexual wives. "You know Hans, you met him at so-and-so's" or "Roberto who is staying with me" or one just said "my partner" like a deb dance. Then these fearful gorillas appear. They have no conversation & are not even pretty or not to ONE anyway. . . . What do you do in London?

Unlike these apes, Tony, intelligent and personable, was popular with Angus's friends; still, he spent many an evening waiting with the car while Angus was being lionized at one gala event or another.

Wilson's second volume of stories, *Such Darling Dodos*, was published in 1950. Again, it was greeted with enthusiasm. In the *Sunday Times*, C. P. Snow wrote: "Part-bizarre, part-macabre, part-savage and part-maudlin, there is nothing much like it upon the contemporary scene." Others, such as John Osborne, concurred. Wilson was turning out to be a writer fascinatingly difficult to classify: while he was still (as he was to remain) passionately liberal and nominally left wing, he disliked left-wing self-deception as much as the right-wing variety, and didn't mind exposing his disdain. *Such Darling Dodos* shows a chilly skepticism about progressive ideals and Labour Party dogma. "I was struck then," he later wrote, "by the fact that a mild social revolution had taken place in England overnight. . . . Readers and critics alike responded to this aspect of my stories. Indeed it earned me a reputation for being a 'social satirist,' which seems to me only an aspect of my writing."

Wilson's *Emile Zola: An Introductory Study of His Novels* was published in 1952. He was later to write two other literary biographies, *The World of Charles Dickens* (1970) and *The Strange Ride of Rudyard*

Kipling (1977). Dickens and Kipling and, to a lesser extent, Zola were writers who fascinated him not only in their own right but because, as he was aware, he shared many qualities with them. All three are good biographies, *Kipling* particularly fine, and considering the period it was written, with Kipling's reputation beginning to reach its miserable nadir, particularly sympathetic.

Hemlock and After, Wilson's first novel, was also published in 1952. It is the story of an elderly and popular novelist, Bernard Sands, whose two lives as a married public figure and a secret homosexual lead him into impossible contradictions. Through a combination of selfishness and wrong principle, Bernard fails his wife, children, and ultimately the young man he loves; finally his recognition of his own dark side kills him.

Though the novel seems rather incomplete and awkward compared with the more expert *Anglo-Saxon Attitudes,* which was to follow, it is alive with talent and with the author's own unusual sensibility. It was also of interest in that it dealt with themes that had seldom been handled openly in the English novel. It is one of the first novels to deal with homosexual life, and the homosexual world, quite casually. Wilson was highly flattered when E. M. Forster wrote expressing his interest in the book and discussing various points in it, but his disenchantment with Forster and his values was already beginning. Forster's style of humanism, with its emphasis on the primacy of human relationships, seemed to him inadequate, and as the years went on he came to feel that the elderly Forster, who wielded possibly more moral authority than any other writer in England, should have had the courage to "come out" at long last.

While in early days, at least, Wilson did not advertise his sexual preferences to the public, neither did he make any effort to hide them. A series of homosexual scandals in the 1950s—Guy Burgess's flight to Moscow in 1951, John Gielgud's arrest in 1953, Alan Turing's suicide in 1954, and the Montagu case the same year—were bringing the question of the legalization of homosexuality into the public consciousness. Later in the decade Wilson would serve on the executive committee of the Homosexual Law Reform Society and sign a letter to the London *Times* in support of the recommendations of the Wolfenden report. Throughout the sixties and seventies he would support gay rights, though he didn't like the word "gay" and balked at being referred to on television as Tony Garrett's "lover"—surely at his age, he asked, "friends" would do just as well?

His sexuality at any rate, combined with his peripatetic childhood, gave him a professional advantage, for gay culture cut across class boundaries in a way unknown to straight England. Wilson made full use of the knowledge this afforded him, and indeed, in his mimetic brilliance, his ability to assume the voice of charwoman, spiv, or society hostess, he was unequaled in his generation.

In 1955 Wilson began writing *Anglo-Saxon Attitudes,* a novel that was to be far longer and more complex than anything he had attempted before. Its challenges were such that Wilson resigned his post at the British Museum, thus giving up the financial security that had meant so much to him. It was not a decision he was ever to regret, but because his novels provided an inadequate income, it meant that for the rest of his life he would have to find alternative means of making a living, a process that became more and more difficult as he aged.

Anglo-Saxon Attitudes is indubitably the finest of Wilson's novels. It is the most skillful and controlled, the most firmly focused upon its principal theme, and at the same time the one with the broadest, and most vivid, social scope. "It is because I wanted to create [a] sense of 'life' that I have often used sub-plots and other old-fashioned devices," Wilson later commented. "Some novelists try to make the magic work by taking you deep down inside one person. I try to multiply the worlds I put into the books." In *Anglo-Saxon Attitudes* he succeeded superbly. Its hero, Gerald Middleton, is about as unlike Wilson himself as it is possible to be—an elderly, introverted academic with a distinguished military bearing, and a moral defeatist of long standing. The novel fans out into expanding circles of odd characters: medievalists, archaeologists, a violent Futurist poet, an old-fashioned "county" girl, an aspiring French bourgeoise, a self-deluded television personality. Most memorable, perhaps, is the raffish homosexual waiter Vin Salad and his grandmother, an insinuating charwoman.

Wilson is not afraid of making his creatures appear in a grotesque light, and some readers have disliked what they see as being unremittingly ugly or unpleasant. Wiliam Plomer, for instance, admired Wilson's cleverness but complained that his stories seemed to him "like the work of a hysterical misanthrope and misogynist, screaming like an ape that can't get out of its smelly cage." Wilson resisted this sort of evaluation. "Vulgarities, lack of discrimination, weaknesses . . . appear to me widespread and no more than venial beside the real wickedness of life," he objected. "I really don't know why people find my characters unpleasant. I believe—perhaps it would be different if I were religious—that life is very difficult for most people and that most people make a fair job of it." Be that as it may, *Anglo-Saxon Attitudes* boasts some of the most monumentally, and delightfully, unpleasant characters in modern literature: Ingeborg Middleton, Gerald's maudlin and self-deluding wife, who affects the demeanor of a gigantic and self-pitying baby; the "Quilpish" Yves Houdet, a vulgarian, a bore, and a sadist; Gerald's narcissistic son-in-law Donald Consett, whose nearest approach to a smile is described as a fish seeming momentarily to flash behind his glasses.

The trick that Wilson pulls off is in making these grotesques believable within the atmosphere of his novel. It was a test he would fail in *No Laughing Matter* (1967), possibly his best novel after *Anglo-Saxon Attitudes*. The characters in *No Laughing Matter* (based closely, maybe too closely, on his own family) get so exaggerated, and the prose so mannered, that many readers must have given up early, sated on bile. Wilson was accomplished at producing realistic fiction—*The Middle Age of Mrs. Eliot* is a realistic book, and *Late Call* (1964), the story of an elderly hotel manageress, now retired and living with her upwardly mobile son in a semi-utopian "New Town," is a particularly fine novel in the realistic tradition—but realism as such was not his primary aim. He had no compunction, for instance, about naming two of his gossiping crones Mrs. Wrigley and Mrs. Crawley.

> I have never felt called on to declare allegiance to either fantasy or realism. They proceed from two different levels of my imagination and without their fusion I could not produce a novel. However, if I must choose between two necessities I should consider the "real" as the less essential. . . . The purpose of my book about Zola, who notoriously depended upon exact fact for the stimulation of his imagination, was to show that what mattered was the nature of his imagination, not the facts that stimulated it.

His last two novels, *As If by Magic* (1973) and *Setting the World on Fire* (1980), departed from realism so drastically—and unsuccessfully—as to alienate most of his readers.

With the 1960s dawned "the age of the conference," as Drabble puts it, and Wilson was one of the most energetic conference-goers of the age. Throughout the sixties and seventies he was on the move—sometimes on pleasure trips to the Far East or North Africa, but usually on some sort of official business, speaking at writers' conferences or PEN or British Council functions, or serving as a visiting professor in one or another American university. Such engagements were absolutely essential in providing supplementary income. (Wilson, a critical success, had never been a big seller, and with the exception of *Late Call*, which was adapted for television by Dennis Potter, none of his books was sold to the movies or TV during his lifetime.) Drabble's narrative loses a good deal of its drama at this point; at least half of her exhaustive recitation of official dinners and cocktail parties is unnecessary.

But not all of this is dull. One point of interest is Wilson's sheer virtuosity on the podium. As one observer noted, he could "deliver an hour-long lecture at the rate of at least 150 words a minute (that is, very fast) in all some 9000 words, with the aid of nothing but three or four sentences scrawled on a piece of note paper." (Wilson had a couple of successful moments as a television interviewer but was deemed "too queer" to be regularly employed.)

Wilson's conference-going was to influence his political orientation. As early as the 1940s he had been irritated by left-wing self-delusion, and though he remained a liberal throughout his life his later experiences only confirmed his early skepticism. In 1963 he was horrified, at a writers' conference in Leningrad, by the obvious lies and veiled threats being conveyed by Soviet officials (his own experience and impressions are given to Quentin Matthews in *No Laughing Matter*). From this moment he became markedly anti-Soviet, even detaching himself from the anti-apartheid movement as it clearly became an instrument of Soviet foreign policy. After a 1965 visit to Czechoslovakia, Wilson expressed his deepening disgust with "life at the Communist top—the heavy banquets, the bonhomie, the drink, the carefully dowdy sexy women, the threats veiled in joviality, the chauffeured car."

Wilson's last years were sad ones, though they were launched happily enough with a knighthood in 1980 (Wilson was surprised, and, being "under no illusion that Mrs. Thatcher personally admired his work," thought it probable that she didn't know who he was). But Wilson aged early and was already infirm at seventy. At this juncture he and Tony made a fatally ill-advised decision to move to the South of France. It quickly became evident that Wilson was really ill with what would turn out to be hydrocephalus: his sense of balance was degenerating, and bouts of mental disorientation and paranoid delusions became frequent. Tony became a round-the-clock nurse, for without spare cash they could not afford help.

After a very long and pitiful decline, Angus Wilson died, nearly destitute, on May 31, 1991, at Pinford End House, a nursing home near Bury St. Edmunds. Tony Garrett, who had sought financial help for Angus, refused it for himself. He lived monastically and in 1994 was received into the Roman Catholic church.

Reflecting upon the years of work he had put into his biography of Kipling, Wilson had come to the conclusion that no biographer can really hope to successfully invade another human personality. This epitaph on biography is certainly applicable to Drabble's effort, sustained and impressive though it is. Wilson's personality was obviously a far darker and more complex one than his butterfly surface implied. Drabble acknowledges Wilson's unpleasant aspects, frequently exposed by the hysteria that often came too close to the surface, the sadistic streak, and the depression and insecurity. Nevertheless this dark side repeatedly eludes her, and in the end it is Wilson's sunny, chattering, charming persona that remains so clearly in the reader's mind. Perhaps this is just as well, and will serve to attract new readers to Wilson's eccentric, intelligent fiction.

[*1996*]

Carson McCullers:
The Story of an
Emotional Vampire

To call Carson McCullers an eccentric, as some have done, is one of the great understatements of all time. McCullers was deeply, prodigiously weird. Sensitive and vulnerable to an almost pathological degree (the actress Anne Baxter called her "skinless"), she was also a tough survivor, ruthlessly advancing her own agenda and interests at the expense of those she purported to love: "I always felt Carson was a destroyer," her sometime friend Elizabeth Bowen commented, "for which reason I chose never to be closely involved with her." McCullers was a monstrous egoist who put her own talents second to none. ("I have *more* to say than Hemingway, and God knows, I say it *better* than Faulkner," she once asserted, wrongly.) She was an emotional parasite; even her cousin Jordan Massee, who loved her dearly, admitted that "Carson is more demanding than anyone else I have ever known." Lillian Hellman, who did *not* love her, complained that "Carson burdened everyone who got close to her. If you wanted burdens, liked burdens, you accepted Carson and her affection. I don't like such burdens." As for McCullers's sex life, to this day no one seems to be able to figure out just what she did and didn't get up to, though some have suggested that she and her husband, Reeves McCullers, could be aptly described by that well-known limerick,

There once was a fairy named Bloom
Took a lesbian up to his room.
They argued all night
About who had the right
To do what, and with which, and to whom.

McCullers died in 1967 at the age of fifty, after many years of invalidism brought on by a series of strokes. Her self-mythologizing and downright lying would make the biographer's task a difficult one, as those who knew her were aware. "Our girl was given to saying pretty much anything that came into her head," her friend Edward Newhouse said. "If I were given the choice of writing her biography or being shipwrecked on a desert island with Spiro Agnew . . . well, I don't know." Virginia Spencer Carr, an intrepid Southerner, took on the unenviable job and in 1975 produced a very thorough biography that for all its many faults and occasional lapses of taste and insight must be acknowledged a definitive work and one that throws fascinating and often lurid light on its odd subject. Other, less exhaustive studies have followed.

McCullers left behind very little in the way of autobiographical material and what there is of it—some seventy pages of egregiously unrevealing reminiscences dictated during the three months before she suffered her fatal stroke—should, mostly because of her congenital dishonesty, have been deemed unpublishable. But in today's commercial climate nothing is too thin, too feeble, too irrelevant to be publishable so long as it comes with a famous name attached. And so now, more than thirty years after McCullers's death, the University of Wisconsin Press has decided to take the aborted embryo off the shelf, pad it out with Carson's and Reeves's previously unpublished wartime correspondence and the original twenty-page outline for what was to become *The Heart Is a Lonely Hunter,* and publish the whole shebang as part of the Wisconsin Studies in Autobiography series, under the title *Illumination & Night Glare: The Unfinished Autobiography of Carson McCullers.*

In an interview with Rex Reed not long before her death, McCullers gave her reasons for attempting an autobiography:

> I think it is important for future generations of students to know why I did certain things, but it is also important for myself. I became an established literary figure overnight, and I was much too young to understand what happened to me or the responsibility it entailed. I was a bit of a holy terror. That, combined with all my illnesses, nearly destroyed me. Perhaps if I trace and preserve for other generations the effect this success had on me it will prepare future artists to accept it better.

Fat chance! And in any case, though McCullers's early success cannot have improved her character or her always fragile emotional state, it did not make her a holy terror: she was already that, long before her first fiction was published.

Carson McCullers was born Lula Carson Smith in 1917 in Columbus, Georgia, where she spent the first seventeen years of her life. Like many another precocious child, she was abetted by a doting parent, in this case her mother, Marguerite, who when still pregnant informed her friends that secret prenatal signs indicated that the child was destined to be a great artist. Carson's relationship with her mother was to be intense and avidly needy on both sides throughout the two women's lives; in the early years it was tempered by the presence of Carson's rational, quiet father, a jeweler.

Little Lula showed evidence of musical talent, and her mother decided that she should train as a concert pianist. The child, who already longed for fame and notoriety at any cost, went along with the plan happily enough and devoted long hours of every day to her piano studies while her teacher, Mary Tucker, became the first in a long line of people, both male and female, on whom McCullers was to focus her passionate affection and insatiable craving for love.

At the age of seventeen, Carson (she had dropped the Lula four years earlier, much as her adolescent heroine Frankie in *The Member of the Wedding* would transform herself into F. Jasmine Addams) departed for New York, ostensibly to study at Juilliard. But in fact her dreams of a musical career were fading as she discovered a new gift for writing, and once in the city she attended creative writing classes at Columbia and New York universities while supporting herself with a series of unexciting jobs. In 1935 she met Reeves McCullers, an attractive young serviceman from Alabama, as sexually ambiguous as she was herself. They were married in 1937, only a few months after Carson's first published fiction appeared in *Story* magazine.

The roller-coaster aspect of marriage to Reeves, who was to provide both the most supportive and the most destructive relationship of Carson's life, began almost immediately. The "pre-nup" was that Reeves should support them for a year while Carson wrote, and then she would do the same for him. Carson's year of writing produced *The Heart Is a Lonely Hunter* (1940), a stunning success that made her a big-time literary star at the absurd age of twenty-three; after that, of course, it was curtains for any similar ambitions Reeves might have had. Could he have been a good writer? Probably not, but we'll never know. Rather than seizing an equal partnership in the marriage, he accepted the supporting role of helping Carson realize her genius to the fullest. He went to the office, shopped, kept house, and generally ministered to the delicate prodigy, services she grudgingly acknowledged in *Illumination & Night Glare:* "I was completely absorbed in my work, and if the food burned up he never chided me." It would have been surprising if he had chided her, for it was he who did the cooking.

Reeves was also expected to turn a blind eye to Carson's never-ending string of amours, the most serious of which was her infatuation with Annemarie Clarac-Schwarzenbach, a glamorous Swiss intellectual Carson met in 1940. Depressed, Reeves developed an extramarital friendship of his own with the composer David Diamond, to whom he confided his many troubles.

We simply are not husband and wife any more, David. It just doesn't make sense our staying together. When I come home, she either is there or is not there, without any explanation. Sometimes she comes home early in the morning, sometimes not. After all, she sleeps with whom she pleases, sees whom she wants. I'm not a husband any longer.

A strange three-way relationship between Reeves, Carson, and Diamond was soon to develop and to become one of the central events in Carson's life, setting the pattern for her lifelong propensity for triangular situations and providing material for both *The Member of the Wedding* (1946) and *The Ballad of the Sad Café* (1951). It is entirely omitted, however, from this "memoir," along with almost all other material of a very personal nature.

A heavy drinker even at the best of times—as was Carson herself—Reeves now hit the bottle ever harder and began to show signs of the instability that would eventually take over and wreck his life. The couple separated in 1940, after Carson sold *Reflections in a Golden Eye* to *Harper's Bazaar,* and she moved into a brownstone in Brooklyn Heights with George Davis, the literary editor of *Harper's Bazaar,* and W. H. Auden. It was a notorious household that would over the course of a few years come to include Gypsy Rose Lee, Benjamin Britten, Virgil Thompson, Paul and Jane Bowles, Richard Wright, and Oliver Smith, among many others. Carson stayed there less than a year. She and Reeves were divorced in 1941.

She spent the war years working on *The Member of the Wedding* and, on the death of her father, moved with her mother to Nyack, New York. Marguerite Smith spent the rest of her life there, and the house also functioned as home base for the more peripatetic Carson and for her long-suffering younger sister, Rita, who as the only really sane woman in this trio, as well as the least self-indulgent, inevitably had to put in a good deal of time as physical and emotional caretaker.

And as the war drew to an end Carson found herself once again in passionate correspondence with Reeves, who participated in the Normandy landings and fought in France, Luxembourg, Belgium, and Germany. Still "in love"—whatever that meant!—they decided to remarry.

In *Illumination & Night Glare,* McCullers is characteristically shifty about her reasons for remarrying.

> I don't know why I felt I owed such devotion to him. Perhaps it was simply because he was the only man I had ever kissed [a likely story!] and the awful tyranny of pity. I knew he was not faithful to me sexually, nor am I an especially maternal woman. . . . For some reason, certainly against my will, we became deeply involved with each other again and before I really knew what had happened, we were remarried.

Never mind that in 1945 she was writing to Reeves, "Our love for each other is like a sort of natural law, independent of our separate wills, inalterable by circumstances." Reeves's own later rationalization for the remarriage was simpler and more to the point: "I think we are all drones—and Carson is the queen bee."

The second marriage proved even more disastrous than the first. Carson's wave continued to rise, cresting in the Broadway triumph of *The Member of the Wedding,* which won both the New York Drama Critics' Circle and the Donaldson awards. Reeves, whose only real success in life had been in the army (he was highly decorated during World War II), was unable to find a place for himself. His drinking, accompanied now by bouts of paranoia and despair, escalated. In 1952, while the couple was living for a short time in France, his talk of suicide, and even of the two of them making a suicide pact, began to frighten Carson. One day while they were driving to a forest for a woodland walk she looked into the back seat and spied two coiled ropes. In a panic, she got out of the car and hitchhiked home. She never saw Reeves again; not long afterward he succeeded in killing himself.

Like a phoenix, Carson rose renewed and one might almost say refreshed from Reeves's ashes. From this point she spoke of him—as she does in *Illumination & Night Glare*—as though he had been, for her, no more than a strange aberration, and many of her friends were distressed by the constant bad-mouthing she dealt him. Tennessee Williams, normally supportive of Carson in nearly every instance, was especially dismayed: "She spoke of him in the most unkind terms, and it always upset me. Reeves died for her, yet she refused to admit it." Another friend, Simone Brown, said that

> What Reeves did for Carson was beyond human endurance. He loved her too much—just as we all did. Carson had a terrible power of destruction. She destroyed everything around her—everything she loved. Yet she also wanted to give. It was a viperish thing—all involved in a rather unusual cycle of love. One can see it in her works. Certainly *The Ballad of the Sad Café* illustrates that power of destruction.

Although Carson's health was increasingly frail she traveled when she could, enjoying her role as an international celebrity and the hospitality of friends all over Europe and America. She also worked on another play, *The Square Root of Wonderful* (1958). It turned out to be a flop, but it brought her a new lover, the producer Arnold Saint Subber. When she died in 1967 Carson McCullers was physically wasted and had not written anything of substance for fifteen years, but as a literary "personality" she was still at the top of her game.

Simone Brown's comment on McCullers's character and the way it is reflected in the fiction is very much to the point: McCullers had a devouring wish for love, and her love object, once attained, would in turn be devoured and drained by her voracious needs. More than one of her friends characterized her as an emotional vampire. "To know Carson well, as a friend," said Saint Subber, "was an occupation that took 100 percent of your time. Even going to the bathroom was something you shared with her, as you did every intimate detail." Those who stayed friends with her over a period of years and continued to love and be loved by her tended to be those diplomatic souls, like Tennessee Williams or Carson's cousin Jordan Massee, who appeared to provide infinite love and support but in reality drew boundaries and maintained a necessary distance.

Illumination & Night Glare is blandly opaque, almost in the manner of the Andy Warhol diaries. For anyone who knows much about McCullers's life, the omissions are so many, and so obvious, as to make the whole enterprise ridiculous. The publication of what the University of Wisconsin Press is pleased to call a "memoir" serves no purpose: aside from a few charming reminiscences and a couple of interesting thoughts on the creative process, it tells us nothing truthful about this most bizarre of characters. McCullers's friend Robert Walden hoped that she would not be "depicted biographically for posterity cloaked in white or wearing a halo. She was a bitch, and I don't want her coming out looking like an angel." *Illumination & Night Glare* does, unfortunately, make McCullers look more angelic than she was, and it would be a pity if unwary readers took her at her own valuation of herself. The truth is less palatable but more interesting.

[*2000*]

Backstage at
The New Yorker

I. ROSS

The ungainly figure of Harold Ross has played a leading role in a number of memoirs. Notable among these are James Thurber's *The Years with Ross* (1957), an amusing account of *The New Yorker*'s early days, and Brendan Gill's *Here at "The New Yorker"* (1975). Gill, unlike Thurber, was unsentimental about Ross, indeed frequently acid, but he didn't underestimate the founding editor's contribution to the magazine's success. *Ross, "The New Yorker," and Me* (1968) was written by Ross's first wife, Jane Grant, who managed to turn a fascinating subject into a dull book. Ross also made an appearance in Wolcott Gibbs's 1950 play, *Season in the Sun*, whose stage directions insultingly suggested that the actor playing the Ross part should be able to play Caliban or Mr. Hyde "almost without the assistance of stage makeup."

But oddly enough there has been until now no actual biography of Ross, though the forty years since his death have only confirmed his position as the most influential magazine editor of this century. Thomas Kunkel, a newspaperman who has never before written a book, has rectified the situation with a sympathetic, entertaining, and informative study, *Genius in Disguise: Harold Ross of "The New*

Yorker." As his title suggests, Kunkel writes with a mission: to dig Ross, the real Ross, out from under the avalanche of anecdotes that have obscured his talents and made him out to be a charming but absurd "character," a Colorado rube who had no business setting himself up as an arbiter of fashion and taste.

While admitting that Ross was a highly colored individual, Kunkel objects to the cartoonish treatment accorded him by Thurber and Gill.

> This cartoon Ross was said to be aggressively ignorant, unfailingly rude, sexually naive, and generally intolerant. His comic tendencies were exaggerated, his editing acumen trivialized, and his achievements laid to dumb luck and the skill of his bemused, solicitous associates. As with all caricatures, there were nuggets of truth underlying each of these assertions, but on the whole they were rubbish. Even so, this deleterious view of Ross took such firm hold that today, if he is remembered at all, it is as Ross the Wonder Editor, the literary equivalent of the precocious pony at the sideshow who taps out sums with his hoof.

Kunkel's defense of Ross has produced a wonderfully readable biography, but I'm not at all sure that Ross ever really needed defending in the first place. Thurber and Gill might have had some fun at Ross's expense, but they were always aware that he was, if not necessarily a "genius," then an editor of very great gifts. "He had a sound sense," Thurber wrote, "a unique, almost intuitive perception of what was wrong with something, incomplete or out of balance, understated or overemphasized," and almost all of The New Yorker writers "would rather have had the benefit of his criticism than that of any other editor on earth." Gill was admittedly a greater fan of William Shawn, who succeeded Ross, but he never denied the fact that The New Yorker owed everything to Ross's wild energy and pertinacity. He credited

Ross with understanding that the real success of his magazine was due to his own willingness to encourage "people more talented than he to do their work better than they had hitherto known how to do it, largely by being harder on themselves than they had been accustomed to be. Simple enough, but how rare!"

Kunkel attempts to come up with a plausible response to the question asked by Ben Hecht and in fact by nearly everyone who knew Ross: "How the hell could a man who looked like a resident of the Ozarks and talked like a saloon brawler set himself up as pilot of a sophisticated, elegant periodical?" There are two partial answers. First: *The New Yorker*, at least in its earliest days, was not really all *that* sophisticated. Ross's imposition of the editorial "we" and a tone of amused but rather jaded condescension reflected not so much his own sophistication as his idea of what "sophisticated" ought to sound like, and it didn't fool everyone; more than one reader back in the twenties felt that the magazine betrayed its staff's "too-recent escape from Middle-Westernness." True sophistication of the kind Ross sought only came to *The New Yorker* with the arrival, in 1927, of the young writer E. B. White, and with the addition of Katharine Angell (soon to be Mrs. White) to the editorial staff. At that time, though Ross had already come up with many of the magazine's final, successful, ingredients—"Comment," "Talk of the Town," the profile, the one-line cartoon—his real challenge lay in recognizing that White's voice, playful, bemused, and ironic, set exactly the editorial tone he had been looking for, and in effectively setting White to work his magic throughout the magazine. In 1927 Wolcott Gibbs and Thurber also began work at *The New Yorker*, and the magazine of which Ross had long dreamed finally came into existence. In Gill's words, "Ross perceiving that, though the magazine was his, the persona of the magazine must be White-Thurber is what led to its success." This is patently true, though, as Kunkel wittily illustrates, the editor's distinctive personality made its mark on the magazine in the guise of the Thurber Man: King Clode, Walter Mitty, and any number of other beleaguered husbands owe a clear debt to Harold Ross.

Second: it hardly needs saying that Ross himself was not quite as unsophisticated as he liked to make out. Playing dumb was something of an editorial strategy: he never pretended to know something if he didn't, but he often pretended not to know something he really did, posing as the most ignorant reader possible in order to inspire his writers to greater intelligibility. Marc Connelly described this technique vividly:

> After *The New Yorker* was solidly established, Ross, pretending ignorance, would often listen with an imbecilically gaping mouth to something being said by a crony of which he had more knowledge than the speaker. At the conclusion of an incorrect statement he would yell with make-believe fury, "That shows you're a god-damned ignoramus!" and then proceed with lordly politeness to state the facts. However, if a comparative stranger pretentiously said something inaccurate, Ross would merely grunt an acceptant "Uh-huh" and walk away.

Occasionally, of course, and despite his impressive store of general knowledge on all sorts of subjects, Ross's ignorance was only too genuine. Perhaps the most famous Rossism was his query, "Is Moby-Dick the man or the whale?" but my own favorite is when, not knowing he was dealing with a quotation, he edited "nature red in tooth and claw" to read, for some obscure reason of his own, "nature red in claw and tooth."

To pretend ignorance was part of Ross's obsessive quest for clarity in his magazine, a hard-fought campaign which must on occasion have driven his writers half mad. As A. J. Liebling put it, clarity "is a fine and necessary quality, but you can go just so far with it. You cannot make subtlety or complexity clear to an extraordinarily dull reader, but Ross in editing would make himself *advocatus asinorum.*" Liebling estimated that of the scores of marginal questions Ross scrawled on every manuscript, perhaps 2¾ percent would actually improve the article. (This editorial technique did not die with Ross: the poet Donald Hall remembers the manuscript of a profile he was working on being sent back by William Shawn with 150 queries and notes on a single page.) In Liebling's own assessment, it was not Ross's pursuit of clarity that made him a great editor, it was his attention to the entire product, the fact that he took everything seriously, from fiction to fashion notes. For example, wrote Liebling, "he knew no more of horse racing than a hog of heaven, but he knew how to find and keep Audax Minor, G. F. T. Ryall, whose tone is precisely right for *The New Yorker.*"

Perhaps the real secret of Ross's success lay in his willingness to be infinitely adjustable in accepting the evolution of his brainchild into something very different from what he had planned. The triumphant *New Yorker* of the thirties and forties, after all, was not exactly the publication that Ross had envisioned when he launched the magazine in 1925. Ross conceived it first and foremost as a humor magazine. His own tastes and experiences pointed him in that direction. As a private in World War I he had (with a group that included Alexander Woollcott and John Held, Jr.) edited the enlisted men's newspaper, *Stars and Stripes;* upon demobilization he launched *The Home Sector,* a weekly magazine for the ex-GI; after that he did a stint as co-editor of *Judge,* a "wheezy and out of step" humor magazine. He had for years been bothered by the moribund nature of what passed for humor in popular magazines, and he hoped to revolutionize the genre by producing a quality publication in which humor would be of paramount importance and whose "general tenor," according to Ross's prospectus, would be "one of gaiety, wit and satire." Ross succeeded beyond his own dreams in revolutionizing American humor: perhaps his greatest legacy (and that of the magazine's brilliant and original art director, Rea Irvin) is the invention and perfection of the modern cartoon, which under Irvin and Ross changed from the corny "he said/she said" illustrated gag to an economical one-line medium of real art and real wit, with image and word intrinsically linked.

But as the Jazz Age drew to an end, and New York and the world entered a more serious era, it became evident that humor was no longer *The New Yorker*'s principal raison d'être. During the depression, it's true, the magazine's writers—with the notable exception of White—had failed to catch the right tone. "Let's let the other magazines be important," Ross would say, using "important" as a euphemism for "dull." The facetious man-about-town editorial manner jarred with the city's obvious poverty and despair, and the magazine was accused of "sitting out" the depression. But as the thirties progressed and the international situation grew increasingly grave, the magazine's writers responded with a new sense of seriousness and political engagement; even the fiction changed in tone as the carefree note struck by early contributors like Thurber, Robert Benchley, S. J. Perelman, Clarence Day, and Dorothy Parker gave way to more serious work by writers such as Cheever, Shaw, and O'Hara, work which we now think of, in fact, as "*New Yorker* fiction."

Ross, an isolationist and a conservative, accepted the fact that his best writers were quite otherwise, and following the urging of Shawn, who had joined the magazine's staff in 1933, gave them a free rein to write what they thought important. The war years saw *The New Yorker* definitively take its place as a forum for serious political writing, thanks to the war coverage of Liebling, Janet Flanner, Molly Panter-Downes, Rebecca West, and others. This is not to say that Ross did not occasionally chafe at the high seriousness that had overtaken his "comic paper." His discomfiture was still apparent in 1946 when John Hersey's powerful essay "Hiroshima" weighed in at 31,000 words. Ross knew that the article was as important as anything he had yet published and would create a sensation; he knew that for maximum impact it should be published in full rather than serialized; but he could hardly bear to do the dirty and bump cartoons, Newsbreaks, "Talk of the Town," and the other regular features that week to make room for it. As Kunkel writes, "gutting the issue to run 'Hiroshima' amounted to the final capitulation, the ultimate admission from its editor that his onetime comic sheet was now so serious and, alas, so respectable that it could comfortably publish the most sober testament he had ever read." Ross made the admission and gutted the issue (in the process getting rid of Hersey's original, pretentious title, "Some Events at Hiroshima"). There can be little doubt that he did the right thing, though times have changed to such a degree that one now looks back with regret to a time when *The New Yorker* did not take itself quite so seriously, when the editor actually believed the dissemination of humor, rather than of editorial opinion, to be his real mission in life.

Thomas Kunkel tells Ross's story in an engagingly fresh and slangy language, a style not unlike that of Ross's own letters and memos, and the result is that genuine sense of sympathy between writer and subject which is always to be desired but not by any means always to be found. Kunkel crams his book with fascinating details, from the invariable lunch menu of the magazine's publisher, Raoul Fleischmann (two martinis straight up, a dozen oysters on the half-shell, and ice cream), to the explanation for Janet Flanner's mysterious pen name Genêt (it was Ross's notion of how "Janet" might sound in French). Kunkel's easy acknowledgment of Ross's many shortcomings is appealing, and he achieves real delicacy in writing of Ross's tragicomic domestic life: Ross shared many tastes and interests with his first wife, Jane Grant, a *New York Times* reporter who was instrumental in getting *The New Yorker* off the ground, but his subsequent two wives were good-looking lowbrows with whom he had little in common, and both marriages were short-lived. "Marriage was probably not his natural state," said Clifton Fadiman. "His natural state was talking with guys at a bar or at dinner. He was very male—*very* male."

Ross was by nature antipathetic to feminism (claiming that his marriage to Jane Grant had failed because "I never had one damned meal at home at which the discussion wasn't of women's rights and the ruthlessness of men in trampling women"), and though he was clearly a sucker for a pretty face he had no sincere interest in women or in women's concerns.

Kunkel's book is important as the first serious biography of a major figure in twentieth-century letters, but not as an effort to convince the world that Harold Ross was a misunderstood genius. "Genius" is always a fraught, subjective term, and though Ross certainly had greatness of a kind, the word "genius" as applied to him is not only dubious but irrelevant. He was a phenomenon; he had tremendous influence on every aspect of magazine publishing and writing. But his memory has never really been in need of polishing, for in fact Ross long ago captured the public imagination, not because of his absurdity but because of his attractions. Ross embodied the American Dream: rough-hewn, plainspeaking, masculine; a Western gee-whiz guy who despised college men and society sophisticates yet created a publication that was the last word in sophistication; an anti-intellectual in the real American tradition who was able to beat the intellectuals at their own game. As Thurber knew, Ross was as magnificent and uncompromising as a great character of fiction; he could have stepped straight from the pages of Mark Twain. His new biographer does him every justice.

II. SHAWN

The New Yorker has become as much a sacred cow for the American mainstream as it is for the cultural elite. This fact has just been demonstrated by the top-priority press treatment given to Tina Brown's departure from the magazine and S. I. Newhouse's choice of

David Remnick as editor. The changeover was awarded a front-page spread in the *New York Times* and a page six cartoon in the *Post*, among other choice spots; it's hard to imagine any other periodical in this country arousing such curiosity about its behind-the-scenes doings. The whole fuss is nothing, though, compared with an even more seismic event in the magazine's life: its 1985 takeover by Newhouse and his ouster of longtime editor William Shawn, the man who for many years personified and defined *The New Yorker*.

The avid interest taken in two new chronicles of Shawn's tenure, published a decade after its actual end, shows that the aftershocks are still being felt. Since these books were written by Lillian Ross and Ved Mehta, two of Shawn's writers and closest colleagues, unwary readers might well pick them up under the impression that they will deliver original or insightful views of the magazine and its revered, famously fastidious editor. But they will be disappointed.

Ved Mehta, who came to the magazine as a young writer in 1960 and stayed on until Tina Brown slammed the door on him some thirty years later, has written *Remembering Mr. Shawn's "New Yorker,"* a chronicle of his own experience. Mehta openly idolizes Shawn, for all the right reasons, and for the wrong ones as well.

"Like editors from an earlier period," Mehta writes of Shawn, "he thought that his job was to educate readers by exposing them to thought-provoking material, irrespective of how many of them would actually read it." This is true, and it was Shawn's great strength. But Mehta is constitutionally incapable of disinterest: he tells his tale obtusely, from the narrow point of view of a needy author seeking approbation from the editor he has cast as both father figure and psychoanalyst. In the process he bestows on that editor unconditional and frequently irrational love.

In fact Shawn was a fine editor without being a perfect one, and his detractors were no philistines, though Mehta would like to believe this to be the case. Shawn's finicky editorial policies annoyed any number of readers and made many who were essentially in step with the magazine—natural *New Yorker* readers as it were—neither entirely surprised nor entirely sorry at his firing. One of the cleverest of Shawn's critics was Tom Wolfe, who memorably attacked the editor in a 1965 article in the soon-to-be-defunct *Herald Tribune.* Entitled "Tiny Mummies! The True Story of the Ruler of 43rd Street's Land of the Walking Dead!" Wolfe's piece presented the magazine as a morgue and Shawn as its reigning mortician.

Shawn and his writers did not laugh off the attack, for it was recognized that while Wolfe had gone over the top, he had also hit on a certain truth. *The New Yorker*'s articles were indeed too long, too boring, too polite, too genteel. Shawn's ruthlessly thorough editing took the juice out of pieces; even great literature, it was said, would not have survived his nitpicking. (I was once told of an in-office joke at *The New Yorker,* which proposed twenty immortal lines as they might be edited and improved by the magazine: it led off, I remember, with "It was the best of times, and, ironically, it was the worst of times.")

"Notes and Comments" as conceived and executed for many years by the inimitable E. B. White was a marvelous invention, but as White *was* inimitable, why keep trying to duplicate his distinctive voice, bemused and slightly supercilious, for decades after his departure from the magazine, as though his successors were attempting to channel him from beyond the grave? And what about the magazine's quixotic stand against four-letter words? It was one thing during the prudish Harold Ross's day, but as the Shawn era progressed into the sixties and beyond, the circumlocutions and euphemisms became downright silly: Pauline Kael's rage when Shawn tried to replace "ass" with "derrière" in her work, or "crap" with the ridiculous "ordure," was more than understandable.

It is worth quoting Mehta at some length on his first meeting with Shawn, during which they discussed the possibility of the young man's doing a piece about his recent return to India:

After a moment, [Shawn] said, "I don't think that your article sounds like a *New Yorker* piece—although I don't know what that is. But if you write it, and want to send it to me, I would be glad to read it and help you revise it. I would also think of a magazine that might be interested in publishing it."

I felt a little disheartened. In some part of my mind, I had thought that his listening to me with complete attention meant that he would accept the article. I wanted to ask how I could go about writing an article for *The New Yorker*—for him. But I realized that if I did I would come off sounding like a child who was asking his father to do his homework.

Instead, I said, "How long do you think the piece should be?" . . .

"You should not worry about that. You should simply write it to its natural length—whatever that is," he said.

The simplicity of his answer dazzled me. I came away feeling that everything about Mr. Shawn and *The New Yorker*'s offices was magical.

It is easy enough for a third party to read between the lines of this exchange, although Mehta does not. First of all, he doesn't seem to realize, even these many years later, that Shawn's prevarication was simply a polite way of being noncommittal. In later years Mehta would be puzzled when Shawn would claim to be interested in a piece but would nevertheless decline to give the writer an expense account or an advance: for example, "He had adroitly ducked my question about expenses. Perhaps he thought that being concerned with money was corrupting to the sanctity of a writing project, and that the matter should be left out until the project was brought to fruition." On the other hand, the reader suspects, perhaps Shawn was simply unwilling to commit money to a piece he wasn't very excited about!

Second, Shawn's "You should not worry about that. You should simply write it to its natural length," while no doubt being music to

Mehta's ears, typified an editorial policy that resulted in countless pieces of lengthy and undisciplined nonfiction and alienated a great many readers. The work of writers like Kael, and Mehta himself, would have been vastly improved if the authors had been held firmly to a maximum word count. It is certainly possible that each piece has a natural length; but the author is not always the fittest person to decide what that length might be. The editor is.

But giving writers their heads was a part of the soothing, sanatoriumlike environment Shawn fostered for his creative staff. Charles McGrath, Shawn's onetime deputy and designated successor at the time of his firing, wrote in an amusing article for *The New York Times Book Review* that Shawn's self-effacing persona encouraged writers to project all their hopes and needs upon him. "Not a few," he noted, "compared the process to psychoanalytic transference." *The New Yorker*'s writers (maybe all writers!) have over the decades been a notoriously neurotic lot, with a disproportionate number of alcoholics, schizophrenics, manic- and unipolar depressives, and just plain eccentrics. For his own reasons, Shawn assumed the role of father, and like greedy children his writers took and took and took: "Of all the scores of writers Bill dealt with over the years," Lillian Ross writes, "including some who were old friends, only [J. D.] Salinger would go out of his way to be helpful to Bill without asking for anything in return."

Mehta sees Shawn as a model of almost saintly self-denial. But Mehta is a poor interpreter of the people and events he describes. Reading, again, between the lines of Mehta's book and of the many other accounts that have been written of Shawn's editorship, it is not difficult to discern that while Shawn was no doubt a man of moral rectitude, kindness, and generosity, he was also a control freak of the deepest dye. In his light and timeless memoir *Here at "The New Yorker,"* Brendan Gill wrote that "Shawn's delicacy is a negative brute force that gets greater results than Ross's positive one"; Charles

McGrath, in the article quoted above, noted that Shawn "had an iron will, and he was not without a subtle appreciation of his own power." The recollections of Jeremy Bernstein, who wrote many essays on scientific subjects during the Shawn administration, were recently published in the *Los Angeles Times Book Review* and are of great interest: he gets more insight about his subject into his three pages than Ved Mehta does in his 414. Especially telling is Bernstein's description of Newhouse and Shawn entering the Rose Room at the Algonquin together, just after Shawn's dismissal.

> I wanted to study their entrance. Mr. Shawn's politeness, which at times verged on aggression, was notorious. You could not get through a door or into an elevator behind him. He would simply stand there until you went first. The entrance to the Rose Room was sufficiently constricted so that one of them had to enter first. . . . When they reached the entrance to the Rose Room, Newhouse put his arm firmly around Mr. Shawn's shoulders and propelled him through first. If you knew what you were watching, everything you needed to know was in that gesture.

It is certainly a good thing for a magazine editor to be detail oriented, but Shawn carried micromanagement to an extreme that was in the end to spell doom for his own tenure and for the magazine he had recreated in his image. For one thing, he lacked the easy ability of his predecessor, Harold Ross, to delegate; he eventually took so much upon himself that his presence in nearly every step of the editorial process became dangerously essential. As a result of, and growing out of, this failing came Shawn's fatal inability to settle upon a successor. In his mid-seventies, long past the mandatory retirement age of sixty-five that had been waived in his case, he dithered over first this candidate and then that; by the time he finally found (in McGrath) one whom his staff was willing to accept, it was too late: Shawn's goose was already cooked.

It was perhaps in his obsessive concentration upon editorial matter that Shawn made his greatest blunder. He was so worried about his own successor, the future editor, that he entirely neglected to worry about an equally or perhaps even more important successor: that of the publisher, Peter Fleischmann. Fleischmann and his father, Raoul, *The New Yorker*'s founding publisher, had always directed the business end of the magazine in a highly eccentric fashion, letting the editors run the show entirely their own way. This was not out of carelessness or lack of interest but the result of a calculated bet on the editors' gifts, and it was a bet that had paid off handsomely.

By the early 1980s, though, Peter Fleischmann was showing signs of running down. His health had been failing for years, and he lacked a capable and interested heir. In retrospect it seems obvious that Fleischmann would simply be compelled, then or very soon, to sell his controlling interest. It would have been something of a miracle if he had sold it to any publisher who would have continued to let the editorial department call each and every shot. Why didn't Shawn admit to himself that such a sale must be imminent? He didn't; and when Fleischmann sold to the highest bidder, rather than, for example, to Warren Buffet, who had at one time wished to buy the magazine and would almost certainly have proved less meddlesome than Newhouse, Shawn was entirely unprepared.

The *New Yorker* staffer who can claim a more intimate knowledge of Shawn than any other is Lillian Ross, who arrived at the magazine more than fifty years ago, hired, along with three other young ladies, because of the dearth of male civilian talent toward the end of World War II. Shawn himself—at that time the managing editor—took them on in defiance of his boss's wishes: Harold Ross "took a dim view of working with women, who were—he was quoted to us as saying crossly—'trouble'," Lillian Ross writes in *Here But Not Here*, her recent memoir. Trouble—and how! For as she recounts in this stunningly trashy book, she and Shawn would soon embark on a forty-year love affair that infinitely transcended, she claims, any residual joy he derived from his marriage. "He said that his real self was not in his home. He said that his presence in his home was a deception, that he made efforts to be with his children, but that he felt like a failure with them. . . . If I left him, he said, it would change nothing in his home. If I left him, he literally could not live."

Now to me this sounds not like some extraordinary and unconventional declaration of love but like very much the sort of thing that a married man, who intends to stay married, only too often says to his mistress. Whatever his reasons, Shawn (who one would have thought already had enough on his plate, between his wife Cecille, their three children, and *The New Yorker*, his true wife) decided that keeping up with a full-time mistress and a second establishment, including a child (a Norwegian boy adopted by Ms. Ross), was a worthwhile expenditure of energy.

Lillian Ross's Shawn, sadly, is as one-dimensional as Ved Mehta's, though this time it is a different dimension. Lillian Ross's Shawn is not the happy family man described by Mehta (and many others) but a lonely, hungering soul. He is not the avid editor taking a visceral joy in his work as described by Mehta (and again, by many others) but a frustrated poet who sees his job as "the ultimate cell," "a man whose individual, creative gifts were obscured and thwarted by his success. He was a tormented man, a man who had the desires of a poet but the duties of a caretaker, and a muse, of poetics." "I am there, but not there," he would say about his marriage.

I'm not suggesting that Ms. Ross is inventing any of this. It is probably all true. But the fact is that in her very different way she is as obtuse, because as self-absorbed, as Mehta. Shawn was simply too wily a customer for either writer to capture. He could live out one side of his personality—the artist, the adventurer—with Ms. Ross, and he did so. His marriage, and his work, obviously fulfilled different needs, and were compartmentalized accordingly.

"After forty years," gushes Ms. Ross, "our love-making had the same passion, the same energies (alarming to me, at first, in our early weeks together), the same tenderness, the same inventiveness, the same humor, the same textures as it had in the beginning." Much of the memoir is in this vein—Ross, like Mehta, could certainly benefit from some of Shawn's editing these days—and publishing it while Cecille Shawn (aged ninety-two) is still alive is either extremely tasteless or pointedly vindictive, despite Ms. Ross's many protestations of sympathy for Cecille and her claims that she, as "the other woman," never envied the official wife for a minute.

Ms. Ross left *The New Yorker* with Shawn; she returned, after his death, to work for Tina Brown, and in her acknowledgments she openly admits that she began her memoir at the behest of a *New Yorker* editor, Katrina Heron, and that she is "indebted to Tina Brown for her unwavering encouragement, her moral support, her creative participation, and, most of all, for her cheerful understanding of love." If the *schlockfest* that follows was truly written with the advice and encouragement of *New Yorker* editors, that fact alone is proof that Brown's *New Yorker* was not what Shawn's was. William Shawn, whatever his faults, would never have let it get by an initial edit.

[*1995, 1998*]

Iris Murdoch,
Drawing-room Philosopher

ONE: Flavia says Hugo tells her that Augustina is in love with Fred.

TWO: "So you've got used to it at last."
"What an odd way of putting it."
"Well, it is startling, I am startled."
"Because it is so sudden."
"Because of what it is."
"Yes, it is like nothing on earth."
"We are like nothing on earth."
"We are made divine. Let us be worthy."
"We shall be."
"To say we are sure may seem rash."
"And naïve."
"But we are sure."

THREE: He paid the taxi man. He rang the bell of the third floor flat. He pressed open the front door and began to climb. He heard Rosalind's door opening above—and the pain now came back and the fear, the *awfulness* of the situation, its bottomless void, suddenly something out of Shakespeare, the dreadful peril of the Bard himself. He heard her door opening above and thought, I will recall this.

*Q*uestion: Two of the preceding quotations are from Iris Murdoch novels, and one is a parody of Murdoch by Malcolm Bradbury. Which is the parody?*

It is easy enough to laugh at such stuff, but it should be remembered that only a writer with a strong individual style is worthy of parody; as Hemingway observed, the better the writer, the more easily parodied he is likely to be. Murdoch, whatever her excesses, is undoubtedly one of the more original stylists of her time. She has also proved to be one of the most consistently interesting and entertaining writers of the last half-century.

A philosopher who has spent many years as a professor at Oxford, where she has been a Fellow of St. Anne's College since 1948, Murdoch infuses her novels with philosophy yet refuses to be labeled a "philosophical novelist." "The consideration of moral issues in the novels may be intensified by some philosophical consideration," she has said, "but on the whole I think it's dangerous writing a philosophical novel. . . . My novels are not 'philosophical novels.'"

Anyone but the most passionate Murdoch fan would be forced to challenge that statement. All of her novels are to some extent philosophical ones. Those in which Murdoch's pure imaginative powers take precedence over her philosophical or theoretic agenda, such as *A Fairly Honorable Defeat* or *The Sea, The Sea,* are complete works of art, whereas those which give the agenda center stage, like *The Green Knight,* are inferior ones. Murdoch's work could, by the unsympathetic reader, in fact be described just as the novels of her writer character Arnold Biffin were so cruelly described in *The Black Prince:* "Jesus and Mary and Buddha and Shiva and the Fisher King all chasing round and round dressed up as people in Chelsea."

But most Murdoch enthusiasts (and there are many, especially in

---

*Answer: ONE. TWO is from *The Green Knight;* THREE is from *Jackson's Dilemma.*

England) read her not for her highbrow credentials, her lifelong professional interest in Plato, or her authority on Sartre and existentialism but because she happens to be a master of drawing-room comedy, a genre that has lost little of its appeal despite the rapidly waning number of drawing rooms and of educated, leisured people to make witty remarks in them. From *Under the Net* (1954) to *Jackson's Dilemma* (1996), Murdoch has continued to set her stories within a rather anachronistic version of the upper middle class.

Her characters are intellectuals, high-level civil servants, artists. With the exception of certain "dropouts" from bourgeois society, such as Jake Donoghue in *Under the Net*, they live lives of enviable material ease, able to devote the larger part of their waking hours to the cultivation of their intellectual interests, their relationships, and their souls. The general level of erudition can be downright absurd: fateful meetings occur at philology conferences or Latin Mass Society dinners; guests at a dinner party will discuss Tolstoy over the soup, Turgenev over the main course, and redemptive suffering over coffee. *A Fairly Honorable Defeat* contains a typical Murdochian lovers' spat, "when Axel had let Simon hold forth for some time about the Titian Pietà in the Accademia before pointing out that it had been finished by Palma Giovane, a fact which Simon certainly ought to have known"—occasioning considerable humiliation for the unfortunate Simon.

These highly stylized lives seem to have been affected neither by postwar austerity nor by the *nouveau riche* social whirl of the Thatcher years. Murdoch makes a few bows to contemporary events like AIDS, but her own "period" was obviously the fifties and sixties, and her novels continue to reflect its way of life. A staggering amount of social drinking goes on: no anemic Chardonnays for these folks but vast quantities of neat whisky or, for the Americanized characters, martinis, and no nonsense about alcohol abuse either. A man hitting a woman—or a woman hitting a man—is a common feature of life, and no heavy weather is made over it. Murdoch's schoolchildren continue to learn Latin and Greek as a matter of course, and usually contrive to be fluent in three or four other languages as well. Even in the 1980s and 1990s her teenagers, somewhat fantastically, address one another as "my dear," and young girls reaching the age of sixteen or so still "put up their hair."

The kind of high artificiality in which Murdoch deals is not for everyone. In a review of *Nuns and Soldiers*, Christopher Ricks gave vent to his irritation:

> If you took away the words "a sort of" or "a kind of" the throb would be audibly hollow. . . . Let me string together the formulae—and every single one of them until the end of this review is taken verbatim from *Nuns and Soldiers*. . . . For her admirers, this novel will be a sort of sacred area, characterized by a kind of happy authority, a kind of intelligent pity, a sort of passionate anarchism, a kind of professional detachment, a kind of elated sadness, etc. etc.

I find this tic less annoying than Murdoch's habit of placing every tenth word within quotation marks, but I believe that both result from the practice of philosophical writing, in which the author must be careful about making uncompromising statements that allow for no qualification. In fact, Murdoch's artificiality can, to the receptive reader, constitute a pleasure in its own right, a manifestation of control, exactitude, and occasionally an exquisite preciosity; it is a refreshing experience to read the work of an author who actually uses words like "pendant" and "couchant" without the slightest self-consciousness.

Social comedy supposes an emphasis upon sexual struggle, and this Murdoch depicts with uncanny intelligence. The self-delusions of lovers and spouses and the petty ignoble deceits they visit on one another are exposed with ruthless honesty; the complexities of the married state are never underestimated. "All married people are unhappy," says one of her characters; true, in Murdoch's work (though she herself has been "happily" married for many years to the critic John Bayley), but such unhappiness does not necessarily imply that the partners would be better off apart. In *The Philosopher's Pupil*, friends observing the violent marriage of brutal George McCaffrey and his stoic wife Stella who "thought that Stella lived in hell were not wrong; but like all those who do not, they failed to understand that hell is a large place wherein there are familiar refuges and corners." Charles Arrowby in *The Sea, The Sea* eavesdrops on Hartley, the old flame he obsessively loves, and her husband Ben; he hears Ben bullying and Hartley cringing, but fails to consider the rather unsavory pleasures that such habitual playacting can bring, for it turns out that Hartley and Ben, while fundamentally unhappy, are nevertheless perversely comfortable within the patterns of their forty-year marriage. "Outsiders who see rules and not the love that runs through them are often too ready to label other people 'prisoners,'" Charles observes, unwittingly describing his own misconstructions to a T.

Murdoch is that rare thing, a woman writer who is hard to classify as a "woman writer." She moves effortlessly between male and female points of view; if anything she seems more comfortable, more authoritative, in the male role. Many of her novels are written in the first person with a male narrator, and they are wholly convincing—to this female reader, at any rate. She is especially adept at depicting the male's method of coldly deciding on which side his bread is buttered and acting accordingly, while at the same time dignifying his selfish decision with illusions of good intentions and right action.

A Severed Head, one of Murdoch's early novels (later turned into a play by Murdoch and J. B. Priestley), is especially rich in such hypocrisies. Martin Lynch-Gibbon, a wine merchant and amateur historian (author of "Sir Eyre Coote and the Campaign of Wandewash"), shilly-shallies between his middle-aged wife Antonia—one of those glossy, avid women who populate Murdoch's fictional world—and his emotional young mistress, Georgie. He finds himself thrown off course by a sudden passion for the enigmatic Honor Klein, but though Martin no longer loves either Antonia or Georgie, he finds himself unable to let them go. He is quite capable of assessing the women dispassionately, taking note, for example, of "the great crystalline tears which [Antonia] used," while simultaneously endowing his own feelings for the two with a self-regarding nobility: "my old love for Antonia, so warm and radiant with golden human dignity, and . . . my love for Georgie, so tender and sensuous and gay."

All of Murdoch's "heroes" wallow in such self-deception, but not all to Martin's extreme degree, and some are quite conscious of their motives, like Jake Donoghue in *Under the Net.* "I was deeply moved," he states at one point. "Yet at the same time I took the thing with a grain of salt. I had often known myself to be moved in the past, and little had come of it." *Under the Net,* despite its serious foundations, is the most farcical of Murdoch's novels, and exhibits an earthiness that her later style, distilled and refined, comes close to losing. Much has been made of Murdoch's debt, in this early novel, to Beckett, but it is in fact more Wodehouse than Beckett, and a large portion of the plot—Sacred Sammy the bookie; the theft of Marvelous Mister Mars, the brilliant canine movie star; the socialist rabble-rouser Lefty Todd proselytizing to toga-clad extras at the Bounty Belfounder film studios—is pure Wodehouse, and very funny. Though such broad farce is not a genre Murdoch was to pursue, a certain strain of it infuses all her work, notably *The Black Prince* and *The Sea, The Sea,* where the passive narrators are persecuted by friends and relatives, like a couple of Bertie Woosters with no Jeeves to protect them.

Murdoch's comedy, though fine in its own right, is nevertheless kept always at the service of a serious theme. Murdoch is perhaps less a philosophical novelist than a religious one. Her main concern is with the death of Christian principles in the West and with the necessity of finding an alternative religious system to take their place.

Through the characters who act as mouthpieces for her own thoughts, such as Brendan Craddock in *Henry and Cato* or Father Damien in *The Green Knight*, Murdoch reiterates fictionally what she has stated in her nonfiction and in interviews: that she believes neither in a personal God, nor an afterlife, nor in the divinity of Christ, but feels that Christianity nonetheless is still central, if only because it happens to be the particular and traditional form which worship has taken in her own country. "The fact is that to lose Christianity would be a most terrible thing," she has said. "The figure of Christ is so compelling. This is what we're so lucky to have."

In Murdoch's fiction, the characters who live in the greatest peril are not those who confront the possibility of evil but those who exist in ignorance of any religious tradition, without the vocabulary or the frame of reference to create a spiritual life for themselves. The young artist Jessica Bird in *The Nice and the Good*, for example, was like most of her fellow students, "entirely outside Christianity. Not only had she never believed or worshiped, she had never been informed about the Bible stories or the doctrines of the Church in her home or school. . . . She was in fact an untainted pagan, although the word suggested a positivity which was not to be found in her life." This is a type that has become increasingly common in the thirty years since this novel was published, for in rejecting Christianity *in toto* we have rejected, along with it, two thousand years of our culture's moral, ethical, and mystical thought and are left with few building blocks toward a viable system of practical spirituality or ethics.

Contemporary philosophy has failed to fill the void. "Kant believed in Reason and Hegel believed in History," wrote Murdoch in her book *The Sovereignty of Good.* "Modern thinkers who believe in neither, but who remain within the tradition, are left with a denuded self whose only virtues are freedom, or at best sincerity, or, in the case of the British philosophers, an everyday reasonableness." Freedom she disposes of as being in most cases illusory, hence existentialism, in which she took an early interest, is finally "an unrealistic and over-optimistic doctrine and the purveyor of certain false values," in which "an unexamined sense of the strength of the machine is combined with an illusion of leaping out of it."

Original sin, though not in its literal Augustinian form, she accepts as a reality that twentieth-century intellectuals have denied to their peril. Of all modern thinkers only Freud, she believes, has presented "what might be called a doctrine of original sin." It is significant that in several of her novels one or more of her characters posit a Freudian explanation for unusual or destructive behavior. In *The Black Prince*, for example, both Francis Marloe and Bradley Pearson himself offer Freudian readings of Pearson's erratic conduct, and in *A Severed Head* the narrator, Martin, ventures an opinion that unacknowledged homosexual urges can explain his ambivalent attitude toward Palmer Anderson. With skill, Murdoch makes us understand that while these theories are convincing and at least partly true, they do not begin to approach the entire "truth." All theories, insofar as they are formulaic, are the property of "that sad crew of semi-educated theorizers who prefer any general blunted 'symbolic' explanation to the horror of confronting a unique human history." As the narrator of *The Philosopher's Pupil* states, "We are in fact far more randomly made, more full of rough and contingent rubble, than art or vulgar psycho-analysis leads us to imagine. The language of sin may be more appropriate than that of science and as likely to 'cure.'"

Murdoch has declared her novels to be more Buddhist than Christian in outlook: Buddhism attracts her because it accepts the possibility of having religion without God, a certainty which many of her characters—people with leftover Christian ideals but unable to believe in a personal God—are seeking. Tuan in *Jackson's Dilemma* searches for evidence of the existence of "Religion without Mysticism, Mysticism without Religion"; Michael in *The Bell* helplessly states, "There is a God, but I do not believe in Him." Many of Murdoch's characters strive after some Christian-derived ideal of "good." Most fail, or achieve only a modest improvement; some, like the ex-priest Brendan Craddock in *Henry and Cato*, go farther down the difficult path. Good, to Murdoch, is an end that we *must* seek, even though it is probably impossible.

What, then, she asks, is to be made "of the command 'Be ye therefore perfect'? Would it not be more sensible to say 'Be ye therefore slightly improved'?" Improvement is certainly to be preferred to no improvement, but the search should not end there. In practical ethics Murdoch sees "good" as the eradication of the self or the ego: "Goodness is connected with the attempt to see the unself." Murdoch's novels illustrate this credo again and again. In *The Green Knight*, the groping and unenlightened but well-meaning Bellamy seeks a life of contemplation in a monastery while his wiser correspondent, Father Damien, urges him to forget about his own soul and do some unromantic and aesthetically unappealing social work at a local home for battered wives. And John Ducane in *The Nice and the Good*, trapped in a seaside cave and faced with almost certain death by drowning, is given a vision of the human ego as wholly ignoble, a greedy and rapacious rat.

> He thought, If I ever get out of here I will be no man's judge. Nothing is worth doing except to kill the little rat, not to judge, not to be superior, not to exercise power, not to seek, seek, seek. To love and to reconcile and to forgive, only this matters. All power is sin and all law is frailty. Love is the only justice. Forgiveness, reconciliation, not law.

Murdoch's characters, then, can be seen as stationed at various points along a continuum between real evil—like Julius King in *A Fairly Honorable Defeat*—and some form of good, or enlightenment. One might predict that the bad characters, like Milton's Satan, would be more interesting and amusing than the good ones, and on the whole this is true: Julius, for example, who represents Satan in the scheme of

179

the novel and plots to break up two happy ménages, often talks a good deal of sense and is far more vivid than his dim, dull opposite number Tallis Browne, who represents Christ in the struggle between good and evil.

Whatever the ethical value of dimness and passivity, they tend to be fatal to fiction. The virtuous Ann Peronett in *An Unofficial Rose,* who out of pure unselfish propriety turns her back on the possibility of happiness with the man she loves to offer herself to the brute she married, seems infuriating rather than admirable, and provides a soft center for what is otherwise a remarkably fine and entertaining novel. Fiction's real strength is in fact the depiction not of pure states of good and evil but of nuances between the two: hence by far the most vivid character in *A Fairly Honorable Defeat* is neither the demonic Julius nor the passive Tallis, nor even Morgan, who symbolizes the human soul torn between them, but a less symbolically loaded character, the sweet-natured homosexual Simon Foster, who survives Julius's machinations and keeps his lover not through any act of unusual nobility but simply by proving not quite as weak and malleable as the arrogant Julius had predicted. The dimness of Tallis indicates an artistic failure: Christ himself, after all, was not dim but by far the most vibrant character in the Gospels, as well as being the wittiest.

Murdoch's novels—and in particular the gloomy *Henry and Cato,* which reads like a mixture of *Brighton Rock, The Heart of the Matter,* and *The Power and the Glory*—sometimes resemble those of Graham Greene, with theological speculation breaking in, often obtrusively, upon a gripping narrative. Like Greene, Murdoch can take perfectly fine characters and turn them into boring representatives of "the good" or mouthpieces for her own theories. Edgar Demarnay in *The Sacred and Profane Love Machine,* for instance, begins as one of Murdoch's most wonderful creations, weeping cravenly and nagging the bereaved Monty Small for a relic of Monty's late wife, whom he had always worshiped. Halfway through the novel, however, the foolish, appealing Edgar disappears and the character becomes a mere repository for Murdoch's own pet views, his vivid and idiosyncratic dialogue disappearing to make way for Murdoch's distinctive idiolect.

"Let it all go, Monty. The resentment and the jealousy and the reliving it all. Sophie is dead and you must *respect* her death, and that means not tearing away at a memory of her personality. Death changes our relation to people. Of course the relation itself lives on and goes on changing. But you must at least try to make it a good relation and not a rotten one. Sophie is dead and you are alive, and your duty is the same as any man's, to make yourself better."

Though this turning of real people into symbolically loaded stock figures mars Murdoch's work—at its worst it can infect her novels with the brittle pretentiousness of T. S. Eliot's *The Cocktail Party*—it is usually kept under control and made an organic part of the larger narrative. Murdoch's novels, especially the pre-1980 ones, hold together and hold up, while those of Graham Greene look, in retrospect, increasingly synthetic: while his "entertainments," such as *This Gun for Hire* and *The Third Man*, endure as classics of their genre, Greene's "serious" work, now that the rather gimmicky novelty of its style is novel no longer, appears forced and artificial.

Murdoch sees the contemplation of great art as a remedy for spiritual failure, and manages to incorporate this theme into almost all her novels. In *The Nice and the Good* the self-delusions of the characters are exposed by Bronzino's uncompromising painting *Venus, Cupid, Folly and Time*; *Hamlet* infuses Bradley Pearson's consciousness in *The Black Prince*; in *An Unofficial Rose* a Tintoretto masterpiece restores and refreshes Hugh Peronett while serving as a symbol of potential freedom for his son Randall. "The greatest art is 'impersonal' because we are not used to looking at the real world at all," Murdoch has written. Art is valuable insofar as it is impersonal, insofar as it diverts the beholder from his "self." Dora Greenfield in *The Bell* goes to the National Gallery to cleanse her soul: "It occurred to her that here at last was something real and something perfect. . . . Here was something which her consciousness could not wretchedly devour, and by making it part of her fantasy make it worthless. . . . When the world had seemed to be subjective it had seemed to be without interest or value. But now there was something else in it after all."

Murdoch, then, parts company with Plato, of whom she otherwise considers herself a follower, on the role of art and the artist. "For both the collective and the individual salvation of the human race," she writes, "art is doubtless more important than philosophy, and literature most important of all. . . . It is the role of tragedy, and also of comedy, and of painting to show us suffering without a thrill and death without a consolation."

[1996]

The Better James Baldwin

Anyone familiar with the fiction and nonfiction of James Baldwin is aware that the formative influence upon his life and career was his stepfather. Baldwin was an illegitimate child; when he was three years old his mother married David Baldwin, a Southerner who had come to New York as part of the great stream of black migration north after World War I. The elder Baldwin labored in a Long Island factory during the week and preached in Harlem storefront churches on Sundays. As a preacher he was passionate but hardly successful; his increasingly bitter harangues were off-putting to his congregations, and he descended, over the years, to ever smaller, grimier, and more insignificant houses of worship.

Young Jimmy was never told that David Baldwin was not his real father, a fact he discovered quite by accident when he was a teenager. He was in effect the eldest Baldwin child in what was to become a large family. David Baldwin's was a powerful, brooding presence that cast a pall over the entire household. "He looked to me, as I grew older," James Baldwin wrote, "like pictures I had seen of African tribal chieftains: he really should have been naked, with warpaint on and barbaric mementos, standing among spears." He was "the most bitter man I have ever met," who emanated "absolutely unabating tension. . . . I do not remember, in all those years, that one of his children was ever glad to see him come home."

Baldwin portrayed his stepfather in all his rage, violence, and religious hypocrisy as the preacher Gabriel Grimes in his first novel, *Go Tell It on the Mountain,* and in that novel he also described his own temporary religious conversion, his experience, as a teenager, of being "saved." He acknowledged that his decision, at the age of fourteen, to become a child preacher was a way in which he could confront his stepfather on his own terms and his own turf, and beat him there. This task turned out to be almost pathetically easy, for David Baldwin's simmering rage and hatred, never far below the surface, made him an unpopular preacher while Jimmy, endowed with the charm of youth and with the verbal glibness that was later to mar so much of his writing, made an immediate hit.

It was only a few short years before the younger Baldwin came to recognize his father's brand of religion—and by extension his own—for what it was: a justification of, and consolation for, the cruelties and injustices that black Americans felt powerless to change, and the sublimation of the debilitating anger that threatened at every minute to overpower them: "a dread, chronic disease, the unfailing symptom of which is a kind of blind fever, a pounding in the skull and fire in the bowels. Once this disease is contracted, one can never be really carefree again. . . . There is not a Negro alive who does not have this rage in his blood—one has the choice, merely, of living with it consciously or surrendering to it."

David Baldwin had surrendered to it long since, a process his stepson vividly imagined in *Go Tell It on the Mountain.* "Hating and fearing every living soul including his children who had betrayed him, too, by reaching towards the world which had despised him," the elder Baldwin went, over the years, from being merely an angry man to one who was literally mad. Laid off from his job, he took to sitting all day at the kitchen table, gazing out of the window and shouting Old Testament curses; eventually he refused to eat, claiming that his family was trying to poison him, and wandered in the streets until he was committed to a state mental institution. Raving and paranoid to the end, he died of tuberculosis just before his stepson's nineteenth birthday.

To James Baldwin his stepfather remained, throughout his life, a fearsome example of what the same "dread, chronic disease" might work on him or on any of his black friends. The picture of David Baldwin was never far from his mind, and when, as a young essayist and fledgling novelist, he decided in 1948 to leave New York for Paris, he looked on the move as a flight, a necessary measure to keep him from going the same way. "By this time . . . I was mad, as mad as my dead father. If I had not gone mad, I could not have left." "I knew the tension in me between love and power, between pain and rage, and the curious, the grinding way I remained extended between these poles—perpetually attempting to choose the better rather than the worse."

The story of James Baldwin's career is in essence the story of that attempt. The question is whether or not he succeeded in it. I believe that the attempt was real—was, in fact, profoundly earnest—but that over the long run he failed; that, although he knew enough to choose "the better" initially, he lacked the stamina and the courage for the long-term effort. The Library of America's editions of Baldwin's essays and early novels, both volumes selected and edited by Toni Morrison, offer the opportunity to assess the career as a whole.

In *Collected Essays*, Ms. Morrison has brought together the published collection, *Notes of a Native Son* (1955), *Nobody Knows My Name* (1961), *The Fire Next Time* (1963), *No Name in the Street* (1972), and *The Devil Finds Work* (1976), and thirty-six previously uncollected pieces. With the fiction, however, she has exercised far greater control: she has included only the first three novels, *Go Tell It on the Mountain* (1953), *Giovanni's Room* (1956), and *Another Country* (1962), as well as the short-story collection *Going to Meet the Man* (1965). Omitted, in other words, are not only Baldwin's plays, *Blues for Mister Charlie* and *The Amen Corner* (both 1964), but his three later novels, *Tell Me How Long the Train's Been Gone* (1968), *If Beale Street Could Talk* (1974), and *Just Above My Head* (1979). The omission of these novels is an act of mercy, both to Baldwin and the reader, for they are fatuous, meandering, unedited rehashes of his earlier themes, and their inclusion would have done Baldwin's current reputation far more harm than good.

The ultimate power of a serious novel, as opposed to that of a comic one, lies in its level of sincerity, the intensity with which it is felt. A great novel, though it does many other things as well, always communicates a potent emotional force. *Go Tell It on the Mountain*, published when Baldwin was twenty-nine, is a good novel, possibly a great one; it reaches a level of fine emotional honesty that none of his other fiction, not even the popular *Giovanni's Room*, would find. It is his most autobiographical piece of work and at the same time his most imaginative; it is the only one, I believe, that lives up to his dictum that "all artists, if they are to survive, are forced, at last, to tell the whole story, to vomit the anguish up. All of it, the literal and the fanciful."

Go Tell It on the Mountain tells the story of the Baldwin family as James Baldwin knew it, and its history as he imagined it. Most of it takes place during a cathartic session of shouting, singing, and testifying in a Baptist church in Harlem, during which the collective history of the Grimes family is related in an interwoven series of flashbacks. Young John Grimes—James Baldwin at the age of about fourteen—provides the central consciousness as he observes the goings-on in church with the sensible cynicism of extreme youth. His stepfather, Gabriel, dislikes him and justifies the dislike by identifying the boy with Sin, in this case the sexual sin of his mother. John, like Baldwin, finds himself "saved" at the end of the novel, but as in Baldwin's case the experience is spurious, a dishonest method of incorporating emotional crisis or of finding a way to bear what cannot be borne.

The religion of adults, of course, is equally false, and in a series of

186

three stunningly executed flashbacks we learn much about Gabriel Grimes, his wife Elizabeth, and his sister Florence; what they are, and what has brought them to this moment on their knees before a false God. Exposed are Gabriel's own sin and grief, Elizabeth's lost chance for love, and Florence's anger, ambition, and blighted hopes. The language is pithy, the descriptive passages brief and always to the point. There are a few false notes: Richard, John's dead father, is too obviously the father the author would dearly love to have had rather than a real human being like Gabriel or like John himself, and the long sections of singing and prayer go on too long and make their statement too obviously. But as a whole the novel is wonderfully true.

Baldwin certainly endorsed Marx's view of religion as the opiate of the masses. He himself saw it, most specifically, as the opium of the oppressed. In *The Fire Next Time* he wrote:

> The principles governing the rites and customs of the churches in which I grew up did not differ from the principles governing the rites and customs of other churches, white. The principles were Blindness, Loneliness, and Terror, the first principle necessarily and actively cultivated in order to deny the two others. I would love to believe that the principles were Faith, Hope, and Charity, but this is clearly not so for most Christians, or for what we call the Christian world. . . . There was no love in the church. It was a mask for hatred and self-hatred and despair.

What makes *Go Tell It on the Mountain* so remarkably skillful is the way in which it exposes the falsity of this sort of "religious" impulse while at the same time using the metaphors of Christian doctrine to expose real truths. Elisha, a kind and frightened young man who has taken refuge from the world's challenges by becoming a deacon and giving his life to the church, is telling the truth—though it is not quite the truth he understands—when he says "The Devil, he don't ask for nothing less than your life. And he take it, too, and it's lost forever. . . . You in darkness while you living and you in darkness when you dead. . . . [The Devil] got as many faces . . . as you going to see between now and the time you lay your burden down."

Go Tell It on the Mountain is a story of the world Baldwin was born into. The world that he penetrated, and of which he became a central figure, was very different indeed, and his subsequent fiction is accordingly different from that one early novel. The Harlem of his childhood, during the 1920s and 1930s, retained a certain small-town aura: most of its inhabitants came from the South (known as the "Old Country") and brought with them a strong family, church, and neighborhood tradition. At the age of eighteen, Baldwin left this insular community forever and took up permanent residence in bohemia: first Greenwich Village, later Paris, Istanbul, and St.-Paul-de-Vence. Most of his later novels deal with international bohemia, and it is significant that they never captured their world with anything like the immediacy and the unself-consciousness of Baldwin's Harlem novel.

Giovanni's Room, Baldwin's second novel, is generally considered his best or his second best. In its day it created a sensation: an explicitly homosexual work, shocking and revolutionary, it was published at the height of the Eisenhower era. Its novelty factor was so great that assessment of its real merits was inevitably distorted. Now, several decades later, *Giovanni's Room* is not at all shocking. So is it any good?

Baldwin was much taken with Henry James at the time he wrote *Giovanni's Room,* and this obsession is reflected a little too obviously in the novel's structure and themes. The narrator is David, a young, white East Coaster. He has gone off to Paris for the traditional post-college jaunt and then, like his fictional progenitor Chad Newsome, has lingered on, emotionally unprepared to go home and settle down to "real life." His father has begun to lose patience and is cutting off funds. His American girlfriend, Hella, currently traveling in Spain, is making preliminary noises about marriage.

David, like Chad, has become inconveniently entangled, but in his case it is not with a European woman but with a European man, the handsome Italian barman Giovanni. Giovanni is vital, vulnerable, unstable; Hella, on the other hand, is endowed with every virtue of the unexciting, American variety. Which of the two will David choose?

There is no surprise ending, because *Giovanni's Room* is told in flashback by an extremely depressed David the night before Giovanni is to be executed for murder. We are given to understand that in rejecting him he not only ruins Giovanni's life but denies his own nature and gives up every chance of happiness; in effect he sells his soul.

So far from being shocking, *Giovanni's Room* now appears merely a romantic, rather sentimental little novel. It is not without certain virtues: the scenes in the gay bars, and especially the conversations between the *vieilles folles,* are amusing. But the main action is more melodrama than drama, and the characters are nothing but types. David and Hella are mere cyphers, the first manifestations of Baldwin's already atrophying stereotypes of white Americans, while the lovely Giovanni is a cardboard figure, a stage Italian: "It might have been better," David says of him, "if he'd stayed down there in that village of his in Italy and planted his olive trees and had a lot of children and beaten his wife. He used to love to sing. . . ." He is supposed to be "vivid" and "winning," but his dialogue shows none of these traits; we are obliged to take David's unconvincing word for everything.

There is also, of course, the older, sophisticated European, a stock figure in Baldwin from this point on. Here it is the dissipated old queen, Jacques, who advises David to love Giovanni: "Love him and let him love you. Do you really think anything else under heaven really matters? And how long, at the best, can it last? since you are both men and still have everywhere to go? . . . You play it safe long enough . . . and you'll end up trapped in your own dirty body, forever and forever and forever—like me." And then there is the obligatory

Jamesian motif, portentously intoned by Hella: "Americans should never come to Europe . . . it means they can never be happy again. What's the good of an American who isn't happy? Happiness was all we had."

The high artificiality of the dialogue comes as an unpleasant surprise after the relaxed, natural speech of the characters in *Go Tell It on the Mountain*. Perhaps it stems from the fact that David, Hella, and Giovanni are all types, ideas rather than human beings, while Gabriel, Florence, and the other characters in *Go Tell It on the Mountain* are very real. Or perhaps it is because Baldwin still has too little experience with the background, the class, the geographical rootedness he has imagined for them. When Knopf, Baldwin's publishers, received the manuscript of *Giovanni's Room* they were unenthusiastic: Baldwin chose to believe it was because they had him pegged as a rising "Negro writer" who would prove consistently marketable as such, and didn't want him straying into untried territory. But it is possible that they sensed, and were distressed by, a false, stagey quality that was never again to be absent from his fiction.

In writing from the point of view of a white character, Baldwin was experimenting with what he conceived of as a "literature of integration." Almost alone among radical black intellectuals of the period, he praised his friend William Styron's *The Confessions of Nat Turner* (1967), in which the white Southern novelist took on the persona of a black narrator, the leader of a tragic slave uprising. Baldwin felt strongly that Styron was to be respected for having even attempted this imaginative leap; it was, perhaps, not so different from the leap he himself had essayed with *Giovanni's Room*. Now that we are able to view both books at several decades' remove from the brouhaha that attended their publication, it is evident that Baldwin's attempt was less successful than Styron's—at least from my own, admittedly white, point of view.

And Baldwin's fiction continued to deteriorate: *Another Country*, his next novel, has all the faults of *Giovanni's Room* without its virtues of economy, structure, and good editing. This rambling book deals with a group of artistic Greenwich Villagers—gay and straight, white and black, male and female—and their various love affairs, and it is a mess: an undisciplined, immature, stupefyingly talky piece of work. Every character sounds exactly like every other character, and they all sound like Baldwin, even the children. The "dialogue" is downright comical:

> It would be wonderful if it could be like that; you're very beautiful, Eric. But I don't, really, dig you the way I guess you must dig me. And if we tried to arrange it, prolong it, control it, if we tried to take more than what we've—by some miracle, some miracle, I swear—stumbled on, then I'd just become a parasite and we'd both shrivel. So what can we really do for each other except—just love each other and be each other's witness? And haven't we got the right to hope—for more? So that we can really stretch into whoever we really are?

The semicolons, the dependent clauses, the qualifications: it all sounds a little like Henry James oddly transformed into a stoned hipster.

Baldwin saw himself as following in the tradition of James and addressing the American condition rather than simply the black condition. To a certain extent he did so in his first two novels and, far more effectively, in his essays of the fifties and sixties. He was certainly capable of delivering home truths: some of his statements and contentions are as disturbing today as they were when first published. For instance:

> The real role of the Negro leader, in the eyes of the American Republic, was not to make the Negro a first-class citizen but to keep him content as a second-class one.

When the American people revile . . . the Haitian, Cuban, Turk, Palestinian, Iranian, they are really cursing the nigger, and the nigger had better know it.

The only time you'll hear nonviolence admired is when black men preach and practice it. Whites admire violence in themselves.

And America, he wrote, is "a society much given to smashing taboos without thereby managing to be liberated from them."

These provocative statements would seem elegantly to refute Norman Mailer's remark that Baldwin was incapable of saying "fuck you" to the reader. But as time wore on, Baldwin's work becomes increasingly studded with silly and meaningless generalizations. *The Fire Next Time,* a long essay about Elijah Muhammad and the Black Muslim movement, is his last really good piece of nonfiction: from that point on he began to go over the top. *No Name in the Street,* his 1972 essay collection, shows Baldwin's transformation from a thinking, reflecting human being to a virtual automaton, a sort of Charlie McCarthy dummy who could be relied on to spew out whatever fashionable radical opinion was currently most fashionable and most radical.

In middle age Baldwin claimed cynically that he had once been "the Great Black Hope of the Great White Father." Here he was referring to the reputation he began to enjoy after the publication of his influential essay "Everybody's Protest Novel," which appeared in *Zero* in 1949 and was anthologized six years later in *Notes of a Native Son.* This essay was in essence an oblique attack on Richard Wright—the first of several father figures Baldwin was to slay symbolically—which compared Wright's *Native Son* with *Uncle Tom's Cabin,* lumping them together in the category of "protest novel." It was a thoughtful piece of work which is perhaps even more pertinent today than when it was written.

The avowed aim of the American protest novel is to bring greater freedom to the oppressed. They are forgiven, on the strength of these good intentions, whatever violence they do to language, whatever excessive demands they make of credibility. It is, indeed, considered the sign of a frivolity so intense as to approach decadence to suggest that these books are both badly written and wildly improbable. One is told to put first things first, the good of society coming before niceties of style or characterization. Even if this were incontestable—for what exactly is the "good of society"?—it argues an insuperable confusion, since literature and sociology are not one and the same; it is impossible to discuss them as if they were. . . . The failure of the protest novel lies in its rejection of life, the human being, the denial of his beauty, dread, power, in its insistence that it is his categorization alone which is real and which cannot be transcended.

This essay epitomizes Baldwin's early thinking. He was determined to escape his own categorization as a "Negro writer" as he had escaped ghettoization in a purely black community: in the Village, and later in Paris, he cultivated a wide circle of friends, both black and white. As a civil rights activist and spokesman, he declared himself an integrationist, a follower of King, and initially rejected the credo of the separatist Black Muslims. He wrote again and again of the possibility, indeed the necessity, of regenerative love between members of the races.

Yet by the late sixties Baldwin had lost his spark of freshness and optimism forever, and had taken to the pernicious habit of "categorization" far more enthusiastically than Richard Wright ever did. He repeatedly expressed his newly developed opinion that "white Americans are probably the sickest and certainly the most dangerous people, of any color, to be found in the world today," and his essays, fiction, and the Broadway play *Blues for Mister Charlie* all illustrate that notion. He invented his own America, a country blighted by "an emotional poverty so bottomless, and a terror of human life, of human touch, so deep, that virtually no American appears able to achieve any viable, organic connection between his public stance and his private life."

What caused this depressing turnaround? Probably a combination of factors. Genuine political disillusionment certainly entered into it; the murders of King and Medgar Evers shocked him deeply. Also his schedule and his habits, which had never been conducive to concentrated periods of work, became even less so as he aged. His drinking grew heavier, his hours later, his social life increasingly frenetic; terrified of solitude, he surrounded himself at all times with an entourage of acolytes and gigolos.

There was also an attention-getting element to Baldwin's displays of bitterness and rage, an attempt to seem more-radical-than-thou, for the fact remained that he was not taken entirely seriously by the militant branch of the Black Power movement. It must have been deeply humiliating to him when Eldridge Cleaver wrote that Baldwin's work contained "the most grueling, agonizing, total hatred of the blacks, particularly of himself, and the most shameful, fanatical, fawning, sycophantic love of the whites that one can find in the writings of any black American writer of our time."

Baldwin's later work is written as though to refute this truly unfair claim and to assert to the world his own radical credentials. Over and over again he schematizes America, dividing it into whites (self-deluding, infantile, ignorant, sexually cold) and blacks (passionate, sensual, sophisticated, knowing). His two stock white characters are the Southern redneck, like Lyle in *Blues for Mister Charlie,* and the lily-livered liberal, like Richard in *Another Country.* His stock black character is, above all, the passionate, tortured, and sensual artist. Where once he had stated his faith that the country could only be healed through love, real love between any black and any white was now deemed impossible. No white, however desperately he tried to bridge the gap, however abjectly he might grovel or abase himself, could ever understand a black or redeem the crimes of his own race, or even be allowed to have an opinion on the subject. Whites were always wrong, always implicated in the crime of racial bigotry.

Baldwin eventually depicted White America as more than just a sick society; he claimed that it was in fact a conspiracy. In his saner days he had stated his views eloquently: "The world in which people find themselves is not simply a vindictive plot imposed on them from above; it is also the world they have helped to make. They have helped both to make and to sustain it by sharing the assumptions which hold their world together." Now, however, he descended into paranoid raving. Society's ills were not simply a result of failings like ignorance, apathy, and prejudice but of an active, well-organized plot hatched by white supremacists—that is, by all whites.

Whites, thinking "If you can't beat them, stone them," dumped drugs into the ghetto.

The educational system of this country is, in short, designed to destroy the black child. It does not matter whether it destroys him by stoning him in the ghetto or by driving him mad in the isolation of Harvard.

Therefore, in a couple of days, blacks may be using the vote to outwit the Final Solution. Yes. The Final Solution.

I yet contend that the mobs in the street of Hitler's Germany were in the streets not only by the will of the German State, but by the will of the western world, including those architects of human freedom, the British, and the presumed guardian of Christian and human morality, the Pope.

In *The Fire Next Time*, Baldwin had considered Elijah Muhammad's call for a separate black nation in America to be the ultimate segregation. He thought about it carefully: after all, he wrote, "If this sentiment is honored when it falls from the lips of Senator Byrd, then there is no reason why it should not be honored when it falls from the lips of Malcolm X." But he concluded that "the Negro has been formed by this nation, for better or for worse, and does not belong to any other—not to Africa, and certainly not to Islam. . . . We, the black and the white, deeply need each other here if we are really to become a nation."

Yet in later years Baldwin's own philosophy became even more intransigent and impossible than that of the Black Muslims. At least they had a solution to propose; he, it seemed, had none. He had dismissed his earlier ideas about love and mutual connection as naive, but he had nothing with which to replace them, and while he still insisted that America was both black and white and must remain so, all his work, fiction and nonfiction, implicitly denied the possibility of merging and connecting. As Baldwin aged—he died in 1987 at the age of sixty-three—his writing and his statements became increasingly irrational until it seemed that his worst nightmare had come true: he, like his stepfather, had gone mad.

If Baldwin had a literary idol, it was probably Henry James; but as a writer and as a cultural influence, Baldwin was in fact much closer, at least in his better work, to the Englishman E. M. Forster than he was to James, his compatriot and fellow exile. Forster and Baldwin shared an almost religious faith in the sacramental and redemptive nature of love, and specifically of the sexual act. They also shared, and propagated, a simplistic and nonsensical stereotype of Anglo-Saxon culture as frozen, anti-sensual, emotionally out of touch, and unnatural, and a corresponding, sentimental notion of non-Anglos as elemental, natural, and free: Forster's prototype of the sexy Mediterranean corresponds perfectly to Baldwin's prototype of the brilliant and intense Harlem jazz musician. Both homosexuals, the two writers idealized male characteristics and male friendship and showed only a token interest in women and a cursory understanding of them.

Like Forster, Baldwin was, at least in the beginning, an idealist. The extraordinary rage with which he reacted to the inadequacies of human behavior presupposes an idealism about what human behavior might or should be which few people of his high intelligence share; only an idealist could finally end up so bitter, so disappointed by the vagaries of the human animal.

Again like Forster, Baldwin believed that art and social criticism are, and should be, inextricably linked. In "The Creative Process," an essay published in *Creative America* in 1962 and not previously anthologized, Baldwin brilliantly explored the role of the artist:

> Society must accept some things as real; but [the artist] must always know that the visible reality hides a deeper one, and that all our action and all our achievement rests on things unseen. A society must assume that it is stable, but the artist must know, and he must let us know, that there is nothing stable under heaven. One cannot possibly build a school, teach a child, or drive a car without taking some things for granted. The artist cannot and must not take anything for granted. . . .

For as long as he took nothing for granted, Baldwin made a substantial contribution to the literature and the cultural dialogue of his time. It was when he broke his own rules and started to assume, started to take for granted, that his contribution sadly ceased to be valid.

[*1998*]

Saul Bellow on Top

I remember reading, some years ago, a piece by James Atlas—I think it was in the *New York Times*—about biography. He had recently abandoned the project of writing a biography of Edmund Wilson some five years after signing a book contract. He had dawdled and eventually tanked, he said, because while he admired Wilson's work he couldn't bring himself to like the actual man. The decisive moment came, I seem to remember, when Atlas read a love letter in which Wilson compared his current mistress's feet to little cream cheeses.

There's no question that that might turn the strongest stomach, and Atlas's decision to reject Wilson in favor of a subject with whom he felt himself to have much more in common, Saul Bellow, is perfectly understandable. Bellow and Atlas came from the same place—the Jewish Northwest Side of Chicago—and the novelist belonged to the same generation and social milieu as the biographer's parents: the two men, as Atlas put it, were *"experience-near."*

The problem is that even after having devoted a decade of his life to research and composition, Atlas doesn't seem to like Bellow any better than he did Wilson; his *Bellow* is a distinctly hostile book, surprisingly so, considering that it deals with a man the author purports to revere. Not that there isn't a great deal for a well-meaning biographer to be hostile about. Even at his best Bellow is magisterially arrogant; at his worst, when the perpetual and ill-concealed rage and pride bubble up to the surface, he is deeply unsympathetic.

A sense of destiny is a useful thing in someone who aspires to an artistic career, giving that Darwinian edge that helps him not only scramble to the top but stay there; it does not always make, though, for a very attractive personality. Recalling Bellow as a young man, Alfred Kazin showed the embryonic Nobel laureate in a sharp light:

> He was measuring the world's power to resist *him*, he was putting himself up as a contender. Although he was friendly, unpretentious, and funny, he was ambitious and dedicated in a style I had never seen in an urban Jewish intellectual; he expected the world to come to him. He had pledged himself to a great destiny. He was going to take on more than the rest of us were.... As Bellow talked, I had an image of a wrestler in the old Greek style, an agonist contending in the games for the prize. Life was dramatically as well as emotionally a contest to him. In some way I could not define, he seemed to be always training for it.

Other friends have described Bellow with just such ambivalence. His longtime crony and intellectual mentor Edward Shils remarked that Bellow's vocation as an artist served as both "a form of self-enhancement and an expression of resentment against most of the rest of mankind for not appreciating his own intrinsic qualities." Philip Roth, essentially a friend and artistic ally of Bellow's, described him unflatteringly (in the person of the fictional Abravanel in *The Ghost Writer*) as inhabiting his own "egosphere."

A self-regarding man, then, whose least appealing qualities have seeped into his imaginative work, damaging it as fiction. Egoism, excusable and maybe even necessary in an artist, transcends itself in his case and becomes high narcissism, so that the barrier between the autobiographical characters (Charlie Citrine, Moses Herzog, Benn Crader) and the other people in the novels becomes impermeable: *Herzog*, for all its fun and readability, is one of the most solipsistic books in the English language. Rage and self-pity can be powerful tools—Roth, for example, wields them like fine surgical knives—but in Bellow's case they tend to get out of the author's control and take over the novels. Misogyny too can be artistically effective, so long as the author is aware of his own skewed vision: Roth again, and Updike, and Kingsley Amis, have long demonstrated this; but Bellow's misogyny is shrill and hysterical, and entirely without self-knowledge. His hatred and fear of women leads one to suspect that he has never troubled to get to know one too well.

But if to future generations Bellow will not, perhaps, prove the great writer he has aspired to be, he still cuts a considerable figure, with a fierce intelligence that from time to time compensates for his constant self-mythologizing:

> I have begun in old age [he wrote recently] to understand just how oddly we are all put together. We are so proud of our autonomy that we seldom if ever realize how generous we are to ourselves, and just how stingy with others. One of the booby traps of freedom—which is bordered on all sides by isolation—is that we think so well of ourselves. I now see that I have helped myself to the best cuts at life's banquet.

Emotional honesty is not Bellow's strong suit: as Atlas proves in example after example, he has always been a master of self-exculpation, blaming every misfortune—failed novels, bad reviews, broken marriages, disaffected children—on forces outside his own control. Still, he is capable of an occasional self-laceration that goes some way toward redeeming his faults. Here, for instance, he blames himself (and by extension his generation of New York Jewish intellectuals) for his failure, in the 1940s, to respond to the Holocaust:

> I was too busy becoming a novelist to take note of what was happening in the forties. I was involved with "literature" and given over to preoccupation with art, with language, with my struggle on the Amer-

ican scene, with claims for the recognition of my talent or, like my pals of the *Partisan Review*, with modernism, Marxism, New Criticism, with Eliot, Yeats, Proust, etc.—with anything except the terrible events in Poland. Growing slowly aware of this unspeakable evasion I didn't even know how to begin to admit it into my inner life.

The problem in reading Bellow is that this sort of honesty is too rare to temper the constant, self-justifying refusal to see a situation from any position but his own. His novels, as a result, generally revolve around a central character with many of the author's own features, surrounded by a sorry parade of losers.

Bellow was a first-generation American, a Russian Jew, and the story of his meteoric and self-transforming career is emblematic of the general trajectory of Eastern European Jews in twentieth-century America. A photograph included by Atlas in the biography shows Bellow's maternal grandfather in Russia, with a long beard, dressed in tatters and painfully thin; his fine, almost beautiful features, though, are recognizably those of the novelist. Sixty-five or so years later the old man's bathing-suited grandson, as shown in another photograph, tanned, fit, and movie-star handsome, embraces a striking blonde on the beach at Martha's Vineyard. The contrast couldn't be more obvious, and, as Atlas shows, Bellow was not only a beneficiary but a prime mover in the cultural shift that made it possible.

As a student he had been discouraged from pursuing graduate studies in English by the guardians of the dying Anglo-Saxon tradition, who told him that no Jew could ever really hope to understand English literature. Later, when he was beginning his apprenticeship as a novelist, "The question wasn't only what he should write but *how* he should write. In 1938 [when Bellow was twenty-three], American novels written by Jews—as opposed to more ethnic Jewish-American novels such as Ludwig Lewisohn's *The Island Within* or Abraham Cahan's *The Rise of David Levinsky*—didn't exist."

And yet only a few years later the deck had been reshuffled, largely due to the efforts of a brilliant generation of writers, artists, and intellectuals like Bellow. His early novel *The Victim* (1947), though not very successful, noticeably reflected the shift: a contemporary critic thought it "the first attempt in American literature to consider Jewishness not in its singularity, not as constitutive of a special world of experience, but as a quality that informs all of modern life, as the quality of modernity itself." And by 1956, with *Seize the Day*, it was no longer necessary, as Leslie Fiedler pointed out, "to label Bellow a Jewish novelist, for he emerges at the moment when the Jews for the first time move into the center of American culture, and he must be seen in the larger context." By the end of the century, with Bellow firmly ensconced as the elder statesman of American fiction, Jewish writers and, to a large extent, a recognizably Jewish sensibility had become the mainstream itself.

Solomon Bellow, known in the family as Shloime or Shloimke and later as Saul, was born in Lachine, a working-class town outside of Montreal, in 1915. He was the first of his family to be born in the New World: his older siblings Zelda, Moïshe (later Maurice), and Schmule (later Sam) had emigrated from Russia with their parents, Abraham and Liza, in 1913. In Canada Abraham Bellow failed at one trade after another, including, finally, bootlegging. The Bellows moved on to Chicago in 1924, where they settled in the mostly Polish and Jewish Northwest Side, a neighborhood that Saul Bellow would celebrate and idealize in *The Adventures of Augie March*. It was a community whose values would influence the author for the rest of his life—"The whole neighborhood seemed dedicated to the pursuit of culture," Atlas writes—and for which the novelist has shown more real feeling than for any human love object. As his nephew Marvin Gameroff has put it, "He can't form permanent attachments. His fidelity is to the past."

Bellow attended Tuley High School, where he made some of the most important friends of his life, including the brilliant but unstable

Isaac Rosenfeld, who was to be an alter ego and competitor for him until Rosenfeld's premature death at the age of thirty-eight: "They had a sense of mutual destiny," remarked their friend Edith Tarcov. It was a moment of high political passion, and while Bellow paid lip service to the issues of his day, dutifully hanging around the Young People's Socialist League, it was widely acknowledged that he was not much of a joiner nor, in fact, a particularly political animal at all. "For all his radical bravado and angry manifestos, politics fit poorly with Bellow's hunger to experience life's intellectual, aesthetic, and sensual pleasures," Atlas argues, convincingly.

Bellow graduated from Tuley in January 1933; his mother died of cancer a month later. As he has admitted, he never really got over her death. It made him, in the words of his character Moses Herzog, "mother-bound" and almost certainly contributed to his disastrous relations with women, the long string of broken marriages and relationships that were to cause so much unhappiness.

After a semester at a junior college, Bellow entered the University of Chicago. Though the University would provide the closest thing he ever had to a home as an adult—he spent more than thirty years teaching in its prestigious Committee on Social Thought—his student career there was not especially distinguished: his grades were mediocre and his literary talent went unrecognized. The experience also sowed the seeds of a lifelong love affair with the institution's Great Books culture that did not prove an unmixed blessing for his fiction. One of Bellow's most infuriating stylistic tics is compulsive intellectual name-dropping: if there's an opportunity for a reference to Heidegger or Kant, however far-fetched and irrelevant to the story, he will grab at it. "Philosophy," as Atlas puts it, "then and later, was one of the unfortunate legacies of Bellow's immersion in the University of Chicago Great Books culture. His heroes shared a penchant for belaboring ideas. They were the products of a provincial Chicago boy's effort to show that he wasn't provincial."

When Abraham had financial difficulties he pulled his son out of school and put him to work in a coalyard (an experience he was later to draw upon for *Augie March*), but eventually the boy scraped together enough money to complete his B.A., transferring to Northwestern University. He claimed to dislike the place, referring to Evanston as "a wax museum of bourgeois horrors," but as Atlas points out he throve there; the professors were receptive to his talents and encouraged his writing. He double-majored in English and anthropology, graduated in 1937, and went on to the University of Wisconsin to take up a graduate fellowship in anthropology.

This venture lasted only a semester. His dissertation, for one thing, refused to progress: "Every time I worked on my thesis, it turned out to be a story," he said. He had also fallen in love with Anita Goshkin, a campus radical from the University of Chicago; during the Christmas vacation they married, and Bellow abandoned his fellowship.

He had now decided to become a writer and embarked on the life he would describe in his 1944 novel *Dangling Man*. It was a daring step for a married man with no other means of support and no encouragement from his family: Abraham Bellow, whose other two sons were taking the first steps in what were to be long and infamous careers as Chicago power brokers and real estate tycoons, was frankly disgusted with his youngest. "You write, and then you erase. You call that a profession? *Was meinst du* 'a writer'?"

Anita had gone to work for the Chicago Relief Administration, and Bellow picked up what odd jobs he could. A belated windfall from Liza Bellow's insurance company allowed the young couple to spend a few months in Mexico, during which time Saul (he had changed his name sometime around his twenty-first birthday) and Anita embarked on a pattern of fights and infidelities that would characterize and eventually ruin their marriage.

At that time the cultural fountainhead for Bellow and his friends was the *Partisan Review*, and the young Bellow enthusiastically shared in the "culture snobbery" of its stars, Philip Rahv, William Phillips, Harold Rosenberg, Dwight Macdonald, and Meyer Schapiro. When *Partisan Review* accepted his first story, "Two Morning Monologues," for publication in the May–June issue of 1941, it was a triumph of a very particular sort. It was Isaac Rosenfeld, though, who had really stormed the citadel: moving to New York in 1941, he quickly made a name for himself as a literary journalist and bohemian personality. "He was our golden boy, more so than Bellow," wrote Irving Howe. Bellow began spending a good deal of time with Rosenfeld and his wife in New York, making inroads with the *Partisan Review* crowd and playing the disciple to Delmore Schwartz, whom he would later portray with ruthless vividness in *Humboldt's Gift;* he and Anita would even live in New York for a time, though he never felt comfortable there. In 1944 Bellow's eldest son, Gregory, was born, and his first novel was published.

Dangling Man, characterized by Atlas as "a novel about a man idling away his days in a fog of introspection," was received respectfully but without fanfare, and it didn't begin to make Bellow's fortune; neither did his second novel, *The Victim.* He turned the corner, though, when he got a Guggenheim grant (on his third try), which he decided to spend on a year in Paris—a city to whose charms he remained steadfastly resistant. (It was a "culture shrine," he noted derisively; "I was not going to sit at the feet of Gertrude Stein.") He was in any case more focused on Chicago than Paris, for it was at this time that he began work on what was to become *The Adventures of Augie March.*

With *Augie March* Bellow, as Philip Toynbee noted, was aiming directly at no less than the Great American Novel, and to that end he abandoned his earlier fealty to the internal novel—to Flaubert and Dostoevsky—to adopt the more exuberant style of Fielding and Dickens. It was a successful ploy if a little too conscious for all tastes: V. S.

Pritchett criticized Bellow's "self-intoxicating style," and Norman Podhoretz carped that "the feeling conveyed by Mr. Bellow's exuberance is an overwhelming impulse to get in as many adjectives and details as possible, regardless of consideration of rhythm, modulation, or, for that matter, meaning." Bellow himself was later to admit that the rhetoric had got out of his control, excusing himself with the rather disarming admission that "The book just came to me. All I had to do was be there with buckets to catch it."

"There was a lot riding on the book," as Atlas remarks. "If anyone could bring Jewish literature into the American mainstream, it was going to be Saul Bellow. He alone possessed the talent and ambition to transcend the narrow confines of the *Partisan Review* culture." *Augie* paid off in spades, selling in impressive numbers and picking up the National Book Award for 1953. Bellow's next novel, *Seize the Day* (1956), was not a financial success, but it too garnered impressive critical notice.

Bellow was now, at the age of thirty-seven, a star, and availed himself of a star's prerogatives. Many of these were erotic. His marriage had long been in trouble, and Gregory's arrival had not helped it: Bellow wished himself to be nurtured, not to be required to nurture others. He and Anita split up in 1952, and he replaced her almost immediately with the twenty-year-old Sondra Tschacbasov, a Bennington girl from a bohemian family. The couple settled in the village of Tivoli on the Hudson River (Bellow had had a one-year appointment at nearby Bard College). The marriage was a disaster almost from the beginning: Sondra was consumed by uncontrollable rages, which many of their friends believed to have been entirely justified. She was soon carrying on an affair with Bellow's neighbor and disciple Jack Ludwig, a relationship Atlas convincingly suggests was unconsciously abetted by Bellow. Some of his friends had had similar suspicions at the time, with Herbert Gold remarking, only half-jokingly, that Bellow "set it up so that he could write his book."

The book was *Herzog* (1964), a big commercial blockbuster (number one on the *New York Times* best-seller list) that eclipsed his recent and more modest success, *Henderson the Rain King* (1959). *Herzog* was autobiographical in a grossly obvious way, yet it was not emotionally credible unless one accepted the author's distorted vision of events: it is as if Bellow were making use of the old trick of the unreliable narrator while all the time naively believing his narrator to be the soul of probity. Herzog, the self-portrait, crossed the line freely into caricature, while the Sondra and Ludwig characters are cartoon figures, distorted out of any reality by the author's hysterical rage.

Bellow would repeat this public drubbing of a wife he had once claimed to love in later novels: his third wife, Susan Glassman, would turn up as the arch-bitch Denise in *Humboldt's Gift* and the even more dreadful Matilda Layamon in *More Die of Heartbreak;* his fourth, the Rumanian mathematician Alexandra Tulcea, by all accounts a charming and compassionate woman, has recently appeared as the narrator's robotic Nazi ex-wife in *Ravelstein.* Even the long-suffering Anita was unflatteringly portrayed as the nagging Margaret Wilhelm in *Seize the Day.* Only Bellow's fifth and current wife, Janis Freedman, forty-four years his junior, has escaped his literary wrath, possibly because in his dotage he is so very much in need of an attentive consort. "The women in his life remained for him secondary figures who served his own fantasies of them as providers, entrappers, sexual predators: the Enemy," Atlas writes, and it's hard to argue with him. Joseph Epstein, writing about Bellow in the guise of a fictional character named Noah Danzig, amusingly professed himself baffled by Bellow's choice of mates:

> He just didn't seem to get, at least in my view, dollar value. His fame ought to have brought him dazzling and fascinating women, but among the seven or eight he coupled with during the time I knew him, all had rather emphatic flaws: they were hopelessly neurotic or shy or

witless or idiotically subservient to him. He seemed to be searching for uncritical adoration, but was unable to find even that. No wonder Noah Danzig couldn't create convincing women—he knew so few.

During the sixties and seventies Bellow's fame was at its apex, but he found himself out of sympathy with the times and conscious of advancing mental, if not physical, age. Being heckled by a young instructor while superciliously delivering a lecture at San Francisco State ("You're an old man, Bellow," the disgruntled youth yelled; "You haven't got any balls") confirmed his contempt for what he saw as the mindlessness of the student radical movement. His response was *Mr. Sammler's Planet* (1970), an odd, unfocused novel in which an elderly Holocaust survivor, an intellectual living in New York, is confronted with some of the more threatening aspects of contemporary life. Atlas primly condemns the novel as "an outburst of racism, misogyny, and puritanical intolerance," but it is not that—or at least it is something more than that.

It would be fairer to say that *Mr. Sammler's Planet* is an expression of discomfort with the knee-jerk radicalism of the period and a simultaneous expression of discomfort with conventional conservatism. While a number of neoconservatives have claimed the later Bellow as one of their own, his political positions seem to me unclassifiable, and his own idea of himself as "some sort of liberal" is a reasonable one— that is, to people who don't take "liberal" and "radical" to be synonyms. During the Vietnam era Bellow proved hard to corral into the conventional left-wing fold, refusing, for example, to join the widespread excoriation of Lyndon Johnson: "I don't like what J. is doing in Vietnam and S. Domingo, though you and I might not agree in our criticisms," he wrote to Harvey Swados. "But I don't see that holding these positions requires me to treat Johnson like a Hitler. He's not that. . . . Intellectuals, and esp. former Marxists, will really have to decide in the end what they think a government *is*."

In the end Bellow's primary political allegiance was to the feeling, as Atlas puts it, "that *all* forms of authority, including intellectual authority, were suspect" and to the commendable belief that politics had no place in art: when Salman Rushdie, for example, complained that writers had abandoned the task of imagining America's role in the world, Bellow snapped back that "Tasks are for people who work in offices."

More than a decade ago John Updike, with the exquisite cruelty of which he is our preeminent master, observed that "Bellow, at this point in his career, has sat atop the American literary heap longer than anyone else since William Dean Howells." (To add insult to injury, Updike, who personifies the goy establishment Bellow has always hated and feared, is the creator of a long-running character with certain marked resemblances to Bellow, Henry Bech—although personally I have always thought Bech owed more to Nabokov's bumbling Pnin than to Bellow, the ruthless careerist.) But Updike is right in saying that now, at eighty-five, Bellow is our senior *litterateur.* His production, in 1999, of both a daughter and a surprisingly decent novel impressed even his detractors. *Ravelstein,* a barely fictionalized portrait of Bellow's friend and University of Chicago teaching partner Allan Bloom, is not only a fairly good novel but in many ways more appealing than his earlier work, representing something of a breakthrough for its narcissistic author in that it is not, at least not primarily, about himself. It also would seem to indicate the author's mellowing in that it is a highly affectionate portrait.

Now, many readers contend that *Ravelstein,* so far from being a paean to Bloom, is a disguised attack: why else would good friend Bellow have tattled on Bloom, the hero of America's conservative intellectuals, for being a promiscuous homosexual and dying of AIDS? Atlas, while liking *Ravelstein,* can't help but focus on this perfidy; he also, it should be noted, believed that *Humboldt's Gift* was an "act of revenge against the poet [Delmore Schwartz] who had once taunted him so mercilessly in the guise of a tribute." There is something to be said for this view, but I think it is an extreme one, and that the truth is that a straightforward tribute is beyond Bellow: he is simply incapable of presenting a rose without including a full measure of not-so-hidden thorns.

Bellow, who must have been perfectly aware that no intelligent biography of him would be uncritical, managed for years to evade and make life difficult for would-be biographers. He seems to have bowed to the inevitable with Atlas, perhaps assuming that by the time the book was finally published he himself would be dead or at any rate senile; how he must regret his cooperation now. As for Atlas, one wonders how he can bear to have devoted such a large hunk of his professional life to someone he so clearly dislikes. He has produced a readable biography—a compulsively readable one, in fact—but it is one with no sense of joy or discovery, or even any genuine regard for its subject.

[*2001*]

Cockeyed Optimist:
Grace Paley and the
Eternal Feminine

*F*or someone who has produced so small a body of work—three slim books of short stories, now collected in one volume—Grace Paley has garnered extraordinary accolades. The critical response has been almost entirely positive, and for more than thirty years she has become something of a sacred cow. It is universally acknowledged that she is a writer of high principles; in fact she has so thoroughly identified her writing with the various causes she boosts—peace, environmentalism, prison reform, feminism—that it seems churlish or at least in bad taste to criticize it. But putting politics aside, how good a writer is Grace Paley?

It is dangerous to read autobiography into fiction, but in this case it is safe to say that Paley writes about people like herself. She is a second-generation radical, the daughter of Ukrainian Jews, Isaac Goodside and Manya Ridnyk, who ran afoul of the Russian government for agitating against tsarist oppression at the turn of the twentieth century. They emigrated to the United States in 1905; Isaac became a doctor, and Grace was born in the Bronx in 1922.

Paley's fictional alter ego is Faith Darwin (loaded name!), like Paley a divorced mother of two, a grassroots political activist in her New York neighborhood, and a writer. Faith appeared toward the end of Paley's first collection of stories, *The Little Disturbances of Man* (1959), and began so thoroughly to permeate the author's fictional world that her next collection, *Enormous Changes at the Last Minute* (1974), was made up not of discrete fictional pieces but of quasi-fictional fragments united by Faith's vision, which is sometimes central and sometimes marginal to the action. Characters from the first volume were reintroduced until the reader gradually realized they were all inhabitants of the same New York City neighborhood, connected by their acquaintance with Faith. *Later the Same Day* (1985) took the technique even further.

Recent analyses of Paley's work have suggested that she developed this style to subvert the linear narrative method of the dominant "patriarchal" culture, rejecting traditional fictional forms of closure in favor of a more fluid, open-ended, and hence "feminine" fiction. I'm sure this is indeed Paley's intention; she (or rather, Faith) says as much in "A Conversation with My Father":

> "I would like you to write a simple story just once more," he says, "the kind Maupassant wrote, or Chekhov, the kind you used to write. Just recognizable people and then write down what happened to them next."
>
> I say, "Yes, why not? That's possible." I want to please him, though I don't remember writing that way. I *would* like to try to tell such a story, if he means the kind that begins: "There was a woman . . ." followed by the plot, the absolute line between two points which I've always despised. Not for literary reasons, but because it takes all hope away. Everyone, real or invented, deserves the open destiny of hope.

Paley may have a point—few would claim that the short-story form should have been frozen forever with Chekhov and Maupassant—but in practice her exploratory divergences from the "absolute line" often lead her down a blind alley. Stories like "Politics," "Northeast Playground," "Love," "Anxiety," and "Listening" meander aimlessly, not so much fiction as strings of subjective observations, cozy aphorisms on sex, love, and life.

The stories tend to be about women. In Paley's world men hover on the margins, dropping in for food, sex, and companionship but generally absent from the real business of life, which is child-rearing, housekeeping, and political action. They are rogue wanderers on the earth—this identity is symbolized by Faith's ex-husband, an explorer—while women are the ones who put down roots. For happiness, Faith requires

> three or four best women friends to whom she could tell every personal fact and then discuss on the widest deepest and most hopeful level, the economy, the constant, unbeatable, cruel war economy, the slavery of the American worker to the idea of that economy, the complicity of male people in the whole structure, the dumbness of men (including the preferred man) on the subject. By dumbness, she meant everything dumbness has always meant: silence and stupidity.

Apparently the very fact of their gender, particularly of motherhood, imparts an earthy wisdom to women; even when they are patently making a mess of their own lives (Faith, for example, acknowledges her weakness for unreliable men), they laugh wryly, confident that they possess an intrinsic moral superiority to men. Faith says her destiny "is to be, until my expiration date, laughingly the servant of man." But why should she be? Faith and her friends are big on political action, but they take little of it on the home front, seldom questioning their function of ministering to the bodily needs of the male. Indeed, they relish the role.

Paley is a feminist but denies being a "feminist writer." Yet she has also stated that "all of art is political; if a writer says this is not po-

litical, it's probably the most political thing that he could be doing."
More spurious is her assertion that art's function is "to make justice in
the world" so that "it almost always has to be on the side of the un-
derdog." One might have thought that in a few trips to the Met, for
example, she would have come across some very great art created
without that guiding principle; but if Paley's vision is often a narrow
one, it is because her own view of history has of necessity been formed
by the two defining political events of her own life and her parents':
the persecutions of late tsarist Russia, and the Holocaust.

Paley's work has many strengths. She has a perfect ear for the ca-
dences of New York (especially Jewish New York) speech; humor is
always present, though untouched by irony; she can stunningly portray the pain and fear of motherhood. When she gets away from Faith
and her women friends and immerses herself imaginatively in an alien
character, she is capable of strong and vivid prose. "The Loudest
Voice," the story of a little Jewish girl who gets the lead part in the
school Christmas play, is an excellent, cohesive story; so is "Goodbye
and Good Luck," an aging woman's look back on her lifelong love affair with a glamorous leading man in the Yiddish theater. "Zagrowsky
Tells" is a near hit: a pharmacist who discriminated against black cus-
tomers in the sixties is now bringing up his own half-black grandson,
the child of his schizophrenic daughter. The story is written with
touches of virtuosity and might be the best of the collection were it not
for the intrusive presence of Faith, who argues with Zagrowski and
smugly points out the moral, as if it weren't obvious enough.

At her best, Paley is able to dish up poetic and humorous slices of
life oddly reminiscent of that most *un*feminine writer, William
Saroyan. Occasionally she even rises above this and achieves real
simplicity and power, as with this excerpt from "The Immigrant
Story": the narrator is telling about his father, who has left Poland for
New York City, leaving his wife and three young sons to follow when
he has found work.

214

Meanwhile, in Poland famine struck. Not hunger which all Americans suffer six, seven times a day, but Famine, which tells the body to consume itself. First the fat, then the meat, the muscle, then the blood. Famine ate up the bodies of the little boys pretty quickly. My father met my mother at the boat. He looked at her face, her hands. There was no baby in her arms, no children dragging at her skirt. She was not wearing her hair in two long black braids. There was a kerchief over a dark wiry wig. She had shaved her head, like a backward Orthodox bride, though they had been serious advanced socialists like most of the youth in their town. He took her by the hand and brought her home. They never went anywhere alone, except to work or the grocer's. They held each other's hand when they sat down at the table, even at breakfast.

But Paley inevitably follows up such affecting material with stories that are just plain silly, like "The Long Distance Runner," in which Faith visits the Brighton Beach building she grew up in (now in a black neighborhood) and is, most improbably, taken in and protected for three weeks by a plucky welfare mother; or like "Northeast Playground," where eleven welfare mothers who have rejected their men bring their children to play together: "What a wonderful calm unity in this group!" Faith gushes. Or like "Enormous Changes at the Last Minute," where an aging bourgeois woman and a cab driver/poet/musician/commune-dweller come together to make a baby and make a song; or like "Politics," where a group of neighborhood mothers sing a protest song to the Board of Estimates; or like "Listening," where Faith is devastated when a lesbian friend accuses her of having written only of heterosexual life and never about "my woman and woman, woman-loving life." It is this side of Grace Paley, unfortunately, that tips the scale: the cockeyed optimist who too often lets her good intentions overpower her good writing.

[1994]

John Barth:
Scheherazade's Exhaustion

Ezra Pound's exhortation to "make it new" has proved to be one of the most destructive aesthetic formulae ever to come along. Had he had an inkling of what grotesque lengths his successors would resort to in their feverish quest to make it new and ever newer, he might have hesitated, for Pound was no disrespecter of literary traditions.

And while Pound, Eliot, and Joyce certainly set out to revolutionize Western literature, it is doubtful whether they meant to end it. Yet for the better part of a century, the experience of reading the great modernists has had a paralyzing or deleterious effect on younger writers. After *Finnegans Wake*, what next? In a well-known 1967 essay in *The Atlantic*, John Barth coined a term which still has resonance: "The Literature of Exhaustion." Joyce and the other major modernists, he wrote, had given future writers nowhere to go. There seemed no way to make literature more innovative, newer, more "modern." There seemed no way now to astonish, at least not to the extent that the modern masters had astonished.

As a result we have witnessed a century-long effort by the highbrow and the would-be avant-garde toward a state of permanent revolution. In the hands of second- and third-rate talents, the quest for innovation at any cost has produced results that can be seen as depressing or laughable, depending on your mood. Unfortunately a few genuinely gifted writers (and artists) have fallen victim to the same delusion. Among these, one of the most notable is John Barth himself, who in a thirty-year career has evolved from a mannered but prolifically talented author to a self-indulgent windbag, a stuck record repeating the same notes *ad nauseam* in book after book after book.

As Barth never allows his readers to forget, his muse, or model, is Scheherazade. He has declared the conceit of the tale-teller telling stories for her very life to be the ruling metaphor for his identity as an artist: "Narrative equals language equals life: To cease to narrate . . . is to die." From a metaphorical point of view this is acceptable—maybe; but as the years go on Barth, always an encyclopedic, repetitive, and lavish writer, has apparently come to take it literally. "About my fiction," he has offered, "my friend John Hawkes once said that it seems spun out of nothingness, simply so that there should not be silence." This is a charge Barth accepts with no small degree of satisfaction, even going so far as to dub the phenomenon "Scheherazade's terror."

This particular wellspring of creative activity would seem to offer more to the author—writing as therapy, perhaps—than to the reader. Writing for the sake of mere writing, writing simply as a means of filling silence or making conversation, would obviously, in the manner of cocktail-party chatter, stress style at the expense of substance. And this has indeed proved to be the case. While Barth's early books—*The Floating Opera* (1958), *The Sot-Weed Factor* (1960), *Giles Goat-Boy* (1966), and *Lost in the Funhouse* (1968)—were (if you can excuse the postmodern excesses of extreme and self-conscious narrative complexity, artificiality, and a kind of dogged and not always very funny "playfulness") interesting pieces of work which displayed almost excessive imaginative powers, each book succeeding his novel *Sabbatical: A Romance* (1982)—*Tidewater Tales* (1987), *The Last Voyage of Somebody the Sailor* (1991), *Once Upon a Time* (1994), and *On with the Story*—has given evidence of an imaginative shriveling, as Barth compulsively plays out minor variations on the themes that obsess him.

"When I was writing *Once Upon a Time*," Barth said in an interview, " . . . I hoped it would be the last go-round, the last riff, the last re-orchestration of some riffs I have been playing for forty years in my fiction, the story of Scheherazade, the sailing quest motif." If only it had been! For *On with the Story* is little more than another riff, more tedious because more familiar and repetitive, on *Once Upon a Time*'s self-involved musings. It is a novel disguised as stories, in actuality a frame story or story cycle, like Barth's favorites *The Thousand and One Nights* and *The Decameron*. It features a narrator and listener remarkably like Barth and his wife, and, in the individual "stories," many other characters also remarkably like Barth. Since this is a postmodern work, there is a lot of punning and linguistic playfulness. There is also a lot of sailing and travel, each journey involving some sort of spiritual search. And the narrator, in a variation on the Scheherazade pattern, spins out his stories to prolong not his own life but that of his mate.

So: a happy, compatible couple in late middle age checks into a luxurious tropical hotel—their "last resort." It appears that the wife has been diagnosed with a fatal illness. Between meals, tennis, swimming, and sex (and in this book we are treated to a bit more sensitive, middle-aged, married sex than is really quite appetizing) the husband tells stories to the wife in an attempt to postpone The End, narrative equaling life.

Unfortunately Barth is ultimately more interested in narrative than in life. The form of *On with the Story* is constructed to include the formal structures of narrative itself, and the stories within it are not distinct entities but reflected versions of one another, with characters and motifs jumping their frames from one tale to the next. It is an interesting and sometimes brilliantly executed conceit, and of course Barth is nothing if not intelligent: *On with the Story* provides the pleasures of a complex puzzle or mathematical proof. But all the life of the book is in its gamesmanship; of passion or of *real* narrative force there is little, and when such a thing threatens to enter the rarefied atmosphere Barth has established, he is always there with an authorial nudge to remind us that the story is really only an imaginative construct. After all, as he has said elsewhere, literature

> is an artifice. . . . And so far as wanting our readers to forget that they are reading a novel, we [that is, writers like himself] are more inclined (but then, so was Scheherazade, so was Sophocles and so was Shakespeare) to remind the reader from time to time that *this is a story. . . .* You're enthralled, you're spellbound, if we are doing our work right, but . . . do not confuse this with reality. Art ain't life.

Well, duh. Barth has been known to boost his own high intellectualism with subtle putdowns of his fellow-Chesapeakian James Michener, a quintessentially "popular" writer, and to imply that Michener's readers get so wrapped up in the story as to confuse its fiction with reality. But let's be serious: even the most benighted Michener fan doesn't really forget that he is reading a novel; likewise, it is awfully arrogant of Barth to think (if he really does) that his own readers are dumb enough to need the authorial intrusions with which he peppers his novels to remind them of his presence. Every time Barth begins to tell a genuinely compelling tale—and he can do so when he wants to—he breaks it off, *delectatio interruptus,* with some first-person digression, as though he can't bear to allow his readers the unworthy, unintellectual pleasure of losing themselves within a story. But could anyone reading a Barth novel ever forget he is reading a novel, or rather, "literature"? Certainly not in the face of prose like the following, from *On with the Story:*

> Supreme in this category of human constructions to be farewelled—
> so much so, to this fareweller, as to be virtually a category in itself—

was that most supple, versatile, and ubiquitous of humanisms, language: that tool that deconstructs and reconstructs its own constructions; that uses and builds its users and builders as they use, build and build with it. Ta-ta language, la la language, the very diction of veridiction in this valley valedictory. Adieu, addio, adios, et cetera und so weiter; he could no more bear to say *good-bye* to you than to say to those nearest dearest, in particular the nearest-dearest, so to say, themof: He meant the without-whom-nothing for him to bid farewell to whom must strain the sine qua non of language even unto the sinequanonsense.

This is the work of someone who has fallen so deeply in love with his own voice that fiction is at an end; all that remains is a narcissistic celebration of self. Barth is far more interested in his own cogitations on art and narrative form than he is in any of his characters.

Which means that his characters tend to be uninteresting to the reader as well, and far too often are merely stand-ins for himself. This has been commented upon before, to disingenuous expressions of annoyance from Barth. Autobiographical connection-making is, he says, "finally impertinent. It beggars [the author's] capacities of invention and transmutation." In that case, why repeatedly invent and transmute middle-aged, male fiction writers who are divorced and happily remarried, teach at universities, and enjoy sailing on Chesapeake Bay? Is the reader supposed to eschew all connections of character with author? Is he not even to be allowed the pleasure of trying to figure out, as with Philip Roth's novels, which facets of the character are autobiographical and which are not?

"Fiction has always been about fiction," Barth has said. This is a problematic statement, rather easy for Barth to make from his lofty position as postmodern professor of literature and writing. Studied in depth, and in context with the entire history of literature, it can indeed be demonstrated that fiction is "about fiction." Yet I doubt that

Chaucer with *The Canterbury Tales,* or Richardson with *Clarissa,* or Conrad with *Lord Jim* were overwhelmingly conscious, during composition, of writing "about fiction." Before the modernist movement only a very few great authors, Sterne or Cervantes or Flaubert, for instance, demonstrated a Barthian preoccupation with form for its own sake. Yet Barth does not hesitate to make the questionable assertion that fiction that "aspires to become part of the history of fiction is almost always about itself."

Barth is consciously writing for the ages, and there seems no doubt that he aspires for his own fiction to become part of the history of fiction. Whether it will or not is another story. In my opinion, his later work is likely to appeal to the reader who shares Barth's narcissism and is primarily interested in literature insofar as it reflects his own erudition and displays his abilities to pick up references and paradoxes. In *On with the Story* Barth deplores writers who, like Keats, die too young, and their opposite numbers, those who go "on being and being *after* one's pen has gleaned et cetera: not so much a pity as simply pathetic." Barth is making a fair bid to join the latter category. "The Literature of Exhaustion" is still a meaningful phrase, but thirty years on it seems not so much the genre that is exhausted but the overtaxed powers of innovation in Barth and some of his contemporaries.

[*1996*]

Rohinton Mistry:
A Butterfly on the
Dung Heap

Rohinton Mistry is not a household name, but it should be. The fifty-year-old Toronto resident, originally from Bombay, has long been recognized as one of the best Indian writers; he ought instead to be considered simply one of the best writers, Indian or otherwise, now alive.

Mistry is not especially prolific, but his development has been swift and steady. His first book, *Swimming Lessons and Other Stories from the Firozsha Baag* (1987), was a wryly humorous series of interlocking tales rather in the manner of his countryman R. K. Narayan, or at least identifiable within that gentle fictional tradition. The stories recreate the environment of Mistry's upbringing: the insular world of *petit bourgeois* Parsi families living in a decaying Bombay apartment block, who struggle, sometimes desperately, to hold on to their precarious livelihoods and dwindling status, and dream of emigrating to Canada—"not just the land of milk and honey," as one of Mistry's characters, fed up with Bombay's foul stinks, puts it, but "also the land of deodorant and toiletry."

Mistry's own experiences are reimagined in those of his characters. "After finishing college in Bombay or elsewhere in India," he has commented, "one had to go abroad for higher studies. If possible, one

222

had to find a job after finishing a master's or a Ph.D. in the States or in England, find a job and settle in the country. That's how success is defined by Indians. So that is why I say that coming to Canada was in some ways decided for me."

Mistry, three times short-listed for the Booker Prize, has certainly achieved success, though perhaps not in the terms defined by his Parsi family. After earning a university degree in mathematics and economics he moved to Canada, where he took a job as a clerk in a Toronto bank. Over the next few years he worked his way up to middle management, but boredom and dissatisfaction led him to pursue part-time studies in literature at the University of Toronto. He was over thirty when he began writing; *Swimming Lessons* was published when he was thirty-five.

Mistry is well aware of a certain duplicity necessary in his chosen role as observer, recorder, and interpreter of the insular culture of his youth, and has written about it with understanding: in the title story of *Swimming Lessons* he juxtaposes a young Indian writer's experiences in Canada with the reactions of his parents back in Bombay as they read his stories for the first time. Initially they are excited: the father, opening the manuscript, hugs his wife,

> saying our son is a writer, and we didn't even know it, he never told us a thing, here we are thinking he is still clerking away at the insurance company, and he has written a book of stories, all these years in school and college he kept his talent hidden, making us think he was just one of the boys in the Baag, shouting and playing the fool in the compound. . . .

But when they read the stories they are not sure what to think:

> In the stories that he'd read so far Father said that all the Parsi families were poor or middle-class, but that was okay; nor did he mind that the seeds for the stories were picked from the sufferings of their

own lives; but there should also have been something positive about Parsis, there was so much to be proud of . . . what would people reading these stories think, those who did not know about Parsis—that the whole community was full of cranky, bigoted people; and in reality it was the richest, most advanced and philanthropic community in India.

Cranky and bigoted is not a bad description of the inhabitants of the Firozsha Baag, but the characters are cranky and bigoted not because they are Parsis but because they are struggling human beings; as in all the best fiction, the reader comes to understand the particularity of the fictional world, in this case Parsi Bombay, while at the same time recognizing its universality. John Galsworthy wrote of Sinclair Lewis's quintessentially American *Main Street* that "every country, of course has its Main Streets"; it can be said with equal justice that every country has its Firozsha Baags.

Mistry's second book, *Such a Long Journey* (1991), was a novel that expanded on the material of the short stories, but this time Mistry drew the characters' lives into the larger political picture: the novel is set in 1971, during the war over Bangladesh. Gustad Noble, the central character, is a kind, sane man who despite his best efforts to hold his family together finds that the forces of destruction are more than he can cope with: his little daughter falls mysteriously ill, his teenaged son rejects his values and ambitions, and he himself is drawn against his will into the morass of crime and corruption fomented by Indira Gandhi's secret police.

Swimming Lessons and *Such a Long Journey* were the work of a miniaturist: controlled, disciplined, tightly contained within one claustrophobic community. Coming on the heels of these two lovely but essentially regional books, *A Fine Balance* (1996) was a surprise: big, panoramic, intensely dramatic, bursting out of the bounds Mistry had previously set for himself. It invited comparisons with Dickens and Tolstoy; this high praise is not exaggerated, and I would add Victor Hugo to the list, for *A Fine Balance* is, among other things, a modern *Les Misérables*.

The Literary Review, with some justice, called *A Fine Balance* "the India novel, the novel readers have been waiting for since E. M. Forster." The book is set in 1975: Forster's India, the raj of King George V where Britons and Indians hovered awkwardly on either side of an unbridgeable gap, has become Mistry's, the "Goonda Raj" of Indira Gandhi, where Hindus are separated from Muslims, Parsis from Sikhs, and the immemorial laws of caste facilitate the brutal exploitation of the helpless by the powerful, in which exercise the corrupt government leads the way. Under these circumstances Forster's all-important act of connecting is possible only on an individual, and always tenuous, level.

Mistry builds his sprawling epic around the experiences of four central characters: Dina, a fortyish Parsi widow; Maneck, a young man who has come to study in the city from his idyllically beautiful hill station; and two Hindu tailors, Ishvar and Omprakesh, uncle and nephew, who have fled their native village after Om's father, an untouchable who dared to challenge the rigid caste rules of the countryside, was murdered along with his wife.

Dina, struggling to maintain independence from her overbearing brother, takes Maneck in as a paying guest and employs the two tailors to produce garments for Au Revoir Exports, a shoddy clothing company for which she acts as middleman. The four characters begin their association filled with mutual suspicions engendered by age-old prejudices, but as time goes on and they find themselves having to join forces against a hostile, dangerous world, they finally become a family in the best sense of the word.

A lot of nonsense has been written by literary critics about "the human spirit," tempting one to point out that the human spirit has always been remarkable more for greed and rapacity than for the exalted qualities the term usually celebrates. Yet occasionally a book does come along that rekindles our affection for the human race, and *A Fine Balance* is one of them. While the suffering it describes should be unbearable to read about, the reading experience is in fact strangely joyful. We can only reflect, with the author, that "Where humans are concerned, the only emotion that made sense was wonder, at their own ability to endure," and notice that those of Mistry's characters who retain this ability are those who have also retained their sense of humor. Mistry has a very finely developed feeling for the absurd: there is hardly a page in all of his fiction that isn't funny on one level or another, and the people in his books whose spirits survive, however grim the circumstances, are those who can crack a joke. What makes the final pages of *A Fine Balance* heartbreaking is not the fact that we see the protagonists' lives so hideously diminished, but that in spite of it all they are still laughing.

Some readers were disturbed by an ending they saw as unremittingly dark, but Mistry himself disagreed with this interpretation, as he made clear in an interview. "Given the parameters of my characters' lives, given who they are, how can you expect them to have any more happiness than they have found? I think that the ending is a hopeful one: the human spark is not extinguished. They continue to find humor in their lives. This is an outstanding victory in their case. . . . There are thousands and thousands of Ishvars and Oms in India today, people who keep going relentlessly in spite of the odds, and this is why I am hopeful."

Family Matters, Mistry's most recent novel, charts the effects of religious bigotry and blind adherence to tradition as they work their insidious way through generations of a family. In the prime of his life, Nariman Vakeel was compelled by his parents and their orthodox Parsi circle to give up the woman he loved, a Catholic Goan, and marry the more appropriate Yasmin, a Parsi widow with two children, Jal and Coomy. "No happiness is more lasting than the happiness that you get from fulfilling your parents' wishes," a family friend tells him, and he allows himself to believe this lie. The subsequent loveless marriage blights the family for decades.

Many years later, with Nariman a helpless old man, the ill effects of his capitulation to religious tradition are still playing themselves out within his family. Jal and Coomy, now middle-aged and emotionally stunted, still live together in Nariman's flat in the misnamed Chateau Felicity apartment building. Roxana, Nariman's and Yasmin's daughter, is married to a kind man, Yezad; they live with their three children in cramped circumstances, struggling to get by. When Nariman is crippled by a broken ankle combined with Parkinson's disease, he moves in with Roxana and her family, setting off a fateful chain of events that ends with the retreat of the gentle, liberal Yezad into the same baneful religious orthodoxy that has damaged the family since Nariman's original marriage.

Religion comes to Yezad as a sweet, seductive trap. During a time of unbearable family tensions, the Zoroastrian fire-temple seems a sanctuary, a visible embodiment of detached tranquility.

How calming, thought Yezad, to watch all this, to let the peace of the moment fill the room. Why did it have such a timeless quality? How comforting, to see the figure in the flowing white robe, see him moving, unhurried . . . with the cumulative grace of generations and centuries, so that it was encoded in blood and bone. . . .

He stood absorbed for a few moments, then felt it was churlish— churlish to refuse to bow before a sight so noble in its simple beauty. If he did not bend now, for this, what would he bend for?

The distortion of the religious impulse into an instrument of prejudice and exclusion propels the novel and its characters, and indeed everywhere in Mistry's work a retreat into ritual indicates a spiritual impoverishment. In *Family Matters* Parsi fundamentalism wrecks the family's harmony and pollutes the very air in the family homes, while in the outside world, Hindu fundamentalism, in the form of Shiv Sena thugs, wantonly ruins the lives of thousands. The thoughtful Nariman, an old-fashioned humanist, is especially wary of the threat posed by zealotry: he admonishes Coomy, for example, for referring to acts of God, observing that she "was getting into the bad habit of burdening God with altogether too much responsibility: 'And that is good for neither God nor us.'"

One of the strongest features of Mistry's novels—and the reason his work is so reminiscent of Dickens and the other great nineteenth-century writers—is his broad, even audacious use of big metaphors. *Family Matters* and *A Fine Balance* are masterly in the way they imbue certain lives, or deaths, with meaning. Nariman's wife and lover, for instance, are perversely joined in death as they have been, much against their wills, during their lives. One of Mistry's most memorable characters is the powerful Beggarmaster in *A Fine Balance*, a terrifying fusion of cruelty and compassion. Beggarmaster literally buys beggars, often children, sends them to doctors for "professional modifications"—that is, he has limbs amputated or eyes put out—and sets them up on streetcorners, then claiming a cut of their weekly takings. A figure of nightmare, in fact; yet he cares for his beggars with the utmost vigilance, and functions as an honorable protector and insurance system in an anarchic world where the police have become more a threat than a refuge. Beggarmaster's star beggar is Shankar, a legless, fingerless man who propels himself about on a rolling platform. In a plot twist that only Mistry, or Dickens, could have come up with, Beggarmaster and Shankar turn out to be half-brothers. The revelation of this fact, and the striking, even emblematic, manner of the two men's deaths, is the sort of dramatic tour de force a reader can never forget.

For fiction writers, it is always more valuable simply to write well than to be profound or "important." Mistry is one of the rare authors who are able to be both important *and* good. Major writers differ from minor ones, even great minor ones, in their ability to handle the Big Questions: death, family, the passing of time, the inevitability of loss, God or the corresponding God-shaped hole. Mistry does all this in a style entirely his own. He also manages, with gentle insistence, to focus our attention on what we have and what we are constantly in the process of losing. Children leave; families disintegrate; love somehow slips away; moments of happiness, too often unrecognized at the time, soon vanish into the past. Material well-being is fragile: as Beggar-master pointedly remarks, "People forget how vulnerable they are despite their shirts and shoes and briefcases, how this hungry and cruel world could strip them, put them in the same position as my beggars." Immaterial goods are just as evanescent; even memory fragments and fades. "Losing, and losing again," one of Mistry's characters insists, "is the very basis of the life process, till all we are left with is the bare essence of human existence." Mistry's work illustrates the comment only too effectively; and yet this essence, seen through his eyes, is still beautiful.

Index

Index

Index

McCaffrey, George, 175
McCaffrey, Stella, 175
McCullers, Carson, biographical details, 149;
    death of, 148, 153; destructiveness of,
    153; dishonesty of, 148; divorce of, 151;
    egoism of, 147; extramarital affairs of,
    150, 151; love, craving for, 150; marriage
    of, 150; neediness of, 154; remarriage of,
    152; success of, 152
McCullers, Reeves, 147, 148, 150, 151, 152;
    suicide of, 153
Macdonald, Dwight, 205
Macdonald, Ramsay, 101
McEwan, Ian, 132
McGrath, Charles, 166, 167
Madame de Pompadour (Mitford), 95, 96
Mailer, Norman, 192
Main Street (Lewis), 224
Malcolm X, 196
Malraux, André, 5
Man in Full, A (Wolfe), x
Manic depression, 55, 56; and writers, 57
Mann, Thomas, 129
Marcus, Jane, 51, 53
Marie Antoinette, 132, 134
Marler, Regina, 58
Marloe, Francis, 178
Mary Queen of Scots, 134
Massee, Jordan, 147, 154
Mathilde, Marquise de Morny ("Missy"), 5,
    11, 12, 13, 18
Matisse, Henri, 45
Matthews, Marcus, 134
Matthews, Quentin, 145
Maugham, W. Somerset, 95, 130
Maupassant, Guy de, 10, 212
Mauriac, François, 81
Maxwell, William, 118, 120, 121, 122, 123
Mehta, Ved, 163, 164, 165, 166, 167, 169,
    170
Member of the Wedding, The (McCullers),
    150, 151, 152
Metcalfe, Baba, 103, 105
Metcalfe, Fruity, 103
Michener, James, 219
Middle Age of Mrs. Eliot, The (Wilson), 134,
    138, 144
Middleton, Gerald, 137, 142
Middleton, Ingeborg, 138, 143
Milton, John, 45
Minor, Audax, 159

Mistry, Rohinton, 222, 229; biographical
    details, 222, 223; humor of, 226;
    metaphors, use of, 228
Mitford, Deborah, 89
Mitford, Diana, 89, 93, 94, 98, 107; arrest of,
    105; education of, 99; Hitler, introduction
    to, 104; and the Holocaust, 106; in Paris,
    99, 100; marriage of, 100; and Sir Oswald
    Mosley, 102, 103, 105; in Munich, 103,
    104; prison, release from, 105, 106
Mitford, Jessica, 89, 91, 93, 107
Mitford, Nancy, 83, 87, 89, 98, 99, 105, 140;
    biographical background, 90, 91; death
    of, 97; France, love of, 95; illness of, 96;
    love affairs of, 91, 92, 94, 95; marriage of,
    93; parents, relationship with, 91;
    political conscience of, 93, 94; as
    socialist, 94; and World War II, 94
Mitford, Pamela, 89
Mitford, Tom, 89, 98, 104, 106; death of, 107
Mitford, Unity, 89, 93, 103, 104, 106; death
    of, 107
Modernists, 216
Molière, 116
Monroe, Marilyn, 54
"Mood," 70, 71
More Die of Heartbreak (Bellow), 207
Morrison, Herbert, 105
Morrison, Toni, 185
Mortimer, Raymond, 89, 95
Mosley, Charlotte, 89–90
Mosley, Lady Cynthia ("Cimmie"), 101, 102,
    103, 105
Mosley, Diana, 64. *See also* Diana Mitford.
"Mosley Manifesto," 102
Mosley, Nicholas, 106
Mosley, Sir Oswald, 89, 93, 97, 98, 100, 101,
    102, 103, 104, 107; arrest of, 105; death
    of, 106; health, deterioration of, 105; and
    the Holocaust, 106; Diana Mitford,
    marriage to, 105
"Mother's Sense of Fun," 138
Motion, Andrew, 98
Moyne, Lord, 105
Mozart, 116
Mr. Fortune's Maggot (Warner), 113
Mr. Norris Changes Trains (Isherwood), 126
Mr. Sammler's Planet (Bellow), 208
Mrs. Dalloway (Woolf), 48, 54, 71
Muhammad, Elijah, 192, 195
Munich, 103

236

Index

Index

A NOTE ON THE AUTHOR

Brooke Allen grew up in New York City and studied at the University of Virginia and Columbia University, where she received a Ph.D. She then worked in the theatre for some years and with wildlife conservation organizations, and as managing editor of *Grand Street* and *Common Knowledge*, both literary quarterlies. Ms. Allen's criticism has appeared frequently in the *New York Times Book Review*, the *Atlantic Monthly*, *The New Criterion*, the *Hudson Review*, and the *New Leader*, among other publications. This is her first book. She lives in Brooklyn with her husband, the photographer Peter Aaron, and two daughters.